Study Guide

for

Carson, Butcher, and Mineka

Fundamentals of Abnormal Psychology and Modern Life

prepared by

Sarah Piazza

Allyn and Bacon
Boston London Toronto Sydney Tokyo Singapore

TABLE OF CONTENTS

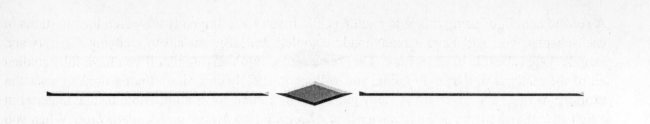

PREFACE

Many students are surprised by and often taken aback by the scope and depth of the field of Abnormal Psychology. They may hope and expect to learn about why their roommate panics before taking exams, but they do not yet realize that answering that question is extremely complicated. Not only is it complicated, but the answer one gives depends on the model of abnormal behavior one subscribes to—whether biological, psychosocial, or sociocultural. The features of these models have to be understood first; only then can one properly evaluate the nature of a particular disorder and what factors might cause and sustain it. Furthermore, as in all fields of study, understanding Abnormal Psychology today presupposes knowledge of basic historical trends in the study of abnormal behavior. For all of these reasons, studying Abnormal Psychology will take real work on your part. Engaging in that work will reap benefits on many different levels. After taking this class, not only will you be able to assess your roommate's panic attacks and perhaps your own issues in a more sophisticated way, but you will also have a solid foundation for a future career in which knowledge of this material may be of value (e.g., in general medicine, nursing, teaching, business, and so on). And, needless to say, you will be much better able to consider whether to pursue a career as a mental health professional.

Using a study guide as an aid to learning is beneficial for at least two reasons. First, it allows you a "second chance" at studying the material in the textbook. Carefully reading each chapter, while highlighting important passages and key terms and concepts judiciously, is an essential first step to studying the text. Yet at the end of this step, many students feel overwhelmed; the chapters are highly rich in information. Using the study guide after reading each chapter forces you to organize the information, and in so doing you will begin to *master* the information. Instead of simply passively absorbing the material by reading it, you will be asked in the study guide to learn actively, which has been shown to be significantly more effective than passive learning. Answering questions about chapter material, whether they are multiple-choice or short-answer, will help you assess and rectify areas of weakness in your understanding of the material. Because every question in this study guide is followed by a page reference, you will always be able to find the answer to the question that may be causing you difficulty.

A second benefit of using this study guide is that if you have diligently answered the questions in each chapter, you will have a ready-made complete and efficient aid to studying for tests and exams. One caveat is in order here. Do not be fooled into thinking that if you have fully studied all of the material in the study guide, you will automatically do well on the portions of tests and exams covering text material. A study guide simply cannot cover all possible factual material in a text as comprehensive as *Fundamentals of Abnormal Psychology and Modern Life*. When you study for tests and exams, look back at your original highlighting of material from the chapters, and you will no doubt notice areas of content that were not covered in the study guide. You will need to study these areas as well!

HOW TO USE THIS STUDY GUIDE

Each chapter in this Study Guide consists of eight or nine sections.

1. Chapter Overview

This is a brief summary of the textbook chapter. It should refresh your memory for the chapter and place the chapter in the larger context of Abnormal Psychology. It should also suggest why the topics covered in the chapter are important and interesting.

2. Chapter Outline

The chapter outline is a reproduction of the headings and subheadings found in the textbook chapter. An outline is a useful tool for organizing the many bits of information you have picked up from your first reading of the textbook chapter. A challenging exercise would be to try to "fill out" the details of the outline, once you have thoroughly studied.

3. Learning Objectives

What information should you be able to take away with you once you have studied the textbook chapter? This section offers important questions you should be able to answer if you have completely studied the textbook chapter. These questions are not intended to be answered, but merely to serve as guides that direct and focus your studying.

4. Terms You Should Know

This is a list of the major terms introduced in the textbook chapter. Each term is tagged with the page number (or numbers) on which it was first presented. In the space provided, write out a brief definition of each term.

5. Names You Should Know

Choosing which names are important for you to know is a challenging and inherently subjective task. No one expects that you should know every author of every study discussed in the textbook chapter. Yet there are names associated with every topic in Abnormal Psychology with which professionals in the field are familiar. The goal in compiling this section was not to inundate you with names but rather to suggest the names of those who have made a substantial contribution to the topic under study. Sometimes, names of people who simply *inspired* study were included. For example, Phineas Gage was a 19th-century laborer whose profound head injury motivated research into brain injuries and their potential consequences for personality. Be advised that your professor's list of important names may not coincide exactly with the list in this Study Guide. If you think a name of importance was omitted here, by all means learn it anyway! In a few chapters, the "names you should know" section was omitted, for lack of relevant names. All names to know have been tagged with page numbers.

6. Concepts to Master

These questions are meant to assess your conceptual understanding of the topics in each textbook chapter. They are not intended to require fact-filled but rather thoughtful answers. The answer to each question can be found on the page or pages listed after the question, so that you may check your work.

7. Study Questions

In contrast to the previous section, this section requires mastery of detailed information. The format of this section is in large part fill-in-the-blank. Wording is taken verbatim from the textbook with one or more words in a sentence omitted. Each item is tagged with the relevant page number. Infrequently, there is a chart for you to fill in, or a list for you to complete. In a few cases, the type of information to be assessed necessitates a short-answer question. Be warned that as in all aspects of this Study Guide, it is impossible to ask about every topic covered in the textbook chapter.

8. Critical Thinking About Difficult Topics

This section is meant to stimulate your imagination and interest in Abnormal Psychology. You do not need to write out answers to these thoughtful questions, but merely to think deeply about them. In some cases, issues are raised that professionals in the field continue to struggle with. In others, you are asked to integrate material from different textbook chapters. You are even asked now and then to plan a program of research that would provide answers to important and interesting questions that continue to plague professionals in Abnormal Psychology.

9. Chapter Quiz

Each chapter in this Study Guide concludes with a short self-test of multiple-choice items. This test assesses your mastery of the chapter. Not all textbook chapter topics can be represented in every quiz, so never assume that if you have answered every quiz question correctly, your study is complete. Be sure to take this quiz *only* after you have studied all other sections in the Study Guide. Answers to each question can be found on the page or pages listed just after the question.

It is hoped that this Study Guide will help you better to organize and expand your fund of knowledge. Good luck studying!

Much of this Study Guide has been adapted from the work of Don C. Fowles, who is gladly acknowledged. Thanks also to the authors of the textbook, especially Susan Mineka, for writing a text that, unlike so many, never talks down to undergraduates. Thanks also to Lara Zeises at Allyn & Bacon for editorial advice.

Sarah Piazza

| **Chapter 1**
| *Abnormal Psychology Over Time* |

◊ OVERVIEW

You may find it easy to discern abnormal behavior in others—or even in yourself. However, it is far more difficult to accurately describe, classify, and determine what motivates such behavior. Chapter 1 begins by discussing the difficulties of defining abnormal behavior. Various working definitions are presented—along with the flaws in each. Then the task of classifying subtypes of abnormal behavior is discussed, with three possible approaches to classification presented. The frequency of psychological disorders in the general population and how this frequency is measured is discussed. A brief history of ideas about and treatments of abnormal behavior is offered. Next, the types of research methods used by mental health professionals are explored. Chapter 1 closes with a discussion of the unresolved issues surrounding the DSM-IV.

◊ CHAPTER OUTLINE

I.   What Do We Mean By Abnormal Behavior?
     A. The DSM-IV Definition of Mental Disorder
     B. Mental Disorder as Maladaptive Behavior

II. Classifying Abnormal Behavior
     A. Reliability and Validity
     B. Differing Models of Classification
     C. DSM Classification of Mental Disorders
          1. The Five Axes of DSM-IV
          2. Main Categories of Axis I and Axis II Disorders
          3. The Problem of Labeling

III. The Extent of Abnormal Behavior

IV. Historical Views of Abnormal Behavior
     A. Demonology, Gods, and Magic
     B. Early Greek and Roman Thought
     C. Views During the Middle Ages
     D. The Resurgence of Scientific Questioning in Europe
     E. The Establishment of Asylums and Shrines
     F. Humanitarian Reform and Changing Attitudes

1

◊ LEARNING OBJECTIVES

After studying this chapter, you should be able to:

1. Explain why it is so difficult to define "abnormal behavior," and describe different approaches to such a definition. (pp. 3-5)
2. Summarize the key concepts associated with classifying abnormal behavior, and identify three major approaches to classification. (pp. 5-10)
3. Describe the methodologies used to determine the rate of mental disorder in a population and the results of recent major epidemiological studies. (pp. 10-12)
4. Discuss how mental disorders were viewed during the Middle Ages. (pp. 12-16)
5. Describe the inhumane treatment received by mental patients in early "insane asylums" and the resulting humanitarian reforms. (pp. 16-20)
6. Explain how a biological link was established between the brain and mental disorder and how the understanding of psychological factors evolved. (pp. 20-25)
7. Discuss the methodologies and issues involved in research in abnormal psychology. (pp. 26-31)

◊ TERMS YOU SHOULD KNOW

abnormal behavior (p. 5)

reliability (p. 5)

validity (p. 6)

categorical approach (p. 6)

dimensional approach (p. 6)

prototypal approach (pp. 6-7)

comorbidity (p. 7)

symptoms (p. 7)

signs (p. 7)

axes (of DSM) (p. 7)

3

4

unconscious (p. 23)

free association (p. 23)

dream analysis (p. 23)

behavioral perspective (p. 24)

classical conditioning (p. 24)

behaviorism (p. 25)

operant (instrumental) conditioning (p. 25)

sampling (p. 27)

control group (p. 28)

criterion group (p.28)

correlation (p. 28)

causation (p. 28)

experimental method (p. 29)

independent variable (p. 29)

dependent variable (p. 29)

analogue studies (p. 30)

case study (p. 31)

retrospective strategy (p. 31)

prospective strategy (p. 31)

◊ CONCEPTS TO MASTER

1. Name three factors complicating the task of defining abnormal behavior. (pp. 3-4)

2. Why does a classification system need to demonstrate both reliability and validity? (pp. 5-6)

3. List and describe three basic approaches to the classification of abnormal behavior and the general assumptions underlying each approach. (pp. 6-7)

4. Describe the five axes of DSM-IV. (pp. 7-8)

5. Discuss some of the problems associated with labeling. (pp. 9-10)

6. Define epidemiology and contrast the concepts of prevalence and incidence, including the associated concepts of point prevalence and lifetime prevalence. (pp. 10-11)

7. Describe early beliefs in demonology and explain why exorcism was used as a cure. (p. 12)

8. Describe the classification and treatment system developed by Hippocrates. (p. 13)

9. What is mass madness? Describe at least one outbreak of this phenomenon. (p. 15)

10. During the sixteenth century, Teresa of Avila, a Spanish nun who later became a saint, explained hysteria among a group of cloistered nuns as *comas enfermas,* which is translated "as if sick." Explain what she meant. (p. 16)

11. What did Pinel do to provide more humane treatment for the inmates of La Bicêtre in Paris? What effect did these measures have on the patients? (pp. 17-18)

12. Describe the historical development of humanitarian reform and identify some of the reasons it occurred. (pp. 17-20)

13. How did early experimental science help to establish a biological connection in mental disorders? (pp. 20-21)

14. One of the major debates of medical history was between Jean Charcot and the Nancy School. What was the nature of the debate? Which side triumphed, and how did the debate influence modern psychology? (p. 22)

15. What influence did Sigmund Freud's concept of the unconscious have on abnormal psychology as studied today? What was Watson's impact on American psychology? (pp. 23-25)

16. Explain why hypotheses are critical supplements to observations of behavior. (p. 26)

17. Explain why research on groups of people is usually preferred to single case studies and why those groups must be representative of larger populations. (pp. 27, 31)

18. A mere correlation does not imply causation. A manic individual exhibits a euphoric mood, a high level of activity without regard for its consequences that may lead to financial bankruptcy, and a loosening of cultural inhibitions that may be associated with crude and inappropriate sexual advances. Mania is also associated with a high rate of divorce--a stressful life event. How might divorce precipitate mania and how might mania lead to divorce (i.e., consider how the direction of causation might go in either direction)? (pp. 28-29)

19. Explain why some experimental studies are inappropriate for abnormal psychology and indicate how analogue studies have been used in their place. (pp. 29-30)

20. Describe the clinical case study and explain why it is easy to draw erroneous conclusions from this method of research. (p. 31)

21. Compare the advantages and disadvantages of retrospective and prospective research in abnormal psychology. (p. 31)

22. Discuss three major difficulties with the DSM. (pp. 32-33)

◊ STUDY QUESTIONS

What do we mean by "abnormal behavior"?

1. Briefly describe the cases of Albert G., Sue D., and Donald G. (p. 3)

2. The authors of the text maintain that the best criterion for determining the normality of behavior is whether it fosters the well-being of the individual and, ultimately, of the group. According to this view, abnormal behavior is thus defined as _____. (p. 5)

3. How do the authors justify considering promotion of inter-group hostility, destructive assaults on the environment, irrational violence, and political corruption as forms of "abnormal behavior"? (p. 5)

Classifying abnormal behavior

4. Why is classification of abnormal behavior an essential first step in the advancement of the science and practice of abnormal psychology? (p. 5)

5. The authors of DSM-IV intended to follow a _____ approach to classification, but instead created more often than not a _____ model of classification. (p. 7)

6. Identify the five axes of DSM-IV. (pp. 7-8)

Axis I

Axis II

Axis III

Axis IV

Axis V

7. In what ways do Axes IV and V add significant information to that provided by the other three axes? (p. 8)

8. The authors of the text indicate that the process of labeling, no matter what classification system is used, has drawbacks. How might labeling affect the patient labeled with a psychological disorder, the professional treating the patient, and significant others in the patient's life? (pp. 9-10)

The extent of abnormal behavior

9. In Table 1.1, which disorders are shown to be more frequent in women than in men? Which disorders show the opposite pattern? Which disorder occurs at the same rate for both men and women? (p. 11)

10. List and discuss two reasons for the substantial decline in mental hospital admissions over the past 45 years. (p. 12)

Historical views of abnormal behavior

11. Hippocrates is considered the "father of modern medicine" and is credited in your text with five important new ideas that contributed to the development of abnormal psychology. Complete this listing of his important contributions. (p. 13)

   a. He saw the _____ as the central organ of _____ _____ and viewed mental disorders as due to _____ _____.

   b. He emphasized the importance of heredity, predispositions, and head injuries as causes of _____ _____.

   c. He classified all mental disorders into three general categories: mania, _____, and phrenitis (brain fever).

   d. He considered _____ to be important in understanding a patient's personality.

   e. He advocated treatment methods that were far advanced over the exorcistic practices of his time. For the treatment of _____, he prescribed a regular and tranquil life, sobriety, abstinence from all excesses, a vegetable diet, celibacy, and exercise.

13

12. Although Hippocrates was ahead of his time in many ways, he was constrained by his time in other ways. What did he believe to be the cause of hysteria, and what was his recommended treatment? (p. 14)

13. The occurrence of mass madness peaked in the 14th and 15th centuries. Why, according to the text, was mass madness so common during these years? (p. 15)

14. Humanitarian reform of mental hospitals received its first great impetus from the work of _____ of France in 1792. Describe the conditions in asylums (e.g., at St. Mary of Bethlehem, or "Bedlam") prior to 1792. (pp. 16-17)

15. Describe moral management and list five reasons for the abandonment of moral management by the late 1800s. (pp. 18-19)

16. What was the mental hygiene movement, and who was its champion? In what respect was it the antithesis of moral management? (pp. 18-19)

17. What assumption about the origins of mental disorders was thought to be proved by the discovery that syphilis causes general paresis? (p. 21)

18. What specific examples of mental disorders were determined to reflect brain pathology? (p. 21)

19. Describe Kraepelin's process of distinguishing the mental disorders. How did he view their course and outcome? (p. 21)

20. What is the medical model? How does it fare when applied to abnormal psychology? (p. 21)

21. In disagreement with the Nancy School, Charcot insisted that _____ _____ led to hysteria. (p. 22)

22. The Nancy School finally triumphed in its dispute with Charcot, representing the first recognition of a _____ cause of mental disorder. (p. 22)

22. In an important development, Sigmund Freud directed his patients to talk freely about their problems while under hypnosis, during which they usually displayed considerable emotion. This method was called _____. The patients, upon awakening, saw no relationship between their problems and their hysterical symptoms, leading Freud to postulate the existence of the _____. (pp. 22-23)

23. Freud soon discovered that he could dispense with hypnosis by substituting two methods. What were they? (p. 23)

24. According to the behavioral perspective, the role of _____ in human behavior is essential. (p. 24)

25. Watson believed that abnormal behavior was the result of earlier _____ and could be modified through _____ . Skinner, on the other hand, studied _____ conditioning, which may be relevant in the production of certain abnormal behaviors, like _____ . (p. 25)

Research in abnormal psychology

26. To make sense of observed behavior, psychologists generate more or less reasonable _____ to help explain the behavior. For example, a psychologist may observe some symptoms and guess that "schizophrenia" is the entity or hypothetical construct that caused the symptoms. (p. 26)

27. The strategy of intensively studying a single case might yield important leads, but it suffers from a basic difficulty. What is this difficulty? (p. 27)

28. To overcome the limitations of studying the single case, psychologists usually rely on studies using groups of individuals. Explain why in such studies it is desirable to obtain a representative sample. (p. 27)

29. "Correlation does not imply causation." Explain. (pp. 28-29)

30. After each of the following research methods, write one strength and one limitation of the approach:

a. case study method (p. 31)

b. analogue studies (p. 30)

c. retrospective research (p. 31)

d. prospective research (p. 31)

───────────◆───────────

◊ CRITICAL THINKING ABOUT DIFFICULT TOPICS

1. The authors of the text argue for a definition of abnormal behavior as maladaptive behavior and conclude that their definition would include "destructive assaults on the environment" (p. 5). Consider the case of an executive of a manufacturing company whose factory discharges pollutants into the air or water that are (a) perfectly legal, (b) within the range of common practice, (c) extremely costly to eliminate, but (d) harmful to the health of a significant number of individuals in the long run. Is his or her behavior indicative of a "mental disorder" (pp. 4-5)? Try to think of other instances in which there is a conflict between "rational" reward-seeking behavior that is not in violation of cultural norms, yet which is "in serious degree contrary to the continued well-being . . . of the human community of which the individual is a member" (p. 5). Similarly, consider the case of the "subcultural delinquent" who acts entirely in keeping with the values, norms, and personal loyalties of his or her gang in committing various delinquent acts that are harmful to many members of the larger society. In what sense does such a person have a mental disorder?

2. Do you think that "Road Rage" should be considered a mental disorder? Why or why not? Discuss your answer in reference to conceptual issues of classification.

3. To what degree do differing views of abnormal behavior across history contrast "free will" versus "determinism"? That is, in some cases the person showing abnormal behavior is said to have acted wickedly (presumably by choice) and, therefore, deserves to be punished. In the other case, an illness is something that happens to a person through natural forces over which the person has no control (determinism) and for which, therefore, the person is not responsible. This contrast is seen throughout this chapter (e.g., in Pinel's argument that "mental patients should be treated with kindness and consideration—as sick people and not as vicious beasts or criminals"), and it can been seen in many discussions of mental illness today. At present, the issue is perhaps most clearly observed in the current debate over alcoholism. Think through the arguments and issues surrounding the opposing views that alcoholism reflects a free choice for which the individual is responsible versus the deterministic view that alcoholism is an illness that happens to the person and for which he or she bears no moral responsibility.

4. Suppose a strong correlation is observed between reported current levels of depression and social skills deficits. What should one conclude? Perhaps depression suppresses one's ability to initiate and sustain relationships with others (i.e., depression may cause social skills deficits). On the other hand, perhaps social skills deficits—present from childhood—have led to depression and loneliness because of the inability to make and keep friends. A third hypothesis is also plausible: Depression in a parent might have led to missed opportunities to develop social skills (e.g., if the parent was too depressed to take the child out on play dates, and so on), as well as a genetic predisposition to develop depression. According to this scenario, a third variable may have caused both current levels of depression and social skills deficits. This example demonstrates that correlation, while important, does not infer causation. Now suppose that a strong correlation is documented between problem drinking and depression. First, finds the possible causes based on this correlation. Then discuss the benefits that accrue from the knowledge that a certain disorder has a certain cause. What is not gained from this knowledge?

5. Table 1.1 shows that women tend to be diagnosed with mood and anxiety disorders more than men. The opposite is true for substance-abuse disorders and antisocial personality disorder. According to the authors, these trends may reflect assessment bias or actual gender differences. Keeping this in mind, should the DSM-IV have differing diagnostic standards for men and women? Consider biological differences (e.g., hormones) as well as the differences in socialization in your answer.

◊ CHAPTER 1 QUIZ

Circle the best of the four answers provided and check them according to answers provided at the back of this study guide. Be sure you understand why each answer is correct.

1. The word *abnormal* literally means behavior that: (p. 4)
    a. deviates from society's norms.
    b. interferes with the well-being of the individual.
    c. is away from the normal.
    d. is undesirable.

2. When different observers agree on the classification of certain abnormal behaviors, the system is said to be: (p. 6)
    a. diagnostic.   c. standardized.
    b. reliable.   d. valid.

3. Widiger and Frances described three basic approaches currently possible for classifying abnormal behavior. Which of the following is *not* one of them? (pp. 6-7)
    a. categorical   c. prototypal
    b. dimensional   d. configural

4. The occurrence of two or more identifiable diagnoses in the same psychologically disturbed person is known as: (p. 7)
    a. synthesis.   c. convergence.
    b. concurrence.   d. comorbidity.

5. The first three axes of the DSM-IV assess: (p. 7)
    a. how well the individual is coping.
    b. stressors that may have contributed to the disorder.
    c. the person's present condition.
    d. the prognosis of the disorder.

6. A diagnosis of mental retardation would be assigned to which axis of the DSM-IV diagnostic system? (p. 7)
    a. Axis I   c. Axis III
    b. Axis II   d. Axis IV

7. Many clinicians object to the inclusion of an _____ diagnosis on insurance forms because it violates the client's confidentiality. (p. 8)
   a. Axis I
   b. Axis II
   c. Axis III
   d. Axis IV

8. A chronic mental disorder can be all of the following EXCEPT: (p. 9)
   a. long-standing
   b. low-intensity
   c. acute
   d. permanent

9. The proportion of those living in a population who ever had a particular disorder (including recovered cases) is known as: (p. 11)
   a. lifetime prevalence.
   b. point incidence.
   c. lifetime incidence.
   d. lifetime comorbidity.

10. According to the National Comorbidity Survey (NCS), the frequency of most diagnosable mental disorders tends to decrease with: (p. 11)
   a. higher socioeconomic status and younger age.
   b. higher socioeconomic status and older age.
   c. lower socioeconomic status and younger age.
   d. lower socioeconomic status and older age.

11. Mental disorders were classified into three categories (mania, melancholia, and phrenitis) by: (p. 13)
   a. Galen.
   b. Hippocrates.
   c. Avicenna.
   d. Paracelsus.

12. Which of the following beliefs did Hippocrates erroneously hold? (p. 13)
   a. The brain is the central organ of intellectual activity.
   b. Head injuries may cause sensory and motor disorders.
   c. The environment is important in mental disorders.
   d. There are basically four types of body fluids.

13. The Greek physician Galen's most important contribution to abnormal psychology was his description of: (pp. 13-14)
   a. the anatomy of the nervous system.
   b. medicinal herbs that could soothe mental patients.
   c. new treatments for the mentally disturbed.
   d. symptoms of common mental disorders.

14. Which of the following is NOT an example of mass madness? (p. 15)
   a. lycanthropy
   b. tarantism
   c. The Black Death
   d. St. Vitus's dance

15. Pinel's and Tuke's moral management in mental hospitals was based on the idea that abnormal behavior is: (p. 18)
    a. a result of sinful living.
    b. due to possession of the devil.
    c. related to an immoral balance of the humors.
    d. the result of severe psychological stress.

16. Which of the following statements about the mental hygiene movement is false? (p. 19)
    a. This movement was based on the belief that mental disorders are caused by biological agents.
    b. Patients' creature comforts increased during this movement.
    c. Patients' psychological and social needs were well met during this movement.
    d. Mental hospitals proliferated during this movement.

17. Emil Kraepelin's early classification system of mental disorders is best described as a _____ model: (p. 21)
    a. dimensional   c. prototypal
    b. categorical   d. psychoanalytic

18. Sigmund Freud directed his patients to talk freely about their problems while under hypnosis, a method that was called: (pp. 22-23)
    a. mesmerism.   c. catharsis.
    b. free association.   d. emotional desensitization.

19. Classical and operant conditioning differ primarily with respect to: (p. 25)
    a. the types of reinforcers involved.
    b. an emphasis on animal versus human subjects.
    c. the number of trials to reach criterion performance.
    d. whether the outcome (reinforcer) is dependent on the animal's behavior.

20. Watson believed that abnormal behavior is caused by: (p. 25)
    a. instrumental behavior.
    b. unconscious emotional material.
    c. inadvertent early conditioning.
    d. brain pathology.

21. The purpose of _____ is to ensure, in effect, that each member of the population has an equal chance of being included in the study's sample. (p. 27)
    a. increasing reliability
    b. hypothesis testing
    c. structured set sampling
    d. random selection

22. Seligman induced learned helplessness in animals by subjecting them to repeated inescapable shock. This study is an example of _____ research. (p. 30)
   a. analogue
   b. clinical
   c. correlational
   d. epidemiological

23. All of the following are problematic for retrospective studies EXCEPT: (p. 31)
   a. the fallibility of a study participant's memory
   b. the preconceived biases of the investigator(s)
   c. the preconceived biases of raters and observers of the study participant
   d. the difficulty in retaining study participants for multiple assessments across many years

24. A psychologist identifies 50 children who have schizophrenic mothers. At adolescence, the researcher compares those who break down with those who don't. This is an example of a _____ study. (p. 31)
   a. case study
   b. comparative outcome
   c. prospective
   d. retrospective

25. Which of the following statements about the DSM-IV is incorrect? (pp. 5, 32-33)
   a. Its categories establish groupings that are clearly and cleanly separated at the boundaries.
   b. While inter-diagnostician reliability is high, the validity of the diagnoses has been questioned.
   c. Its authors have faced pressure to include greater varieties of socially undesirable behavior.
   d. Its definition of mental disorder makes no reference to causal agents.

Chapter 2
Causal Factors and Viewpoints in Abnormal Psychology

◊ OVERVIEW

There are several theoretical models that explain the origins of abnormal behavior. The biological perspective believes several broad physiological causal factors—ranging from brain and biochemical functioning to genetic and constitutional vulnerabilities—impact abnormal behavior. The psychosocial viewpoint—encompassing psychodynamic, behavioral, and cognitive-behavioral models—focuses on the importance of early psychosocial factors as powerful causes of abnormal behavior. The sociocultural viewpoint reminds us that our behavior cannot be fully understood without reference to the influences of the society in which we live. It is now widely recognized that no one model adequately explains every aspect of every form of abnormal behavior. Consequently, the biopsychosocial model assesses and studies the interaction of biological, psychosocial, and sociocultural factors in order to develop a complete understanding of the origins of abnormal behavior.

◊ CHAPTER OUTLINE

I. Causes and Risk Factors for Abnormal Behavior

II. Models or Viewpoints for Understanding Abnormal Behavior

III. The Biological Viewpoint and Causal Factors
    A. Neurotransmitter and Hormonal Imbalances
        1. Imbalances of Neurotransmitters
        2. Hormonal Imbalances
    B. Genetic Vulnerabilities
        1. The Relationship of Genotypes to Phenotypes
        2. Methods for Studying Genetic Influences
        3. Common Misconceptions About Genetic Influences
    C. Constitutional Liabilities
        1. Physical Handicaps
        2. Temperament
    D. Brain Dysfunction and Neural Plasticity
    E. Physical Deprivation or Disruption
    F. The Impact of the Biological Viewpoint

IV.   The Psychosocial Viewpoints
    A. The Psychodynamic Perspectives
        1. The Structure of Personality: Id, Ego, and Superego
        2. Anxiety, Defense Mechanisms, and the Unconscious
        3. Psychosexual Stages of Development
        4. The Oedipus Complex and Electra Complex
        5. Newer Psychodynamic Perspectives
            a) Object-Relations Theory
            b) The Interpersonal Perspective
        6. Impact of the Psychodynamic Perspectives
    B. The Behavioral Perspective
        1. Classical Conditioning
        2. Instrumental Conditioning
        3. Generalization and Discrimination
        4. Observational Learning
        5. Impact of the Behavioral Perspective
    C. The Cognitive-Behavioral Perspective
        1. Attributions, Attributional Style, and Psychopathology
        2. Cognitive Therapy
        3. The Impact of the Cognitive-Behavioral Perspective
    D. What the Adoption of a Perspective Does and Does Not Do

V. Psychosocial Causal Factors
    A. Our Views of the World and of Ourselves: Schemas and Self-Schemas
        1. Why Schemas Are So Important
        2. Predictability and Controllability
    B. Early Deprivation or Trauma
        1. Institutionalization
        2. Deprivation and Abuse in the Home
        3. Other Childhood Traumas
    C. Inadequate Parenting Styles
        1. Parental Psychopathology
        2. Parenting Styles: Warmth and Control
            a) Authoritative Parenting
            b) Authoritarian Parenting
            c) Permissive-Indulgent Parenting
            d) Neglectful-Uninvolved Parenting
        3. Inadequate, Irrational, and Angry Communication
    D. Marital Discord and Divorce
        1. Marital Discord
        2. Divorce or Other Separation
            a) Effects of Divorce on Parents
            b) Effects of Divorce on Children
    E. Maladaptive Peer Relationships

VI. The Sociocultural Viewpoint and Causal Factors
    A. Uncovering Sociocultural Factors Though Cross-Cultural Studies
        1. Universal and Culture-Specific Disorders
        2. Culture and Overcontrolled Versus Undercontrolled Behavior
    B. Causal Factors Within the Sociocultural Environment
    C. Other Pathogenic Social Influences
        1. Low Socioeconomic Status and Unemployment
        2. Disorder-Engendering Social Roles
        3. Prejudice and Discrimination Based on Race, Ethnicity, and Gender
        4. Social Change and Uncertainty
    D. The Impact of the Sociocultural Viewpoint
VII.   Summary

◊ LEARNING OBJECTIVES

After studying this chapter, you should be able to:

1. Explain how diathesis-stress models of the etiology of abnormal behavior and the concepts of protective factors and resilience are related. (pp. 37-39)

2. Summarize the causal factors of abnormal behavior according to the biological viewpoint, including neurotransmitter and hormonal imbalances, genetic vulnerabilities, constitutional liabilities, brain dysfunction, and physical deprivation or disruption. (pp. 40-49)

3. Outline the major psychosocial approaches to abnormal behavior, including the psychodynamic, behavioral, and cognitive-behavioral perspectives. (pp. 49-62)

4. Describe the effects of various psychosocial causal factors, including schemas and self-schemas, early deprivation or trauma (e.g., parental deprivation, institutionalization, abuse, etc.), inadequate parenting styles, marital discord and divorce, and problems with peer relationships. (pp. 63-70)

5. Describe the sociocultural viewpoint, and explain how sociocultural causal factors contribute to abnormal behavior. (pp. 70-76)

6. Explain why the biopsychosocial viewpoint may best fulfill the need for a more unified viewpoint. (pp. 39-40, 76)

◊ TERMS YOU SHOULD KNOW

---

etiology (p. 37)

diathesis-stress models (p. 37)

protective factors (p. 38)

resilience (p. 38)

developmental psychopathology (p. 39)

biopsychosocial viewpoint (p. 39)

synapse (p. 41)

neurotransmitters (pp. 41-42)

hormones (p. 42)

genotype (p. 44)

phenotype (p. 44)

genotype-environment correlation (p. 44)

genotype-environment interaction (p. 44)

family history method (p. 44)

twin method (pp. 44-45)

concordance rate (p. 45)

adoption method (p. 45)

temperament (p. 46)

developmental systems approach (p. 47)

id (p. 51)

libido (p. 51)

pleasure principle (p. 51)

primary process thinking (p. 51)

ego (pp. 51-52)

secondary process thinking (p. 52)

reality principle (p. 52)

superego (p. 52)

intrapsychic conflicts (p. 52)

27

ego-defense mechanisms (pp. 52-53)

psychosexual stages of development (pp. 52-53)

Oedipus complex (pp. 53-54)

castration anxiety (p. 54)

Electra complex (p. 54)

ego psychology (p. 54)

object-relations theory (pp. 54-55)

introjection (pp. 54-55)

interpersonal perspective (pp. 55-56)

interpersonal accommodation (p. 56)

attachment theory (p. 56)

classical conditioning (pp. 57-58)

extinction (pp. 57-58)

spontaneous recovery (pp. 57-58)

instrumental (operant) conditioning (pp. 58-59)

reinforcement (p. 58)

generalization (pp. 59-60)

discrimination (pp. 59-60)

cognitive-behavioral perspective (p. 60)

attribution (p. 61)

schema (p. 61, pp. 63-64)

self-schemas (p. 64)

assimilation (p. 64)

accommodation (p. 64)

◊ NAMES YOU SHOULD KNOW

Carl Rogers (p. 50)

Sigmund Freud (pp. 51-54)

Anna Freud (p. 54)

Otto Kernberg (p. 55)

Alfred Adler (p. 55)

Erich Fromm (p. 55)

Karen Horney (pp. 55-56)

Erik Erikson (p. 56)

Harry Stack Sullivan (p. 56)

John Bowlby (p. 56)

Ivan Pavlov (pp. 57-58)

Edward Thorndike (p. 57)

B. F. Skinner (p. 57)

John Watson (p. 57)

Albert Bandura (pp. 59, 60)

Aaron Beck (p. 61)

---

1. Describe the diathesis-stress model of abnormal behavior. What are some examples of diatheses? Of stressors? (pp. 37-38)

2. Define "protective factors" and "resilience" (p. 38). What are some examples of protective factors? (p. 38)

3. What is a "steeling" or "inoculation" effect? (p. 38)

4. Explain why the diathesis-stress model is a multi-causal developmental model. (p. 39)

5. Describe the biopsychosocial viewpoint, and why may it be a better model of the origins of abnormal behavior than other current models. (pp. 39-40, p. 76)

6. A patient has the delusion that he is Arnold Schwarzenegger. How does this delusion reveal that biological causes must interact with experience? (p. 40)

7. Discuss the five categories of biological factors that are especially relevant to the development of abnormal behavior. (pp. 40-41)

8. Outline the sequence of events involved in the transmission of nerve impulses, and explain how imbalances of neurotransmitters might produce abnormal behavior. How do these processes relate to the mechanisms by which medications used to treat various disorders exert their effects? (pp. 41-42)

9. What is the hypothalamic-pituitary-adrenal-cortical axis, and why is it so important in reference to abnormal behavior? (p. 43)

10. Explain at least two ways in which a genotype may shape and interact with the environment. (p. 44)

11. Summarize the various methods (family history, twin, and adoption) used to study genetic influences on abnormal behavior. (pp. 44-46)

12. Define concordance rate and describe how it is used to disentangle genetic versus environmental contributions to abnormal behavior. (pp. 44-45)

13. What are some common misunderstandings about the impact of genetics on abnormal behavior (p. 46) and about the spate of recent biological advances (p. 49)?

14. What are constitutional liabilities? List two types discussed in your text. (pp. 46-47)

15. Distinguish between gross brain pathology and more subtle deficiencies of brain function and indicate which applies to only a small percentage of people with abnormal behavior. (p. 47)

16. The text documents with several examples the conclusion that dietary deficiencies can have long-term effects (well beyond the period of malnutrition) on psychological functioning. Describe the results reported for former World War II and Korean War POWs and explain the effects of severe malnutrition. (p. 48)

17. Describe the interaction of the id, ego, and superego in Freud's conception of personality. (pp. 51-52)

18. Choose two of the ego-defense mechanisms listed in Table 2.1 and create your own examples of how they might operate. (p. 53)

19. Describe Freud's five stages of psychosexual development. (p. 53)

20. Contrast the newer psychodynamic approaches with the earlier Freudian perspective, including the greater emphasis on ego functions and object relations. Summarize some of the newer psychodynamic perspectives developed by Anna Freud, Otto Kernberg, Harry Stack Sullivan, and John Bowlby. (pp. 54-56)

21. Discuss two of Freud's most noteworthy contributions to our understanding of normal and abnormal behavior and list several criticisms of his approach. (pp. 56-57)

22. Define each of the following terms. (pp. 57-59)

classical conditioning

extinction

instrumental (operant) conditioning

reinforcement

response-outcome expectancy

conditioned avoidance response

generalization

discrimination

23. List the major strengths and weaknesses of the behavioral perspective. (pp. 59-60)

24. Describe Albert Bandura's concept of self-efficacy. (p. 60)

25. Discuss the importance of attributions and schemas to the cognitive-behavioral perspective. (pp. 60-62)

26. How are assimilation and accommodation involved in the processing of new experiences, and which of the two is the basic goal of psychosocial therapies? (p. 64)

27. What are the four categories of psychosocial causal factors that exemplify the psychosocial approach? Explain how each might contribute to the development of abnormal behavior. (pp. 65-70)

28. How are the variables of parental warmth and parental control related to the authoritative, authoritarian, permissive-indulgent, and neglectful-uninvolved parenting styles? What impact is each of these parenting styles thought to have on children's development? (pp. 67-68)

29. List some examples of universal and some of culture-specific disorders. (pp. 71-72)

30. What cultural factors may be responsible for the differences found in over- and undercontrolled behavior problems in Thai versus American children? (pp. 72-73)

31. Outline the major sociocultural factors that contribute to abnormal behavior. (pp. 73-75)

◊ STUDY QUESTIONS

Causes and risk factors for abnormal behavior

1. The _____ leaves an individual vulnerable to developing a disorder, while the _____ is the trigger that leads to abnormal behavior. (pp. 37-38)

2. _____ factors mitigate the adverse consequences of experiencing a stressor and so protect against the development of abnormal behavior. (p. 38)

3. How is developmental psychopathology used in the study of abnormal psychology? (p. 39)

Models or viewpoints for understanding abnormal behavior

4. What two recent paradigm shifts have been occurring in parallel in the study of abnormal behavior? (p. 39)

5. An integrative approach that acknowledges multiple factors in the role of psychopathology and treatment is the _____ viewpoint. (pp. 39-40)

The biological viewpoint and causal factors

6. The electrical nerve impulse travels from the cell body of a neuron to the terminal buttons via the _____. (p. 41)

7. The _____ are the sites where neurotransmitter substances are stored until needed. When the nerve impulse reaches the axon endings, the transmitter is released into the _____, a tiny fluid-filled gap between the axon endings of the _____ neuron and the _____ of the postsynaptic neuron. (p. 41)

8. The dendrite of the postsynaptic neuron has specialized areas called _____ _____ where the neurotransmitters pass on their chemical message. (p. 41)

9. The action of the neurotransmitter substance is time-limited either by deactivation by an _____, such as monoamine oxidase, in the synaptic cleft or by a process called _____, which takes it back into the presynaptic neuron and stores it in the synaptic storage vesicles. (p. 42)

10. _____ is a neurotransmitter that may play a role in psychological disorders like anxiety and depression. (p. 42)

11. Extraverted children may seek the company of others, thereby enhancing their own tendencies to be sociable. This is an example of a(n) _____-_____ _____. (p. 44)

12. If a given disorder were completely heritable, the _____ _____ for identical twins with the disorder would be 100%. (p. 45)

13. Those factors that would affect all children in a family similarly are known as _____ _____ _____. (p. 45)

14. Height is largely genetically determined, and yet nutrition has a strong influence on the height an adult will finally reach. This example illustrates the flaw in which argument? (p. 46)

15. Physical handicaps and temperament are both considered to be _____ _____. (p. 46)

The psychosocial viewpoints: The psychodynamic perspectives

16. The id operates on the _____ principle. (p. 51)

17. The id generates mental images and fantasies referred to as _____ _____ thinking. (p. 51)

18. The ego operates according to the _____ principle. (p. 52)

19. The ego mediates between the demands of the _____ and the moral constraints of the _____; thus, it is often called the executive branch of the personality. (p. 52)

20. Anxiety is a warning of impending danger as well as a painful experience, so it motivates people to reduce it. The ego can cope with anxiety in essentially two ways. First, the ego can cope with anxiety by rational measures. If these are not effective or sufficient, the ego unconsciously resorts to ___-_____ _____. (p. 52)

21. Complete the table about Freud's psychosexual stages of development. (pp. 52-53)

Psychosexual Stage	Age of Occurrence	Source of Gratification

22. A man with aggressive impulses takes up the sport of ice hockey. This is an example of the ego-defense mechanism of _____. (p. 53)

23. Differentiate the Electra complex from the Oedipus complex. What is the role of castration anxiety, and what is considered to be its proper resolution given normal development? (pp. 53-54)

24. What three directions did newer (that is, post-Freud) psychodynamic theorists take? (p. 54)

25. In object relations theory, the focus is not on the ego or on the id. Explain what this approach focuses on. (pp. 54-55)

26. Theorists who share an interpersonal perspective believe that abnormal behavior is best understood by analyzing a person's _____, both past and present. (p. 55)

27. Bowlby emphasized the importance of the quality of _____ _____ to the development of secure attachments. (p. 56)

28. _____ can be seen as the first systematic approach documenting how human psychological processes can result in mental disorders. (p. 56)

The psychosocial viewpoints: The behavioral perspective

29. Behavioral psychologists assert that the data used by psychoanalysts, including material obtained by free association and dream analysis, is unverifiable scientifically. What data do behaviorists prefer? (p. 57)

30. In operant (instrumental) conditioning, initially a high rate of reinforcement may be necessary, but thereafter it is especially persistent when reinforcement is _____. (p. 58)

31. A boy who has been bitten by a vicious dog may develop a conditioned avoidance response in which he consistently avoids all dogs. Why is his avoidance difficult to extinguish? (p. 59)

32. Match the following terms and examples: (pp. 58-61)

Terms	Example
a. Discrimination	____ A person, previously bitten, avoids dogs.
b. Generalization	____ An occasional win at gambling keeps the behavior going.
c. Intermittent	____ A person, beaten as a child by an authority figure, has an involuntary fear of anyone in authority.
d. Reinforcement	____ A child performs a response that in the past produced candy.
e. Conditioned Avoidance Response	____ A child learns that although red and green strawberries look somewhat similar, only red ones taste good.

33. What is observational learning? Describe Bandura's classic series of experiments on this topic. (p. 59)

34. Behaviorists believe that maladaptive behavior develops as a result of two problems. What are they? (p. 59)

The psychosocial viewpoints: The cognitive-behavioral perspective

35. What does the cognitive-behavioral approach consider that behaviorism does not? (p. 60)

36. Describe how attribution theorists view the origins of abnormal behavior. What is a dysfunctional attributional style? (pp. 60-61)

37. How do cognitive theorists (e.g., Beck) view the origins of mental disorder? What is a schema? (p. 61)

38. What is an important consequence of adopting a particular psychosocial perspective? (p. 62)

Psychosocial causal factors
39. What are the four categories of psychosocial causal factors listed in the text? (p. 63)

40. Define the concept of self-schema and explain why it is so important. (p. 64)

41. Abused children suffer from many deficits and are at heightened risk for later aggressive behavior, including abuse of their own children. List four other consequences of parental abuse. (pp. 64-65)

42. Two protective factors for children institutionalized at an early age are entering a _____ home and having _____ _____ at school. (p. 65)

43. Match the following parenting styles with child outcomes: (p. 68)

Style	Child Outcome
a. authoritative	____ impulsive and aggressive; spoiled, selfish, inconsiderate, and demanding; exploitative of others
b. authoritarian	____ disruptions in attachment during childhood; moodiness, low self-esteem, and conduct problems later in childhood; problems with peer relations and academic performance
c. permissive-indulgent	____ energetic and friendly; competent in dealing with others and the environment
d. neglectful-uninvolved	____ conflicted, irritable, moody; poor social and cognitive skills

44. What did Amato and Keith (1991) concluded about the average negative effects of divorce on children? (p. 69)

45. Explain the sequence of events by which a child who fails to establish successful relationships with peers may end up mentally disordered (consider the diathesis-stress model as you answer this). (p. 70)

The sociocultural viewpoint and causal factors

46. Explain why the acute sense of guilt sometimes associated with depression varies across cultures. (pp. 71-72)

47. Discuss the role of subgroups in shaping behaviors. How do conflicting roles from varied subgroups affect an individual? (p. 73)

48. The lower the socioeconomic class, the _____ the incidence of abnormal behavior. What are some causal pathways that might be responsible for this relationship? (p. 74)

49. Discuss the impact of unemployment as a factor in abnormal behavior. (p. 74)

50. What impact has sociocultural research had on detection, treatment, and prevention of mental disorders? (p. 75)

◊ CRITICAL THINKING ABOUT DIFFICULT TOPICS

1. Referring to family history, twin, and adoption methods for studying genetic influences on abnormal behavior, the authors of your text write, "although each of these methods alone has its pitfalls of interpretation, if the results from studies using all three strategies converge, one can draw reasonably strong conclusions about the genetic influence on a disorder" (p. 45). Describe the weaknesses of each method taken alone and explain why convergence across these methods may eliminate alternative interpretations.

2. Freud's theories about the development of personality and disordered behavior were revolutionary and profoundly impacted the study of abnormal psychology. Yet today many believe his views caused more harm than good to the field of abnormal psychology. Consider, for example, the current controversy over repressed memories of early sexual abuse. In what way is this controversy a direct descendant of Freudian theory? How do you think Freud's psychosexual stages, when taken less specifically than he intended them to be, may be useful as a way of conceptualizing the development of the child?

3. We have seen a tragic increase in violent mass shootings in our high schools. In many cases, these murders are planned and carried out by classmates who are described as "loners" and "outcasts," with a fascination for weapons, and so on. List and discuss several biological, psychosocial, and sociocultural factors discussed in Chapter 2 that you believe might adequately explain what motivates these students to commit such crimes. What are some ways such causal factors may be targeted in order to prevent future crimes from occurring?

4. Culture influences both the type of mental disorders that may develop and also how they may be experienced. Is this evidence damaging to the biological viewpoint? Why or why not? Consider the term "sociocultural inheritance" (p. 73) as you answer this question.

5. Consider the psychosocial causal factors detailed in the chapter and describe the kind of childhood you think might be <u>most protective</u> against the later development of abnormal behavior. Support your answer by making reference to the results of empirical studies.

◊ CHAPTER 2 QUIZ

Circle the best of the four answers provided and check them according to answers provided at the back of this study guide. Be sure you understand why each answer is correct.

1. Exposure to stressful events that are handled successfully can foster self-esteem; in other words, some stressors paradoxically promote coping. This is called a(n): (p. 38)
    a. protective effect.
    b. inoculation effect.
    c. genotype-environment correlation.
    d. genotype-environment interaction.

2. After being released into the synaptic cleft, a neurotransmitter may be reabsorbed into the presynaptic axon button, a process called _____. (p. 42)
    a. re-uptake   c. recapture
    b. deactivation   d. active transport

3. A child is introverted. She tends to decline opportunities to play with her peers. Having only minimal social interactions with her peers enhances her introverted nature. This is an example of a (p. 44)
    a. genotype-environment interaction.
    b. genotype-environment correlation.
    c. genotype-phenotype interaction.
    d. genotype-phenotype correlation.

4. All of the following are examples of shared environmental influences EXCEPT: (pp. 45-46)
    a. socioeconomic class   c. poverty
    b. peer group   d. overcrowding

5. Which of the following is true? (p. 46)
    a. Strong genetic effects do not limit the strength of environmental influences.
    b. Genes provide a limit to potential.
    c. Genetic effects diminish with age.
    d. Disorders that run in families must be genetic.

6. Which of the following is NOT a possible consequence of being malnourished early in life? (p. 48)
   a. markedly lowered intelligence
   b. enhanced risk of attention-deficit disorder
   c. lowered resistance to disease
   d. increased vulnerability to accidents

7. According to Freud's psychoanalytic perspective, the source of all instinctual drives is the: (p. 51)
   a. ego.
   b. id.
   c. libido.
   d. superego.

8. The correct sequence of Freud's psychosexual stages of development is: (p. 53)
   a. anal, oral, phallic, latency, genital
   b. latency, oral, anal, phallic, genital
   c. oral, anal, phallic, genital, latency
   d. oral, anal, phallic, latency, genital

9. A mother and wife is being verbally abused by her husband. She hits her son frequently, often with little provocation. According to Freud, she is using the ego-defense mechanism of: (p. 53)
   a. displacement.
   b. reaction formation.
   c. projection.
   d. sublimation.

10. According to object-relations theory, the internal process in which a child incorporates symbolically important people in his or her life is called: (p. 55)
   a. assimilation.
   b. introjection.
   c. accommodation.
   d. secondary process thinking.

11. Who developed attachment theory? (p. 56)
   a. Harry Stack Sullivan
   b. Erik Erikson
   c. Alfred Adler
   d. John Bowlby

12. The form of learning in which an individual learns to achieve a desired goal is called: (p. 58)
   a. classical conditioning.
   b. instrumental (operant) conditioning.
   c. modeling.
   d. avoidance conditioning.

13. The process by which a response conditioned to a stimulus or set of stimulus conditions can be evoked by other, similar stimuli is called: (p. 59)
   a. generalization.
   b. discrimination.
   c. extinction.
   d. intermittent reinforcement.

14. The tendency to explain one's success as due to luck, as compared to hard work, is best categorized as an example of a specific _____: (p. 61)
   a. dysfunctional attribution style.
   b. contributory effect.
   c. proximal schema.
   d. internal representation.

15. A basic goal of psychosocial therapies is _____. (p. 64)
   a. accommodation   c. reduction of anxiety
   b. social skills training   d. assimilation

16. A _____ parental style is likely to produce a child who is impulsive and aggressive, spoiled, selfish, inconsiderate, and demanding, and who will exploit people for his or her own purposes. (p. 68)
   a. authoritative   c. permissive-indulgent
   b. authoritarian   d. neglectful-uninvolved

17. Which parenting style is high in both warmth and control? (p. 68)
   a. authoritative   c. permissive-indulgent
   b. authoritarian   d. neglectful-uninvolved

18. Thai children and adolescents, compared to their American counterparts, suffer from: (pp. 72-73)
   a. more overcontrolled problems but the same number of undercontrolled problems.
   b. more overcontrolled problems but fewer undercontrolled problems.
   c. fewer overcontrolled problems but more undercontrolled problems.
   d. the same number of overcontrolled problems but fewer undercontrolled problems.

19. The lower the socioeconomic class, the higher the incidence of abnormal behavior. For what disorder is this especially true? (pp. 73-74)
   a. depression   c. antisocial personality disorder
   b. social phobia   d. schizophrenia

20. The authors of your text suggest that because most disorders are the result of many causal factors, the model that might best help us understand the causes of and risk factors for abnormal behavior is the _____ model. (p. 76)
   a. psychosocial   c. developmental systems
   b. sociocultural   d. biopsychosocial

Chapter 3
Clinical Assessment and Treatment

◊ OVERVIEW

Chapter 3 opens with a review of commonly used physical and psychological assessment methods that are integrated into a clinical profile of a client. Assessment data allow mental health professionals not only to diagnose clients but also to choose the best treatment for them, as well as to evaluate the progress and outcome of treatment. Therapies are broadly either biological or psychological in nature; each type logically follows from its model of psychopathology, described in Chapter 2. Biologically based therapies are predominately psychopharmacological. Psychologically based therapies discussed include psychodynamic therapies, behavior therapies, cognitive and cognitive-behavioral therapies, humanistic-experiential therapies, and therapy for interpersonal relationships. Despite the large number of therapies offered at present, no single approach to psychotherapy has yet proven capable of handling the entire range of problems seen clinically. Consequently, the inclination to identify strongly with one approach or another is decreasing. Many therapists are familiar with a variety of techniques culled from several therapeutic approaches and use some or others depending on the types of problems a client may be experiencing. Chapter 3 closes with a discussion of the evaluation of treatment outcome, which depends on some of the same assessment methods reviewed at the beginning of the chapter.

◊ CHAPTER OUTLINE

I. Clinical Assessment
    A. The Dynamics of Clinical Assessment
    B. Assessment of the Physical Organism
        1. The Neurological Examination
        2. The Neuropsychological Examination
    C. Psychosocial Assessment
        1. Assessment Interviews
        2. The Clinical Observation of Behavior
        3. Intelligence Tests
            a) The Rorschach
            b) The Thematic Apperception Test
            c) Sentence-Completion Test
        4. Projective Personality Tests
        5. Objective Personality Tests
            a) The MMPI

    b) Advantages of Objective Personality Tests
  D. Integrating Assessment Data
    1. Ethical Issues in Assessment
    2. Incorporating Psychological Test Data into Therapy

II. Biologically Based Therapies
  A. Early Attempts at Biological Intervention
    1. Electroconvulsive Therapy
    2. Neurosurgery
  B. Psychopharmacological Methods of Treatment
    1. Antipsychotic Drugs
    2. Antidepressant Drugs
    3. Antianxiety Drugs
    4. Lithium and Other Mood-Stabilizing Drugs

III. Psychologically Based Therapies
  A. Psychodynamic Therapies
    1. Classical Psychoanalysis
    2. Psychodynamic Therapy Since Freud
    3. Evaluating Psychodynamic Therapies
  B. Behavior Therapies
    1. Guided Exposure
    2. Aversion Therapy
    3. Modeling
    4. Systematic Use of Reinforcement
      a) Response Shaping
      b) Token Economies
      c) Behavioral Contracting
    5. Biofeedback and Relaxation Training
    6. Evaluating Behavior Therapies
  C. Cognitive and Cognitive-Behavioral Therapies
    1. Rational Emotive Behavior Therapy
    2. Stress-Inoculation Therapy
    3. Beck's Cognitive Therapy
    4. Evaluating Cognitive-Behavioral Therapies
  D. Humanistic-Experiential Therapies
    1. Client-Centered Therapy
    2. Existential Therapy
    3. Gestalt Therapy
    4. Evaluating Humanistic-Experiential Therapies
  E. Therapy for Interpersonal Relationships
    1. Couples Counseling (Marital Therapy)
    2. Family System Therapy

IV. How Does One Measure Success in Psychotherapy?
   A. Objectifying and Quantifying Change
   B. Would Change Occur Anyway?
   C. Can Therapy Be Harmful?

V. Summary

◊ **LEARNING OBJECTIVES**

After studying this chapter, you should be able to:

1. Describe the basic elements of clinical assessment, including its nature and purpose and the relationship between diagnosis and treatment. (pp. 80-81)

2. Summarize the various techniques used to assess the structure and function of the brain. (pp. 81-84)

3. Compare structured and unstructured interviews as means of assessing psychosocial functioning. (pp. 84-85)

4. Discuss various tools for the clinical observation of behavior and identify the advantages of each. (pp. 85-86)

5. Explain the difference between projective and objective personality tests, and give examples of each type. (pp. 87-91)

6. Summarize some ethical issues and other considerations affecting the integration of assessment data for use in planning or changing treatment. (pp. 91-93)

7. Describe early attempts at biological intervention, and identify those that are still considered effective. (pp. 93-95)

8. Identify four major types of drugs commonly used to treat mental disorders, and discuss their applications, modes of action, and effectiveness. (pp. 95-102)

9. State the overall assumptions and goals of psychotherapy. (pp. 103-104)

10. Describe the basic goals and techniques of classical psychoanalysis, and trace the developments in psychodynamic therapy since Freud. (pp. 104-107)

11. Describe the principles and techniques of various behavior therapies and cognitive-behavioral therapies. (pp. 107-114)

12. Understand the assumption underlying humanistic-experiential therapies. (pp. 114-115)

13. Discuss the difficulties associated with attempting to evaluate the effectiveness of psychotherapy. (pp. 118-119)

◊ **TERMS YOU SHOULD KNOW**

---

clinical assessment (p. 80)

dynamic formulation (p. 81)

electroencephalogram (EEG) (p. 83)

computerized axial tomography (CAT scan) (p. 83)

magnetic resonance imaging (MRI) (p. 83)

positron emission tomography (PET scan) (pp. 83-84)

functional MRI (fMRI) (p. 84)

neuropsychological assessment (p. 84)

unstructured interviews (p. 85)

structured interviews (p. 85)

self-monitoring (p. 86)

rating scales (p. 86)

intelligence tests (pp. 86-87)

projective tests (p. 87)

Rorschach Test (pp. 87-88)

Thematic Apperception Test (TAT) (p. 88)

sentence-completion test (p. 88)

objective tests (pp. 88-89)

Minnesota Multiphasic Personality Inventory (MMPI-2) (pp. 89-91)

electroconvulsive therapy (ECT) (pp. 93-94)

neurosurgery (p. 94)

prefrontal lobotomy (pp. 94-95)

psychopharmacology (p. 95)

antipsychotic drugs (p. 96, pp. 98-99)

antidepressant drugs (99-101)

antianxiety drugs (pp. 101-102)

psychotherapy (p. 103)

psychodynamic therapy (p. 104)

free association (p. 105)

manifest content (p. 105)

latent content (p. 105)

resistance (p. 105)

transference (pp. 105-106)

countertransference (p. 106)

behavior therapy (p. 107)

systematic desensitization (pp. 107-108)

in vivo exposure (p. 108)

in vitro exposure (p. 108)

aversion therapy (pp. 108-109)

modeling (p. 109)

response shaping (p. 109)

token economy (pp. 109-110)

behavioral contracting (p. 110)

biofeedback (pp. 110-111)

cognitive or cognitive-behavioral therapy (p. 111)

rational emotive behavior therapy (REBT) (pp. 111-112)

stress-inoculation therapy (SIT) (pp. 112-113)

client-centered (person-centered) therapy (pp. 114-115)

couples counseling (p. 116)

marital therapy (p. 116)

family systems approach (p. 117)

conjoint family therapy (p. 117)

structural family therapy (p. 117)

◊ NAMES YOU SHOULD KNOW

Hermann Rorschach (p. 87)

C.D. Morgan (p. 88)

Henry Murray (p. 88)

Starke Hathaway (p. 89)

J.C. McKinley (p. 89)

John Cade (p. 102)

Sigmund Freud (p. 104)

Harry Stack Sullivan (p. 106)

Albert Ellis (pp. 111-112)

Donald Meichenbaum (pp. 112-113)

Aaron Beck (p. 113)

Carl Rogers (pp. 114-115)

Frederick (Fritz) Perls (p. 115)

Virginia Satir (p. 117)

◊ CONCEPTS TO MASTER

1. Explain the difference between diagnosis and clinical assessment and list several components that must be integrated into the dynamic formulation. (pp. 80-81)

2. Describe the five important neurological procedures, explaining what makes each one especially valuable. (pp. 83-84)

   EEG

   CAT scan

   MRI

   PET

   fMRI

3. Explain why neuropsychological assessment is useful in assessment. (p. 84)

4. List, describe, and explain the purpose of the five tests included in the Halstead-Reitan battery. (p. 84)

5. Compare and contrast structured and unstructured assessment interviews. Which is more reliable? (p. 85)

6. Explain the use of rating scales in clinical observation and self-reports. (p. 86)

7. List some assumptions behind the use of projective tests. How do they differ from objective tests? Describe the use of the Rorschach Test and the Thematic Apperception Test (TAT) in clinical assessment. (pp. 87-89)

8. List some advantages of objective personality tests. What is the MMPI-2, and what are its uses in clinical assessment? (pp. 88-91)

9. Define the concept of "empirical keying" and summarize the steps involved in this approach to developing the MMPI. (p. 89)

10. Describe five ethical issues that clinicians should be aware of when evaluating test results. (p. 92)

11. List three reasons why clinicians often fail to incorporate psychological test data into therapy. (p. 93)

12. Describe the discovery and use of electroconvulsive therapy (ECT). (pp. 93-94)

13. Describe the treatment of prefrontal lobotomy and its effects on a patient. (pp. 94-95)

14. Describe the effects and side effects of antipsychotic drugs. (pp. 98-99)

15. Describe the effects and side effects of antidepressant drugs. (pp. 99-101)

16. Describe the effects and side effects of antianxiety drugs. (pp. 101-102)

17. Describe the use of lithium in the treatment of manic disorders, including its effects and side effects. (p. 102)

18. Outline the major features of the therapeutic relationship that enhance psychotherapy and promote better treatment outcomes. Note that these are "common" or "nonspecific" factors in the sense that they have little to do with specific techniques or specific theoretical approaches. (pp. 103-104)

19. Explain how the four basic techniques of psychoanalysis are used in psychodynamic therapies. (pp. 104-106)

Free Association

Analysis of Dreams

Analysis of Resistance

Analysis of Transference

20. Summarize the changes in psychodynamic therapy that have taken place since Freud's time. (p. 106)

21. Evaluate the effectiveness of the psychodynamic approach as a treatment for maladaptive behavior. (pp. 106-107)

22. Explain how behavior therapies differ from psychodynamic therapies. (p. 107)

23. Explain how the behavioral technique of systematic desensitization (a form of guided exposure) works. (p. 107)

24. Compare and contrast in vivo exposure procedures with in vitro (imagined) exposure procedures. Which of the two seems to work better? (p. 108)

25. Describe aversion therapy, and give several examples of its use in treating behavioral disorders. (pp. 108-109)

26. Describe modeling and explain how it can be used in the treatment of mental disorders. (p. 109)

27. Explain what is meant by systematic use of reinforcement and discuss three general techniques based on this plan. (pp. 109-110)

28. Describe biofeedback, list three steps in the biofeedback approach to therapy, and describe several of its applications to maladaptive behaviors. (p. 110-111)

29. List and explain three advantages that behavior therapy has compared with other psychotherapies and indicate why it cannot be a cure-all. (p. 111)

30. What are the two main themes that characterize all cognitive-behavioral therapies? (p. 111)

31. Compare and contrast Ellis' rational emotive behavior therapy (REBT), Meichenbaum's stress-inoculation therapy (SIT), and Beck's cognitive therapy. (pp. 111-113)

32. Compare the outcomes of cognitive-behavioral therapies with those of other psychotherapies and describe some trends in its use. (pp. 113-114)

33. What is the central focus of humanistic-experiential therapies, and what assumption underlies their use? (pp. 114-115)

34. Discuss-client-centered therapy, existential therapy, and gestalt therapy. (pp. 114-115)

35. List some criticisms of the humanistic-experiential therapies. (p. 115)

36. Describe two types of interpersonal therapy and the assumption that underlies both types. (pp. 116-118)

37. List the various sources of information used to evaluate the effectiveness of psychological treatment and describe the limitations of each. (p. 118)

38. Define eclecticism and discuss the relaxing of boundaries between the various schools of psychotherapy. (Highlight 3.7, p. 119)

Clinical assessment

1. For most clinical purposes, knowledge about an individual's _____, _____ _____, personality characteristics, and environmental pressures and resources is more important than a formal diagnosis. (p. 81)

2. The material gained through assessment is integrated into a consistent and meaningful picture, often called the _____ _____, that should lead to an explanation of why the person is engaging in maladaptive behavior and to hypotheses about the person's future behavior as well. (p. 81)

3. An EEG is a graphic record of the brain's _____ _____. Significant divergences from the normal pattern of brain impulses can reflect abnormalities of brain function, such as might be caused by a brain tumor or other lesion. (p. 83)

4. Functional MRI measures changes in _____ _____ (i.e., blood flow) of specific areas of brain tissue which in turn depend on _____ activity in those specific regions. Ongoing psychological activity, such as _____, _____, and thoughts, can thus be "mapped," at least in principle, revealing the specific areas of the brain that appear to be involved in their neurophysiological mediation. (p. 84)

5. Match each subtest of the Halstead-Reitan neuropsychological battery with the correct description of its purpose: (p. 84)

Subtest	Purpose
___ Halstead Category Test	a. Determines if an individual can identify spoken words.
___ Tactual Performance Test	b. Measures the ability to learn and remember.
___ Rhythm Test	c. Measures the speed at which one can depress a lever. Gives clues to the extent and location of brain damage.
___ Speech Sounds Perception	d. Measures attention and sustained concentration.
___ Finger Oscillation Test	e. Measures motor speed, response to the unfamiliar, and ability to learn tactile and kinesthetic cues.

6. The main purpose of direct observation is to learn more about the person's psychological functioning through the objective description of behavior in various contexts. Ideally, such observations would occur in the individual's _____ _____, but they are typically confined to _____ or _____ settings. In addition, many clinicians ask their patients to report their own behavior, thoughts, and feelings as they occur in various natural settings—a procedure called _____. (pp. 85-86)

7. Match the following psychological tests with the appropriate description of each test's purpose: (pp. 86-91)

Psychological Test	Purpose
___ Rorschach Test	a. Scale for rating clinical symptoms
___ Thematic Apperception Test (TAT)	b. Intelligence scale for children
___ Minnesota Multiphasic Personality Inventory (MMPI-2)	c. Intelligence scale for adults
___ WAIS-III	d. Projective test using inkblots
___ WISC-III	e. Projective test using pictures
___ Brief Psychiatric Rating Scale (BPRS)	f. Objective personality test
___ Sentence-Completion Test	g. Test that pinpoints clues to problems, attitudes, and symptoms

8. Place a 1, 2, or 3 in front of the following steps to indicate the sequence in which the step appeared during the construction of the MMPI. (p. 89)

   ___ Scales were constructed.
   ___ Item analyses were performed.
   ___ Items were administered to large groups of normal individuals and psychiatric patients.

9. Complete the chart below that compares the overall strengths and weaknesses of projective and objective tests. (pp. 87-91)

Test	Strengths	Weaknesses
Projective		Interpretations are subjective, unreliable, and difficult to validate; require trained staff to administer and score
Objective	Cost-effective, reliable, objective; can be administered and scored by computer	

10. The following factors should be kept in mind when evaluating test results: (p. 92)
    1. potential cultural bias of the instrument or the clinician
    2. theoretical orientation of the clinician
    3. _____
    4. insufficient validation
    5. _____

Biologically based therapies

11. After awakening several minutes after ECT, the patient has _____ for the period immediately preceding the therapy. With repeated treatments, usually administered three times weekly, the patient gradually becomes _____. (p. 94)

12. The advent of _____ led to a widespread decrease in the use of neurosurgery, especially prefrontal lobotomy. (p. 95)

13. Define psychopharmacology.(p. 95)

14. Fill in the missing information in the following chart that summarizes the four types of drugs commonly used for mental disorders: (pp. 95-102)

Class of Drugs	Biological Effect	Behavioral Effect	Trade Name(s)
Antipsychotic		Reduce the intensity of psychotic symptoms (including delusions and hallucinations)	Thorazine
Antidepressant (Tricyclics)	Produce functional decreases in available norepinephrine and serotonin		
Antianxiety (Benzodiazepines)		Selectively diminish generalized anxiety	
Antimanic or mood stabilizers (Lithium)		Resolve 70% of manic episodes	

15. One particularly troublesome side effect of long-term antipsychotic drug treatment is the development of _____ _____ , a disfiguring disturbance of motor control, particularly of the facial muscles. (p. 99)

16. Why aren't monoamine oxidase (MAO) inhibitors widely used today? (p. 100)

17. Why are the SSRIs currently considered the preferred class of antidepressant drugs? (p. 100)

18. Explain why if antidepressants are discontinued when symptoms have just remitted, there is a high probability of relapse. (p. 101)

19. All antianxiety drugs have the potential of inducing _____ when used unwisely or in excess. (pp. 101-102)

20. There can be no doubt at this point concerning the remarkable effectiveness of lithium in at least partially resolving about ___ percent of clearly defined manic states. (p. 102)

Psychologically based therapies

21. The client's major contribution to the therapeutic relationship is his or her _____. Almost as important is a client's _____ of receiving help. (p. 103)

22. To at least some extent, effective therapy depends on a good _____ between client and therapist. Hence, a therapist's own _____ is necessarily a factor of some importance in determining therapeutic outcomes. (pp. 103-104)

23. Briefly explain how the analyst uses the four basic techniques of classical psychoanalysis. (p. 105)

Technique	How It Is Used
Free association	
Analysis of dreams	
Analysis of resistance	
Analysis of transference	

24. Indicate whether each of the following statements represents a valid criticism of classic psychodynamic therapy by circling the correct response: (p. 106)
   a. It is time-consuming and expensive.   True or False
   b. It is based on a questionable approach to human nature.   True or False
   c. It fails to bring its clients new insights into themselves.   True or False
   d. It neglects a client's immediate problems.   True or False
   e. There is inadequate proof of its effectiveness.   True or False

25. Systematic desensitization begins when a client constructs a(n) _____ _____. (p. 107)

26. Actual exposure is referred to as ____ _____ exposure. It has been shown to be ____ effective than imaginal (in vitro) exposure. (p. 108)

27. Aversion therapy involves modification of behavior by _____, which can be of two types. What are these types? (p. 108)

28. Modeling involves learning skills through _____. (p. 109)

29. Briefly describe each of the following reinforcement techniques: (pp. 109-110)

a. Response Shaping

b. Token Economies

c. Behavioral Contracting

30. What are five advantages of using tokens as reinforcers for appropriate behavior? (p. 110)

31. What are the three steps involved in biofeedback? (p. 110)

a.

b.

c.

32. Respond true or false to the following statements about behavior therapy. (p. 111)

a. The treatment is precise.   True or False
b. Behavior therapy is particularly successful in the treatment of
    Axis II disorders.   True or False
c. Behavior therapy techniques are important in the treatment of
    sexual dysfunction.   True or False

33. What are the two main themes that characterize cognitive-behavioral therapy? (p. 111)
a.

b.

34. Complete the chart below to summarize two different cognitive-behavioral therapies. (pp. 111-113)

Therapeutic Approach	Description
Rational Emotive Behavior Therapy (REBT)	a. This approach was developed by _____. (p. 112)
	b. The REBT therapist disputes irrational beliefs by _____. (p. 112)
Stress-Inoculation Therapy (SIT)	a. Stress-inoculation training usually involves three stages. Briefly describe what happens at each of the stages: (p. 113) 1. Cognitive preparation 2. Skill acquisition and rehearsal 3. Application and practice

35. Beck's cognitive therapy was originally developed in order to treat _____. Instead of accomplishing change through the use of debate and _____, as is common in REBT, therapist and client formulate the client's beliefs and expectations as _____ to be tested. (p. 113)

36. How does Beck's type of cognitive therapy for depression compare with drug treatment? (p. 114)

37. On what major assumption are humanistic-experiential therapies based? (p. 114)

38. Client-centered therapy was developed by _____ and is based on the goal of helping clients accept and _____. Gestalt therapy, on the other hand, was developed by _____ and emphasizes the need to _____ thought, feeling, and action into one's self-awareness. (pp. 114-115)

39. List some techniques that therapists use in couples counseling (marital therapy). (p. 116)

40. The family system approach is based on the assumption that the problem manifested by a(n) _____ is often only a symptom of a larger family problem. (p. 117)

41. Define conjoint family therapy and structural family therapy. (p. 117)

How does one measure success in psychotherapy?

42. Most researchers today would agree that psychotherapy is ____ effective than no treatment. (p. 119)

43. In as many as ____ percent of cases, the client is worse off than if psychotherapy had never been undertaken. (p. 119)

◊ CRITICAL THINKING ABOUT DIFFICULT TOPICS

1. There has been a good deal of criticism of the Rorschach test and other projective tests. Do you think that there is anything valuable to be learned from the projective testing of a person? In other words, knowing what you now know about the questionable reliability and validity of projective testing, would you want to ban its use? Consider the possibility of severely limiting the scope of the conclusions drawn from responses to these measures and ask yourself whether any information of value to the clinician might remain.

2. In his 1997 book *Listening to Prozac*, Peter Kramer expressed surprise and concern that an antidepressant drug that should ameliorate depressive symptoms should also alter one's personality. Is this surprising to you? It seems plausible that those trained under a disease model would expect "medicines" to treat only "diseases" and not to affect other behavior. How might it be possible for pharmacological drugs to exert their primary effect on restructuring brain-behavior relationships, while at the same time affecting symptoms of behavior disorders? Consider the biopsychosocial model as you address this question.

3. Are the psychologically based therapies biased in favor of one or another race, ethnicity, or gender? Consider the client characteristics a successful treatment outcome is thought to depend on. Do any of these characteristics vary according to gender, race, or ethnicity? Think also about the research presented on p. 104 regarding client-therapist ethnic match and mismatch as you answer this question. Also consider that behavior therapies and cognitive-behavioral therapies have sometimes been criticized for being too academically oriented. Do you think that this criticism has merit?

4. The authors of the text modestly conclude, "Most researchers today would agree that psychotherapy is more effective than no treatment" (p. 119). Do you think that this effectiveness has little or nothing to do with the specific treatment offered to a client, but rather stems from the client's characteristics (e.g., abilities, motivations, and expectancies) and response to the general fact of being treated? If so, how do we know that the numerous treatment methods derived from the psychosocial model are at all effective? What kind of research might be conducted to help answer this question?

5. Each of the psychologically based psychotherapies reviewed in this chapter is based on the assumption that specific aspects of its approach determine a successful treatment outcome. On the other hand, many elements of these psychotherapies are common to all of them and often termed "common factors." It has been argued that such common factors account for much of the success claimed by psychotherapy. Consider Ellis' rational emotive behavior therapy (REBT), Meichenbaum's stress-inoculation therapy (SIT), and Beck's cognitive therapy (CT). Which elements are common across these three therapies, and which elements are unique to each?

◊ CHAPTER 3 QUIZ

Circle the best of the four answers provided and check them according to answers provided at the back of this study guide. Be sure you understand why each answer is correct.

1. Which type of mental health professional is trained to handle mild adjustment problems pertaining to education, marriage, or occupation? (p. 82)
   a. clinical psychologist
   b. counseling psychologist
   c. psychiatrist
   d. psychoanalyst

2. A neurological diagnostic aid that reveals how an organ is functioning by depicting areas of differential metabolic activity is the: (p. 83)
   a. PET scan.
   b. CAT scan.
   c. EEG.
   d. MRI.

3. According to the text, the rating scale specifically targeted for depression that has almost become the standard for selecting clinically depressed research subjects is the: (p. 86)
   a. Beck Depression Inventory.
   b. Schedule for Rating Depressive Temperament.
   c. Leeds Depression Rating Scale.
   d. Hamilton Rating Scale for Depression.

4. The aim of a projective test is to: (p. 87)
   a. predict a patient's future behavior.
   b. compare a patient's responses to those of persons who are known to have mental disorders.
   c. assess the way a patient perceives ambiguous stimuli.
   d. assess the role of organic factors in a patient's thinking.

5. Which of the following is not true of projective tests? (pp. 87-88)
   a. Their use has declined over the years.
   b. They tend to be unreliable.
   c. They are highly structured.
   d. They take considerable time to administer and interpret.

6. Some clinicians have criticized the MMPI-2 for being too: (p. 91)
   a. mechanistic.
   b. expensive.
   c. objective.
   d. superficial.

7. All of the following were suggested as possible reasons for the failure to incorporate psychological assessment data into therapy *except*: (p. 93)
    a. lack of training.
    b. theoretical bias.
    c. cost.
    d. insufficient validation.

8. Which of the following caused an immediate decrease in the widespread use of neurosurgical procedures in this country? (p. 95)
    a. a 1951 law banning all such operations
    b. the advent of electroconvulsive therapy (ECT)
    c. the advent of the major antipsychotic drugs
    d. the unusually high mortality rate

9. Antipsychotic, antidepressant, antianxiety, and lithium compounds are all referred to as _____ drugs. (p. 96)
    a. hallucinogenic
    b. mind-expanding
    c. narcotic
    d. psychotropic

10. The unique quality of antipsychotic drugs is their ability to: (p. 96)
    a. calm patients down.
    b. put patients to sleep.
    c. reduce patients' anxiety.
    d. reduce the intensity of delusions and hallucinations.

11. The immediate *short*-term effects of the tricyclic antidepressants serve to: (p. 100)
    a. reduce central nervous system arousal.
    b. reduce intracranial pressure by absorbing cerebral spinal fluid.
    c. increase the availability of lithium in the central nervous system for absorption.
    d. increase the availability of serotonin and norepinephrine in the synapses.

12. Lithium compounds are used in the treatment of: (p. 102)
    a. anxiety.
    b. hyperactivity and specific learning disabilities.
    c. manic disorders.
    d. hallucinations and delusions.

13. According to the text, which of the following is *not* a major contributor to the therapeutic relationship? (pp. 103-104)
    a. client's motivation
    b. clinician's personality
    c. client's expectation of receiving help
    d. client's emotional reactivity

14. All of the following are major therapeutic techniques in classical psychoanalysis *except*: (p. 105)
    a. analysis of dreams
    b. analysis of transference
    c. analysis of resistance
    d. analysis of projection

15. Contemporary psychodynamic approaches to therapy tend to place an emphasis on: (p. 106)
    a. early repressed sexuality.
    b. interpersonal functioning.
    c. long-term treatment.
    d. childhood events.

16. Aversion therapy reduces maladaptive behavior by following it with: (p. 108)
    a. a request for the client to avert his or her eyes from the stimulus.
    b. negative reinforcement.
    c. punishment.
    d. stimuli diverting the client's attention.

17. Which of the following is *not* an example of contingency management (i.e., systematic use of reinforcement)? (pp. 109-110)
    a. token economy
    b. behavioral contracting
    c. response shaping
    d. modeling

18. In which of the following therapies do the therapist and client engage in experiments to disconfirm hypotheses about the client's beliefs and expectations? (p. 113)
    a. SIT
    b. REBT
    c. Beck's CT
    d. Gestalt

19. Stress-inoculation therapy (SIT) has been successfully used with all of the following problems *except*: (p. 113)
    a. Type A behavior
    b. mania
    c. pain
    d. mild anxiety

20. Which of the following is untrue of Gestalt therapy? (p. 115)
    a. It is commonly used in a group setting.
    b. Integrating thought, feeling, and action into one's self-awareness is important.
    c. Unconditional positive regard from the therapist is critical.
    d. Clients are expected to "take care of unfinished business."

21. Happily married couples tend to differ from unhappily married couples in all of the following ways *except*: (p. 116)
    a. using less nonverbal communication
    b. remaining best friends
    c. using more problem-solving behavior
    d. keeping channels of communication open

22. Which of the following problems has structural family therapy been shown to help? (p. 117)
    a. reactive depression
    b. hypochondriasis
    c. anorexia nervosa
    d. schizophrenia

◊ OVERVIEW

Chapter 4 begins with a detailed discussion of stress—a topic of increasing concern as modern life becomes more and more pressured. A definition of stress is followed with discussions of the factors that predispose us to experience stress and how we respond to stress. The authors then turn to the biological and psychological effects of severe stress. Experiencing common life stressors may precipitate what is known as adjustment disorder; experiencing severe or catastrophic stress may cause acute or post-traumatic stress disorder. The reasons why catastrophic stress leads to the development of post-traumatic stress disorder in some people, while others are spared, is taken up next. The kinds of catastrophes that may engender acute or post-traumatic stress disorder are discussed in some detail—including the traumas of rape, military combat, and severe threats to personal safety and security. The chapter closes with an examination of the types of treatments aimed at preventing stress reactions, or limiting their intensity and duration once they have become problematic.

◊ CHAPTER OUTLINE

I.   What Is Stress?
    A. Factors Predisposing a Person to Stress
        1. The Nature of the Stressor
        2. The Person's Perception of the Stressor
        3. The Individual's Stress Tolerance
        4. A Lack of External Resources and Social Supports
    B. Responding to Stress

II. The Effects of Severe Stress
    A. Biological Effects of Stress
        1. Stress and the Sympathetic Nervous System
        2. Stress and the Immune System
    B. Psychological Effects of Long-Term Stress

III. Adjustment Disorder: Reactions to Common Life Stressors

IV. Acute and Post-Traumatic Stress Disorders: Reactions to Catastrophic Events
    A. Distinguishing Between Acute Stress Disorder and Post-Traumatic Stress Disorder
    B. Causal Factors in Post-Traumatic Stress
    C. The Trauma of Rape
        1. Factors Influencing the Experience of Post-Traumatic Stress after Rape
        2. Long-Term Effects
        3. Counseling Rape Victims
    D. The Trauma of Military Combat
        1. Clinical Picture in Combat-Related Stress
        2. Prisoners of War and Holocaust Survivors
        3. Causal Factors in Wartime Stress Problems
            a) Temperament
            b) Psychosocial Factors
            c) Sociocultural Factors
        4. Long-Term Effects
    E. Severe Threats to Personal Safety and Security
        1. Forced Relocation
        2. The Trauma of Being Held Hostage
        3. Psychological Trauma Among Victims of Torture

V. Treatment and Prevention of Stress Disorders
    A. Stress Prevention or Reduction
    B. Treatment of Post-Traumatic Stress Symptoms
        1. Medications
        2. Crisis Intervention Therapy
        3. Direct Therapeutic Exposure

VI. Unresolved Issues: The Abuse of PTSD and Other Stress-Related Diagnoses

VII. Summary

◊ LEARNING OBJECTIVES

After studying this chapter, you should be able to:

1. Define stressor, stress, and coping strategies, and discuss factors that increase or decrease a person's vulnerability to stress. (pp. 123-125)

2. Contrast the two major categories of stress responses, and outline the possible physical and psychological negative effects of severe stress. (pp. 125-129)

3. Characterize the elements of the DSM-IV diagnosis of adjustment disorder, and list some factors that increase the risk of adjustment disorder. (pp. 130; pp. 124-126)

4. List the DSM-IV diagnostic criteria for acute stress disorder and post-traumatic stress disorder, and compare and contrast the two disorders. (pp. 130-134)

5. Summarize the major features of people's reactions to catastrophic events, including rape, combat, and severe threats to safety and security. (pp. 134-142)

6. Summarize the approaches that have been used to treat or prevent stress disorders and evaluate their effectiveness. (pp. 144-145)

◊ TERMS YOU SHOULD KNOW

stressors (p. 123)

stress (pp. 123-124)

coping strategies (p. 124)

eustress (p. 124)

distress (p. 124)

crisis (p. 124)

stress tolerance (p. 125)

task-oriented response (p. 125)

defense-oriented response (pp. 125-126)

personality (psychological) decompensation (p. 126)

general adaptation syndrome (p. 127; Figure 4.1, p. 127)

psychoneuroimmunology (p. 129)

adjustment disorder (p. 130)

acute stress disorder (ASD) (p. 130; Table 4.2, p. 131)

post-traumatic stress disorder (PTSD) (p. 130, pp. 132-134; Table 4.3, p. 133)

disaster syndrome (pp. 132-133)

stress-inoculation training (SIT) (p. 144)

crisis intervention (pp. 144-145)

◊ NAME YOU SHOULD KNOW

Hans Selye (pp. 127-128)

◊ CONCEPTS TO MASTER

1. Compare and contrast the concepts of stressors, stress, and coping strategies, noting particularly the interrelation among them. (pp. 123-124)

2. Describe how the nature of the stressor, an individual's perception of it, his or her stress tolerance, and his or her external resources and supports can modify the effects of stress. (pp. 124-125)

3. Differentiate between *task-oriented* and *defense-oriented* responses to stress. (pp. 125-126)

4. Describe two ego-defense mechanisms that are examples of defense-oriented responses to stress. (p. 126)

5. Describe the three phases of Selye's general adapation syndrome. Compare and contrast these with the three stages of personality decompensation. (p. 127, p. 129)

Phase 1: Alarm Reaction

Phase 2: Stage of Resistance

Phase 3: Exhaustion

6. Describe the effect of stress on the sympathetic nervous system and list four components of the "fight-or-flight" response. (p. 128)

7. What is the impact of stress on the immune system? (pp. 128-129)

8. Describe the symptoms of adjustment disorder. (p. 130)

9. List some examples of the severe stressors that may precipitate either acute or post-traumatic stress disorder. (p. 130)

10. Compare and contrast acute stress disorder (ASD) and post-traumatic stress disorder (PTSD). What is the difference between acute and delayed PTSD, and what is the controversy about the frequency of diagnosis of the latter? (p. 130; p. 140; pp. 146-147)

11. List the three stages of the "disaster syndrome," indicating at which stage post-traumatic stress disorder may develop. Then identify three intense emotions that may complicate the picture. (pp. 132-133)

12. List five areas of life functioning disrupted by rape (McCann et al., 1988). (p. 135)

13. Describe the factors that influence the development of post-traumatic stress after rape. (p. 135)

14. Trace the history of the trauma of military combat from World War II to the present. (p. 136)

15. Describe the results of the study by Laufer, Brett, and Gallops (1985), in which the self-reports of Vietnam veterans were grouped according to three levels of experienced stress. (p. 136)

16. In spite of variations in experience, the general clinical picture of combat stress has been surprisingly uniform for those soldiers who develop it. Describe this clinical picture. (pp. 136-137)

17. Explain why the post-traumatic stress of some prisoners of war and Holocaust survivors is attributed to both psychological and biological stressors. (pp. 137-138)

18. List and describe three types of causal factors in the development of wartime stress reactions. (pp. 138-140)

19. Describe the results of the 1994 study conducted by Basoglu and colleagues in which Turkish activist prisoners who had been tortured were studied. (p. 142)

20. Explain why some noradrenergic brain systems are believed to be involved in producing some of the symptoms of PTSD and how the drug yohimbine was used to test this hypothesis. (Highlight 4.4, p. 143)

21. Describe the relationship of uncontrollable stress-induced analgesia (SIA) to symptoms of PTSD. Explain the roles of unpredictable and uncontrollable stressors in the development of PTSD. (Highlight 4.4, p. 143)

22. Describe the strategies that are useful for prevention or reduction of maladaptive responses to stress. (p. 144)

23. Describe three treatment approaches for patients with PTSD. (pp. 144-145)

24. Explain the unresolved issue of using PTSD and other stress-related diagnoses in court cases. (pp. 146-147)

◊ STUDY QUESTIONS

What is stress?

1. Adjustive demands, also known as _____, create effects within an organism that are known as _____. (pp. 123-124)

2. Why are "crises" especially stressful? (p. 124)

3. The nature of the stressor is known to influence the degree of disruption that occurs. Also disruptive are the person's _____ of the stressor, his or her stress _____, and a lack of external _____ and social _____. (pp. 124-125)

4. What are the two challenges with which a person is confronted in coping with stress? (p. 125)

5. What are the two common types of defense-oriented responses? (p. 126)

6. When are ego-defense mechanisms considered maladaptive? (p. 126)

The effects of severe stress

7. Fill in the phases of Selye's general adaption syndrome: (1)_____; (2)_____; and (3)_____.

8. Describe how severe stress affects the sympathetic nervous system. (p. 128)

9. Describe how severe stress affects the immune system. (pp. 128-129)

10. Personality decompensation under extreme stress appears to follow a course resembling biological decompensation. State the biological response of the individual during each stage. (p. 129)

   Alarm and mobilization:

   Resistance:

   Exhaustion:

Adjustment disorder: Reactions to common life stressors

11. Adjustment disorder is said to be present when a person whose response to a common stressor such as _____, _____, _____, or _____ is maladaptive and occurs within ___ month(s) of the stressor. (p. 130)

12. In adjustment disorder, the person's maladjustment lessens or disappears under what two scenarios? (p. 130)

13. What feature distinguishes acute stress disorder from post-traumatic stress disorder? (p. 130)

14. What feature distinguishes between delayed and acute post-traumatic stress disorder? (p. 130)

15. Describe the behavior that is typical of each stage of the disaster syndrome. (pp. 132-133)

       Shock stage

       Suggestible stage

       Recovery stage

16. Give specific examples of symptoms for three of the four major symptom categories that typify post-traumatic stress disorder. (Table 4.3, p. 133)

   a. The experience of intense fear, helplessness, or horror after the trauma

   b. Persistent reexperiencing of the trauma
     Example:

   c. Persistent avoidance of trauma stimuli and numbing of general responsiveness
     Example:

   d. Persistent symptoms of increased arousal
     Example:

17. Rubonis and Bickman (1991) concluded that _____ percent of people who had experienced disasters showed psychological adjustment problems. (p. 134)

18. What factors determine whether someone develops post-traumatic stress disorder or not? (p. 134)

19. In all cases of post-traumatic stress, _____ appears to be a key causal factor. (p. 134)

20. Discuss how each of the following variables is thought to affect a woman's response to rape: (p. 135)

    a. Relationship to the offender

    b. Age

    c. Marital status

21. According to the government figures presented in your text, the percent of soldiers who suffered combat exhaustion _____ in each successive war from World War II to Vietnam. (p. 136)

22. What is the relationship between the degree of combat exposure and later development of PTSD? (p. 136)

23. Most physically wounded soldiers have shown ____ anxiety or combat exhaustion than those who were not wounded, except in cases of permanent mutilation. (p. 137)

24. Those incarcerated in a POW or concentration camp have been shown to have a higher _____ _____ after return to civilian life. (p. 138)

25. In a study of memory and cognitive performance, Sutker and colleagues (1992) found that POW survivors who had experienced the greatest trauma-induced _____ _____ performed significantly worse on _____ tasks. (p. 138)

26. Personal _____ sometimes stemming from parental overprotection is commonly cited as making a soldier more vulnerable to combat stress. (p. 139)

27. Clarity and acceptability of war goals, identification with the combat unit, esprit de corps, and quality of leadership are sociocultural factors that play an important part in determining a person's adjustment to combat. Describe how each of these has an effect. (pp. 139-140)

28. What is controversial about assessment of the frequency of diagnosis of delayed post-traumatic stress disorder? (p. 140)

29. Refugees face not only the trauma of being uprooted from their homes, but also the stress of adapting to a new and unfamiliar culture. Among those who come to the U.S., the Southeast Asians arriving after 1975 have had the most difficult adjustment. A ten-year longitudinal study of Hmong refugees from Laos found many signs of improvement after ten years in the U.S.: 55% were employed, the percentage on welfare had dropped from 53% to 29%, and symptoms of phobia, somatization, and low self-esteem had also improved. On the other hand, considerable problems remained. What were these? (p. 141)

30. Basoglu, Mineka, and colleagues (1997) found that _____ for trauma is a critical protective factor for lessening the psychological effects of torture. Earlier, Basoglu and Mineka (1992) had found that whether the torture was perceived by the victim as _____ and _____ determined how much impact the torture had. (p. 142)

31. Many of the symptoms of emotional numbing seen in people with PTSD may be caused by _____. (p. 143)

32. Post, Weiss, and Smith (1995) found that soldiers who had been _____ in childhood were more likely to develop PTSD during the Vietnam war. This is because prior experience with stressors can _____ an organism. (p. 143)

Treatment and prevention of stress disorders

33. In general, the more _____ a personality and the more _____ a person's life situation, the more quickly he or she will recover from a severe stress reaction. (p. 144)

34. Many people called to the scene of a disaster to assist victims later experience _____. (p. 144)

35. One strategy to prevent the development of stress is called _____ _____ _____. Describe the three stages of this strategy. (p. 144)

36. Describe three strategies for the treatment of PTSD. (pp. 144-145)

37. What is the most important factor, from the standpoint of legal precedent, in establishing legal justification for the PTSD defense? (pp. 146-147)

◊ CRITICAL THINKING ABOUT DIFFICULT TOPICS

1. According to the authors of your text, "All situations, positive and negative, that require adjustment can be stressful" (p. 124). Thus, such events as getting married, being promoted to a better position, graduating from college, and starting a new and attractive job all constitute positive stress or eustress, as opposed to negative stress or distress. Do you think that positive stressors are as pathogenic as negative stressors? Can you envision a new marriage or a new job having negative consequences without negative stressors also being involved? Consider "interpersonal conflict in marriage" and "inability to cope with new obligations in one's job" as stressors with both positive and negative components.

2. The authors of the text state that in the case of delayed post-traumatic stress disorder, "...the frequency with which this disorder has recently been diagnosed in some settings suggests that its increased use is as much a result of its plausibility and popularity as of its true incidence" (p. 140). If this assertion is true, what does it tell you about the validity of diagnosis? If a diagnosis can be influenced so strongly by plausibility and popularity, should we view diagnoses with some skepticism?

3. "Today's stress can be tomorrow's vulnerability" (p. 123). Explain what this statement means. As you do so, consider the concept of the diathesis-stress model developed in Chapter 2. Cite evidence, some of which is detailed on p. 143, that supports this quotation.

4. "Among returning World War II POWs from the Pacific area, Wolff (1960) found that, within the first 6 years, nine times as many died from tuberculosis as would have been expected in civilian life, four times as many from gastrointestinal disorders, over twice as many from cancer, heart disease, and suicide, and three times as many from accidents" (p. 138). Why do you think this result was obtained? In other words, what possible pathways of causation—biological and psychological—might have operated to produce this effect?

5. Consider the research conducted by Sutker and colleagues (1992) comparing the memory and cognitive performance of POW survivors who had experienced relatively more or less trauma-induced weight loss (p. 138). How might their conclusions bear on the psychological disorder anorexia nervosa? You probably have not studied this disorder yet, so simply refer to your knowledge of anorexia as it is discussed in the media. Think about how difficult it is to treat anorexia. Do you think that extreme weight loss might be a physical cause of anorexia's treatment resistance?

◊ CHAPTER 4 QUIZ

Circle the best of the four answers provided and check them according to answers provided at the back of this study guide. Be sure you understand why each answer is correct.

1. A wedding is likely to cause which of the following? (p. 124)
   a. distress
   b. delayed stress
   c. acute stress
   d. eustress

2. When we respond to stress, we confront two challenges. One is to meet the requirements of the stressor, and the other is to: (p. 125)
   a. protect the self from psychological damage and disorganization.
   b. change the way we think about the problem.
   c. protect the self from a defense-oriented response.
   d. make sure that we do not face a stressor again.

3. Which of the following defense-oriented responses is of the damage-repair type? (p. 126)
   a. denying
   b. intellectualizing
   c. mourning
   d. repressing

4. Which of the following is <u>not</u> a "fight-or-flight" response of the sympathetic nervous system to stressful situations? (p. 128)
   a. heart rate increasing
   b. skin constricting
   c. pupils constricting
   d. blood sugar increasing

5. The alarm and mobilization stage of personality decompensation in the face of trauma is characterized by: (p. 129)
   a. emotional arousal, increased tension, and greater alertness.
   b. exaggerated and inappropriate defensive measures.
   c. lowering of integration.
   d. rigidity as the individual clings to accustomed defenses.

6. A Desert Storm veteran has been experiencing detachment, reduction in awareness of his surroundings, and dissociative amnesia for 3 months. He has not experienced active combat for over 10 years and was symptom-free until 3 months ago. The appropriate diagnosis to make in this case is: (p. 130)
   a. adjustment disorder.
   b. acute stress disorder (ASD).
   c. acute post-traumatic stress disorder (acute PTSD).
   d. delayed post-traumatic stress disorder (delayed PTSD).

7. Which of the following is <u>not</u> one of the stages of the disaster syndrome? (p. 132)
   a. shock stage
   b. suggestible stage
   c. exhaustion stage
   d. recovery stage

8. PTSD is __ likely in women ___ in men. (p. 134)
   a. less...than
   b. more...than
   c. as...and
   d. not...or

9. All of the following were mentioned as factors influencing the experience of post-traumatic stress after rape EXCEPT: (p. 135)
   a. age of victim.
   b. whether offender is known to victim.
   c. socio-economic class of victim.
   d. marital status of victim.

10. One of the strongest emotional components of PTSD in combat veterans is: (pp. 136-137)
    a. sadness.
    b. anger.
    c. anxiety.
    d. guilt.

11. Which of the following is <u>not</u> true of former POWs? (p. 138)
    a. Their post-traumatic stress may be initially masked by relief at no longer being confined.
    b. They suffer a higher death rate after return to civilian life than do civilians.
    c. In one study, 90% of former POWs met PTSD criteria 40-50 years after their release.
    d. Biological and psychological stressors probably interact to produce PTSD in this group.

12. Which of the following causes of combat stress do we know the most about? (pp. 138-139)
    a. constitutional differences in sensitivity
    b. differences in temperament
    c. differences in vigor
    d. the conditions of battle that tax a soldier's stamina

13. Why is it difficult explicitly to relate cases of delayed PTSD to combat stress? (p. 140)
    a. Biological effects are no longer present.
    b. Only rape victims report experiencing delayed PTSD.
    c. Psychological effects are no longer substantial.
    d. There might be other adjustment problems involved.

14. The refugees from _____ have perhaps had the most difficult adjustment to the United States. (pp. 140-141)
    a. Haiti
    b. Southeast Asia
    c. Cuba
    d. Ethiopia

15. All of the following have been found to have protective value against PTSD in survivors of torture EXCEPT: (p. 142)
    a. psychological preparedness.
    b. strong social supports.
    c. strong commitment to a cause.
    d. ignorance about upcoming torture.

16. A stressor to which there is no way to respond to reduce its impact (e.g., by escape or avoidance) is called: (p. 143)
    a. uncontrollable.
    b. unpredictable.
    c. chronic.
    d. severe.

17. PTSD researchers now believe that many of the symptoms of emotional numbing may be caused by: (p. 143)
    a. a psychological defense reaction against remembering the trauma.
    b. stress-induced analgesia (SIA).
    c. prior experience with uncontrollable stressors.
    d. early experiences of physical abuse.

18. According to Vargas and Davidson (1993), which of the following treatments tends to be more effective in improving PTSD symptoms? (p. 144)
    a. both psychotherapy and medication
    b. medication alone without psychotherapy
    c. psychotherapy without medication
    d. both medication and the avoidance of fear-producing situations

19. One strategy to prevent stress is called: (p. 144)
    a. crisis intervention therapy.
    b. direct therapeutic exposure.
    c. stress-inoculation training.
    d. anger management therapy.

20. Definitively proving the existence of PTSD to the satisfaction of the legal system: (pp. 146-147)
    a. would be scientifically unethical.
    b. is exceedingly difficult.
    c. has already been accomplished.
    d. will never be accomplished.

| Chapter 5 |
| *Panic, Anxiety, and Their Disorders* |

◊ OVERVIEW

Chapter 5 opens by considering the response patterns that differentiate fear from anxiety, leading into a discussion of the clinical features, causal factors, and treatment of anxiety disorders. Anxiety disorders—characterized by unrealistic, irrational fear or anxiety of disabling intensity—discussed include specific phobias, social phobia, panic disorder with and without agoraphobia, generalized anxiety disorder, and obsessive-compulsive disorder. Psychosocial and biological causal factors are specified, and treatments of choice are discussed. Throughout, there is a strong emphasis on the role of unpredictability and uncontrollability in the development and maintenance of anxiety disorders. Chapter 5 closes with a discussion of sociocultural causal factors for the anxiety disorders.

◊ CHAPTER OUTLINE

I.   The Fear and Anxiety Response Patterns

II. Overview of the Anxiety Disorders

III. Specific Phobias
    A. Blood-Injection-Injury Phobia
    B. Age of Onset and Gender Differences
    C. Psychosocial Causal Factors
        1. Phobias as Learned Behavior
    D. Biological Causal Factors
        1. Genetic and Temperamental Causal Factors
        2. Evolutionary Causal Factors
    E. Treating Specific Phobias

IV. Social Phobia
    A. Interaction of Psychosocial and Biological Causal Factors
        1. Social Phobias as Learned Behavior
        2. Social Fears and Phobias in an Evolutionary Context
        3. Genetic and Temperamental Factors
        4. Perceptions of Uncontrollability
        5. Cognitive Variables
    B. Treating Social Phobia

3. OCD and Preparedness
4. The Role of Memory
5. The Effects of Attempting to Suppress Obsessive Thoughts
D. Biological Causal Factors
1. Genetic Influences
2. Abnormalities in Brain Function
3. The Role of Serotonin
E. Treating Obsessive-Compulsive Disorder

VIII. General Sociocultural Causal Factors for Anxiety Disorders
A. Cultural Differences in Sources of Worry
B. Taijin Kyofusho

IX. Summary

◊ LEARNING OBJECTIVES

After studying this chapter, you should be able to:

1. Distinguish between fear and anxiety. (pp. 150-152)

2. Identify the major features and causal factors, as well as the treatment approaches, for specific and social phobias. (pp. 153-161)

3. Give the diagnostic criteria for panic disorder with and without agoraphobia, and summarize the different causal factors and treatment approaches for these conditions. (pp. 162-171)

4. Describe the symptoms, causal factors, and treatments for generalized anxiety disorder. (pp. 171-176)

5. Characterize obsessive-compulsive disorder, and summarize its causal factors and treatment. (pp. 176-183)

6. Provide several examples of sociocultural differences in anxiety disorders. (pp. 184-185)

◊ TERMS YOU SHOULD KNOW

neurotic behavior (p. 150)

neurosis (p. 150)

fear (p. 151)

panic (p. 151)

anxiety (p. 151)

anxiety disorder (p. 152)

phobia (p. 152)

specific phobia (pp. 152-154)

social phobia (p. 152; p. 159)

blood-injection-injury phobia (pp. 154-155)

panic disorder (p. 162)

agoraphobia (pp. 163-164)

interoceptive fears (p. 166)

generalized anxiety disorder (GAD) (pp. 171-172)

obsessive-compulsive disorder (OCD) (pp. 176-177)

obsessions (p. 177)

compulsions (p. 177)

body dysmorphic disorder (BDD) (Highlight 5.2, p. 180)

◊ NAMES YOU SHOULD KNOW

David Barlow (p. 151; p. 162; p. 171)

Peter Lang (p. 151)

Susan Mineka (pp. 155-156, 157)

Arne Öhman (p. 157; p. 160)

Albert Bandura (p. 157)

Aaron Beck (p. 161; p. 174)

Donald Klein (p. 165)

David Clark (p. 167)

O.H. Mowrer (p. 179)

◊ CONCEPTS TO MASTER

1. Compare and contrast the concepts of fear (cognitive/subjective, physiological, and behavioral) or panic with anxiety. Be sure to note that both emotions involve three response systems but differ with respect to time orientation. (pp. 150-152)

2. Explain the significance of the fact that both fear and anxiety can be classically conditioned. (pp. 151-152)

3. What is the central feature of all anxiety disorders; that is, what do they have in common? (p. 152)

4. What are the central features of the three major kinds of phobias? (p. 152)

5. List the five subtypes of specific phobias (p. 153)

6. Describe how blood-injection-injury phobia differs from the other specific phobias. (pp. 154-155)

7. Describe the original classical conditioning explanation for the origins of specific phobias and identify the primary criticisms of this hypothesis. (pp. 155-156)

8. Explain how behavioral, biological, and evolutionary views have improved and expanded the basic conditioning hypothesis of phobia acquisition. (pp. 156-157)

9. Describe the most effective treatment for specific phobia. Did such treatment work for Mary in the Case Study? (pp. 157-158)

10. Distinguish between specific and generalized social phobia. (p. 159)

11. Identify the psychosocial and biological causal factors for social phobia, and explain how they interact. (pp. 159-161)

12. Describe the major treatment approaches used for social phobia, and evaluate their relative effectiveness. What treatment did Paul receive in the Case Study? (p. 161)

13. Describe the major diagnostic features of both panic disorder and agoraphobia, and explain how they are thought to be related. (pp. 162-164)

14. Differentiate between panic attacks and other types of anxiety in terms of intensity and time course. (p. 162)

15. How are the locus coeruleus, the central periaqueductal gray, the limbic system, and the prefrontal cortex involved in the various phenomena seen in panic disorder? What other biological causal factors have been implicated in panic disorder? (pp. 165-166)

16. Traditionally, a key feature of panic attacks is that they seem to "come out of the blue." Recent evidence, however, suggests that panic attacks are in fact triggered by bodily sensations. Compare and contrast the closely related interoceptive conditioning and the cognitive model of panic with respect to the triggers of panic attacks and summarize the evidence supporting the cognitive model. (pp. 166-168)

17. Explain how anxiety sensitivity may be involved in the development of panic disorder. (pp. 168-169)

18. Discuss the major approaches to treatment of panic disorder. Which treatment(s) appear(s) to be the most effective? Cite evidence to support your answer. (pp. 169-171)

19. Describe the three-part cognitive-behavioral therapy for panic disorder. (Highlight 5.1, p. 170)

20. What are the characteristic features of generalized anxiety disorder, and what is its typical age of onset? (pp. 171-172)

21. Describe the role of unpredictable and uncontrollable events in the development of GAD, and explain other cognitive factors in GAD. (pp. 173-175)

22. Explain the function that worry may serve for people with GAD and why worry may help maintain GAD. (p. 174)

23. Describe the biological causal factors for GAD. (pp. 175-176)

24. How are benzodiazepines thought to reduce generalized anxiety, and what neurotransmitter(s) may modulate generalized anxiety? (p. 175)

25. Compare and contrast the nature and effectiveness of biological and cognitive-behavioral treatments of GAD. (p. 176)

26. Summarize the major characteristics of obsessive-compulsive disorder. (pp. 176-179)

27. Explain how the behavioral view of OCD has been revitalized by the addition of the concept of preparedness. (p. 179; p. 181)

28. Discuss Body Dysmorphic Disorder (BDD) and why it is discussed in context with OCD. (Highlight 5.2, pp. 180-181)

29. How have cognitive factors been implicated in OCD? (pp. 181-182)

30. Discuss the biological causal factors for OCD. (pp. 182-183)

31. Evaluate the biological and behavioral treatment approaches for OCD. What treatment was used for Mark in the Case Study? (p. 184)

32. What are some examples of cultural differences in sources of worry? (p. 184)

33.   How does taijin kyofusho (TKS) relate to social phobia, and what kinds of cultural forces seem to have shaped it? (pp. 184-185)

◊ STUDY QUESTIONS

The fear and anxiety response patterns

1. Historically, the most common way of distinguishing between fear and anxiety has been to ask whether there is a clear and obvious source of _____. When the source of danger is obvious, the emotion has been called _____. (p. 151)

2. Lang's three components of fear are _____ components, _____ components, and _____ components. (p. 151)

3. Activation of the "fight-or-flight" response is associated with the basic emotion of _____ or _____. (p. 151)

4. The basic fear and anxiety response patterns are highly conditionable to previously neutral stimuli. These neutral stimuli may consist not only of external cues, but also of _____ _____ _____, such as stomach or intestinal contractions or heart palpitations. (p. 152)

Overview of the anxiety disorders

5. Anxiety disorders, which are manifested by _____ fear or anxiety of _____ intensity, are relatively common. According to the results of the National Comorbidity Survey, one type of anxiety disorder, called _____, was the second most common psychiatric disorder among women and the fourth most common among men. (p. 152)

6. Anxiety disorders are thought to have a lifetime prevalence rate of ___% of U.S. women and ___% of U.S. men. (p. 152)

Specific phobias

7. List the three main categories of phobias in the DSM-IV. (p. 153)

8. Phobic avoidance behavior is reinforced in two ways. First, it is reinforced by the reduction in anxiety that occurs each time the feared object or situation is avoided. Second, phobias may be maintained by _____ _____, such as increased attention, sympathy, or some control over the behavior of others. (p. 154)

9. When do blood-injection-injury phobics show their unique physiological response pattern, and when do they fail to show this pattern? (p. 155)

10. Describe the specific findings of Mineka, Cook, and colleagues' experiments supporting the importance of vicarious conditioning of intense fears. (p. 155)

11. Experiencing an inescapable and _____ trauma (e.g., being attacked by a vicious dog) seems to condition fear much more powerfully than the same intensity of trauma that one can _____ or to some extent _____. (p. 156)

12. Evidence supporting the contribution of temperament in the etiology of phobias comes from Kagan's finding that _____ _____ children were at higher risk for the development of multiple specific phobias at 7-8 years old than were _____ children. (pp. 156-157)

13. Primates and humans may be _____ evolutionarily to rapidly associate certain kinds of objects with aversive events. (p. 157)

14. _____ _____, developed by Bandura, may be even more effective than exposure alone in the treatment of specific phobias. (p. 157)

Social phobia

15. Fear of _____ _____ by others may be the hallmark of social phobia. (p. 159)

16. Individuals with _____ _____ _____ fear most social situations. (p. 159)

17. The temperamental variable that appears to be of greatest importance to social phobia is _____ _____. (p. 160)

18. Social phobics have _____ schemas that may play a role in the onset and maintenance of their disorder. (p. 161)

Panic disorder with and without agoraphobia

19. The two features of panic attacks that distinguish them from other types of anxiety are their characteristic _____ and their _____. (p. 162)

20. Panic attacks are referred to as _____ alarms for which there is no obvious trigger, as opposed to a _____ alarm that occurs when one encounters a phobic object. (p. 162)

21. _____ usually develops as a complication of having panic attacks. (p. 163)

22. Abnormal _____ activity in the _____ _____ may play a biological causal role in panic attacks. (p. 166)

23. The key difference between the cognitive model of panic and the interoceptive conditioning (or "fear of fear") model is the importance to the cognitive model of the _____ the person places on bodily sensations, which causes panic attacks to occur when the person makes catastrophic interpretations about certain bodily sensations. (p. 168)

24. A high degree of belief that certain bodily symptoms may have harmful consequences is called _____ _____ and is thought to be a causal factor for panic attacks and perhaps panic disorder. (p. 168)

25. Briefly outline the three aspects of the treatment of cognitive-behavioral therapy for panic disorder presented in Highlight 5.1. (p. 170)

Generalized anxiety disorder

26. Complete the following list of the symptoms characteristic of individuals suffering from generalized anxiety disorder, in addition to the core experience of excessive worry. (p. 171)

a. Restlessness or feelings of being _____

b. A sense of being easily _____

c. Difficulty _____ or mentally going blank

d. _____

e. Muscle tension

f. _____ disturbance

27. Although _____ _____ also is part of other anxiety disorders, it is the essence of GAD, leading Barlow to refer to GAD as the "basic" anxiety disorder. (p. 171)

28. The age of onset of GAD is often _____ _____ _____. (p. 172)

29. According to the psychoanalytic view, the primary difference between specific phobias and GAD is that the defense mechanisms of _____ and _____ are operative in specific phobias, but not so in GAD. (p. 173)

30. People with GAD may have a history of experiencing many important events in their lives as _____ and/or _____. (p. 173)

31. A relative lack of _____ _____ in their environment may help account for why people with GAD are tense and hypervigilant. (p. 173)

32. List the five most common benefits of worrying cited by people with GAD. (p. 174)

    a.

    b.

    c.

    d.

    e.

Obsessive-compulsive disorder

33. In OCD, _____ _____ are designed to neutralize _____ thoughts or distressing images or to _____ some dreaded event or situation. (p. 177)

34. For OCD, there is _____ gender difference, which makes OCD different from most other anxiety disorders. (p. 178)

35. What are the five primary types of compulsive acts? (p. 178)

36. What seems consistent across all the different clinical presentations of OCD is: (a) _____ is the affective symptom; (b) people afflicted with OCD fear that something terrible will happen to themselves or others for which they will be _____; and (c) compulsions usually _____ _____ _____, at least in the short term. (p. 179)

37. Describe the behavioral view of OCD, based on O.H. Mowrer's two-process theory of avoidance learning. (p. 179)

38. People with OCD show impairments in their _____ memory but not in their _____ memory. (p. 181)

111

39. Biological causal factors are more clearly implicated in OCD than in any of the other anxiety disorders. Evidence from twin studies reveals a _____ concordance rate for OCD in monozygotic twins and a _____ rate in dizygotic twins; clients with OCD have abnormally active _____ levels in the orbital prefrontal cortex, the caudate nucleus, and the cingulate cortex; finally, the neurotransmitter _____ is strongly implicated in OCD. (p. 182)

General sociocultural causal factors for anxiety disorders

40. How does TKS differ from the Western diagnosis of social phobia, and what does this tell us about the role of culture in the development of at least some anxiety disorders? (p. 184)

◊ **CRITICAL THINKING ABOUT DIFFICULT TOPICS**

1. In recent years, many prominent researchers have proposed a fundamental distinction between fear or panic, on the one hand, and anxiety, on the other hand (p. 151). Further, this distinction proves important in understanding the differences between phobias and panic, on the one hand, and generalized anxiety, on the other. Have you been making a similar distinction in your everyday usage of the concept of anxiety? If not, how would making this distinction affect how you interpret your social environment? For example, can you identify some individuals who are more anxious, and others who are more fearful? Do some students worry about and prepare for exams in advance, whereas others do not prepare for them but become fearful during them? Can a similar distinction be made in the domain of public speaking?

2. According to both the interoceptive conditioning model and the cognitive model of panic, panic attacks are triggered by internal bodily sensations (pp. 167-168). But in the cognitive model, the meaning attached to the experience of bodily sensations (i.e., that they are catastrophic) is critically important. These catastrophic interpretations are often "just barely out of the realm of awareness" (p. 167). The cognitive model predicts that a panic attack should occur only if catastrophic interpretations are made with reference to a bodily sensation. How might you test the hypothesized difference between the two models if the catastrophic interpretations important to the cognitive model are not always conscious? In other words, how would you know whether someone was indeed making a catastrophic interpretation? In answering this question, it may help to read the evidence supporting the cognitive model presented on p. 167.

3. Examine Table 5.2 (p. 172), which reports gender differences in the lifetime prevalence estimates of the anxiety disorders. Which disorders show the greatest gender differences, and which the smallest? For each disorder, think about why its gender ratio might make sense. Consider the sociocultural explanation offered on p. 165 for the gender difference in panic disorder with and without agoraphobia. Is this explanation plausible to you? Do you think sociocultural factors operate in every case in which a gender difference is present? How might you test whether sociocultural factors or perhaps biological (hormonal) factors are at the root of the gender differences in some of the anxiety disorders?

4. Do you think that obsessive-compulsive disorder (OCD) belongs in the DSM-IV category of the anxiety disorders? Consider the many respects in which it is discrepant from the rest of the disorders. First, there is almost no gender difference in OCD. Second, remember that biological causal factors are more strongly implicated in the development of OCD than in that of any of the other anxiety disorders. Now think about ways in which OCD resembles the other anxiety disorders detailed in Chapter 5. What avenues of research would you suggest as most promising in order to help us understand OCD better?

◊ CHAPTER 5 QUIZ

Circle the best of the four answers provided and check them according to answers provided at the back of this study guide. Be sure you understand why each answer is correct.

1. Which of the following is described at the physiological role as a state of chronic overarousal reflecting readiness for dealing with danger should it occur? (p. 151)
   a. fear
   b. panic
   c. anxiety
   d. fight-or-flight response

2. In the National Comorbidity Survey, _____ were the second most common psychiatric disorders reported for women and the fourth most common for men. (p. 152)
   a. obsessive-compulsive disorders
   b. generalized anxiety disorders
   c. panic disorders
   d. phobias

3. All phobic avoidance behaviors are reinforced by: (p. 154)
   a. increased self-esteem.
   b. reduction in anxiety.
   c. repetition.
   d. generalization.

4. Dental phobia, claustrophobia, and accident phobia may all develop from: (p. 155)
   a. vicarious classical conditioning.
   b. observational classical conditioning.
   c. direct traumatic conditioning.
   d. operant conditioning.

5. Prepared fears are: (p. 157)
   a. innate.
   b. easily extinguished.
   c. easily acquired.
   d. influenced by higher cognitive processes.

6. The most effective treatment for specific phobias is: (p. 157)
   a. exposure alone.
   b. exposure and participant modeling.
   c. exposure and response prevention.
   d. pharmacological.

7. Fear of urinating in a public bathroom is an example of _____: (p. 159)
   a. panic disorder.
   b. specific social phobia.
   c. generalized social phobia.
   d. generalized anxiety disorder.

8. The temperamental variable of greatest importance in the development of social phobia is _____: (p. 160)
   a. introversion.
   b. extraversion.
   c. behavioral inhibition.
   d. sociability.

9. A panic attack is sometimes referred to as a(n) _____ . (p. 162)
   a. true alarm
   c. false alarm
   b. learned alarm
   d. automatic alarm

10. In a study supporting the cognitive model of panic, clients given a cognitive rationale showed _____ physiological responses to a sodium lactate infusion than control clients; they were _____ likely to panic in response to the infusion than were control clients. (p. 167)
    a. stronger; more
    c. weaker; more
    b. stronger; less
    d. weaker; less

11. Which of the following is <u>not</u> typically a part of cognitive-behavior therapy for panic disorder? (Highlight 5.1, p. 170)
    a. exposure to feared situations and feared bodily sensations
    b. deep muscle relaxation and breathing retraining
    c. identification and modification of logical errors and automatic thoughts
    d. carbon dioxide inhalation and/or lactate infusion

12. Barlow refers to the fundamental process in generalized anxiety disorder as: (p. 171)
    a. the alarm reaction.
    c. anxious apprehension.
    b. the fight-or-flight response.
    d. prepared focal anxiety.

13. According to the psychoanalytic view, two defense mechanisms are operative in the phobias, but not in generalized anxiety. These defense mechanisms are: (p. 173)
    a. projection and displacement.
    b. projection and reaction formation.
    c. repression and displacement.
    d. repression and reaction formation.

14. Individuals with generalized anxiety disorder have all of the following EXCEPT: (pp. 174-175)
    a. their attention drawn away from threat cues.
    b. threatening interpretations of ambiguous information.
    c. automatic thoughts revolving around physical injury, illness, or death.
    d. worry that suppresses emotional and physiological response to aversive imagery.

15. The benzodiazepines, drugs that reduce generalized anxiety, probably exert their effects through stimulating the action of: (p. 175)
    a. acetylcholine.
    c. serotonin.
    b. GABA.
    d. norepinephrine.

16. The personality disorders with which OCD most often co-occurs are: (p. 179)
    a. narcissistic and antisocial.
    c. schizoid and schizotypal.
    b. borderline and histrionic.
    d. avoidant and dependent.

17. People with checking compulsions show impairments in: (p. 181)
    a. nonverbal memory.
    b. verbal memory.
    c. attention span.
    d. switching attentional focus.

18. OCD is often successfully treated with clomipramine; this suggests that _____ is implicated in OCD. (p. 182)
    a. dopamine
    b. serotonin
    c. norepinephrine
    d. GABA

19. Taijin kyofusho (TKS) is related to _____. (p. 184)
    a. panic disorder with agoraphobia
    b. generalized anxiety disorder
    c. body dysmorphic disorder
    d. social phobia

| Chapter 6 |
| *Mood Disorders and Suicide* |

◊ OVERVIEW

Mood disorders are alarmingly prevalent, and they are apparently being diagnosed more frequently in recent years. This chapter begins with a review of lifetime prevalence rates of the two types of mood disorders: unipolar mood disorders and bipolar disorders. Unipolar mood disorders include both milder forms of depression, like dysthymia and adjustment disorder with depressed mood, as well more severe depression, which is called major depressive disorder. The biological, psychosocial, and sociocultural causal factors for unipolar mood disorders are then specified.

Bipolar disorders can be distinguished from unipolar mood disorders by the presence of mania—defined as intense and unrealistic feelings of excitement and euphoria. Most typically, periods of mania alternate with periods of depression. Like unipolar mood disorders, bipolar disorders are grouped according to severity. Cyclothymia is the diagnosis made when the disturbance is mild to moderate, while more severe disturbance is referred to as bipolar disorder. Unlike unipolar mood disorders, bipolar disorders appear to be caused principally by biological factors, although psychosocial and sociocultural causal factors are also reviewed.

Finally, the treatments for and outcomes of mood disorders, both unipolar and bipolar, are discussed. Pharmacotherapy, electroconvulsive therapy, and psychotherapy are among the treatments of choice for mood disorders. Chapter 6 closes with a discussion of suicide, a tragic outcome for which depressed individuals are at constant risk.

◊ CHAPTER OUTLINE

I. What Are Mood Disorders?
    A. The Prevalence of Mood Disorders
    B. Depression Throughout the Life Cycle

II. Unipolar Mood Disorders
    A. Mild to Moderate Depressive Disorders
        1. Dysthymia
        2. Adjustment Disorder with Depressed Mood

B. Major Depressive Disorder
   1. Subtypes of Major Depression
   2. Distinguishing Major Depression
   3. Depression as a Recurrent Disorder
   4. Seasonal Affective Disorder
C. Biological Causal Factors
   1. Hereditary Factors
   2. Biochemical Factors
   3. Neuroendocrine and Neurophysiological Factors
   4. Disturbances in Sleep and Other Biological Rhythms
      a) Circadian Rhythms
      b) Sunlight and Seasons
D. Psychosocial Causal Factors
   1. Stressful Life Events as Causal Factors
      a) Chronic Strains
      b) Individual Differences in Responses to Stressors
      c) How Stressors Act
   2. Types of Diathesis-Stress Models for Unipolar Depression
      a) Personality and Cognitive Diatheses
      b) Early Parental Loss as a Diathesis
      c) Summary of Diathesis-Stress Models
   3. Psychodynamic Theories
   4. Behavioral Theories
   5. Beck's Cognitive Theory
      a) Evaluating Beck's Theory as a Descriptive Theory
      b) Evaluating the Causal Aspects of Beck's Theory
   6. The Helplessness and Hopelessness Theories of Depression
      a) The Roles of Attributional Style and Hopelessness
   7. Interpersonal Effects of Mood Disorders
      a) Lack of Social Support and Social Skills Deficits
      b) The Effects of Depression on Others
      c) Marriage and Family Life
   8. Summary of Psychosocial Causal Factors
E. Sociocultural Causal Factors
   1. Cross-Cultural Differences in Depressive Symptoms
   2. A Belief in Self-Sufficiency
   3. Relieving Losses
   4. Demographic Differences in the United States

III. Bipolar Disorders
   A. Cyclothymia
   B. Bipolar Disorder
      1. Features of Bipolar Disorder
   C. Schizoaffective Disorder

◊ LEARNING OBJECTIVES

After studying this chapter, you should be able to:

1. Describe the prevalence and onset patterns of mood disorders, and distinguish between unipolar and bipolar disorders. (pp. 189-191)

2. Summarize the symptoms and causal factors for the unipolar disorders. (pp. 192-214)

3. Summarize the symptoms and causal factors for the bipolar disorders. (pp. 214-221)

4. Describe the treatments that have been shown to be effective with mood disorders. (pp. 222-226)

5. Summarize the risk factors for suicide. (pp. 226-232)

6. Describe the key features of suicide prevention and intervention programs. (pp. 232-235)

◊ TERMS YOU SHOULD KNOW

mood disorders (p. 189)

mania (p. 189)

depression (p. 189)

unipolar disorders (p. 191; Table 6.1, p. 190)

bipolar disorders (p. 191; Table 6.1, p. 190)

dysthymia (p. 192; Table 6.1, p. 190)

adjustment disorder with depressed mood (p. 194; Table 6.1, p. 190)

major depressive disorder (pp. 195-198; Table 6.1, p. 190)

melancholic type (p. 196)

severe major depressive episode with psychotic features (p. 196)

120

mood-congruent psychotic features (p. 196)

mood-incongruent psychotic features (p. 197)

postpartum onset (p. 197)

recurrence (p. 198)

relapse (p. 198)

seasonal affective disorder (SAD) (pp. 198-199)

depressogenic schemas (p. 206)

dysfunctional beliefs (p. 206)

negative automatic thoughts (p. 206)

negative cognitive triad (p. 206)

learned helplessness (p. 208)

attributions (p. 208)

hopelessness theory (p. 208; p. 210)

hypomania (p. 214)

cyclothymia (p. 214; Table 6.1, p. 190)

bipolar disorder (p. 215)

bipolar disorder with a seasonal pattern (p. 215)

rapid cycling (p. 217-218)

schizoaffective disorder (p. 218)

suicide (p. 226)

John Bowlby (p. 193; p. 212)

George Brown (p. 204)

Peter Lewinsohn (p. 205)

Aaron Beck (pp. 205-208)

Martin Seligman (p. 208)

Lynn Abramson (p. 208)

◊ CONCEPTS TO MASTER

---

1. Describe the two key moods involved in mood disorders. (p. 189)

2. What is the major difference between unipolar disorders and bipolar disorders, and how prevalent are the two types of mood disorder? (pp. 190-191)

3. How do the prevalence rates of unipolar and bipolar disorders differ between the genders and over the lifespan? (p. 191)

4. What are the major features that differentiate dysthymia, adjustment disorder with depressed mood, and major depressive disorder? (p. 192; pp. 194-195)

5. Characterize the four phases of response to the loss of a spouse or close family member (as described by Bowlby) and note when prominent anxiety and prominent depression are likely to appear. (Highlight 6.1, p. 193)

6. List the eight symptoms of major depressive disorder. (p. 195)

7. What are the three common subtypes of major depressive disorder? (pp. 196-198)

8. Discuss the current dominant theoretical approach to understanding the overlap between depressive and anxiety symptoms. (Highlight 6.2, p. 197)

9. Distinguish between a recurrence of depression and a relapse. (p. 198)

10. Describe seasonal affective disorder. (pp. 198-199)

11. Summarize the evidence for a genetic contribution to unipolar depression. (p. 199)

12. Trace the history and current status of the monoamine hypothesis of depression. (p. 200)

13. Outline the neuroendocrine and neurophysiological factors in depression. (pp. 200-201; Figure 6.1, p. 201)

14. Define the concepts of circadian rhythms and seasonal variations in basic functions and review their possible involvement in unipolar depression. (pp. 201-202)

15. List the most frequently encountered precipitating circumstances in depression. (p. 202)

16. Summarize the results of research by Brown and Harris, as well as Dohrenwend and colleagues, on the role of stressful life events in unipolar depression. (p. 203)

17. Compare and contrast the diathesis-stress models for unipolar depression based on (a) personality and cognitive diatheses; and (b) early parental loss and/or poor parental care. (pp. 203-205)

18. Discuss the psychodynamic and behavioral theories of the causation of unipolar mood disorders. (p. 205)

19. Describe Beck's cognitive theory of depression involving the concept of the depressogenic schema. (pp. 205-206)

20. Discuss the reformulated learned helplessness and hopelessness theories (Abramson et al.) involving the concept of a pessimistic attributional style. (pp. 208-210)

21. Evaluate the major theories explaining gender differences in unipolar depression. (p. 209)

22. Discuss the evidence for the conclusions that lack of social support and social skills deficits may play a causal role in depression *and* that depression itself produces interpersonal difficulties. (p. 210)

23. Even in those non-Western cultures where unipolar mood disorders are relatively common, depression generally takes on a form different from that customarily described in our society. Describe this different form. (p. 211; p. 213)

24. How does Bowlby's attachment theory explain the links between marital distress, depression, and domestic violence? (Highlight 6.4, p. 212)

25. Describe the symptoms and clinical features of cyclothymia and bipolar disorder, and compare and contrast the two disorders. (pp. 214-218)

26. Discuss the typical course and outcome of bipolar disorder. (pp. 217-218)

27. Describe the symptoms of schizoaffective disorder and explain why some clinicians find this diagnosis controversial. (p. 218)

28. Describe the biological causal factors of bipolar disorders. (pp. 218-219)

29. Describe the pathway by which stressful life events may contribute to the etiology of bipolar disorders. (pp. 219-220)

30. Compare and contrast psychosocial, psychodynamic, and sociocultural causal factors for bipolar disorder. (pp. 219-221)

31. Evaluate the effectiveness of antidepressant medications, electroconvulsive therapy, and mood-stabilizing drugs such as lithium in the treatment of unipolar and bipolar disorders. (pp. 222-224)

32. Describe the three major forms of psychotherapy that have been shown to be effective for treating depression. (pp. 224-226)

33. Who is most likely to attempt suicide, who is most likely to complete suicide, and what are some of the major psychosocial causal factors for suicide? (pp. 227-230)

34. What are the warning signs for student suicide? (Highlight 6.5, p. 229)

35. Compare and contrast biological and sociocultural causal factors for suicide. (pp. 230-231)

36. How is suicidal ambivalence related to communication of suicidal intent? (pp. 231-232)

37. What are the goals of suicide intervention programs, and how successful do they seem to be? (p. 232; pp. 234-235)

38. Compare and contrast the rights of a terminally-ill person who wishes to die with the rights of a suicidal person (who is not terminally ill). (Highlight 6.6, p. 233)

◊ STUDY QUESTIONS

What are mood disorders?

1. The two key moods involved in mood disorders are depression and _____. (p. 189)

2. Recent results from the National Comorbidity Survey found lifetime prevalence rates of major depression at nearly _____% for males and _____% for females. Bipolar disorder is much less common than unipolar mood disorder. Estimates of lifetime risk of bipolar disorder range from _____% to _____%, and there is no discernible sex difference in prevalence rates. (p. 191)

Unipolar mood disorders

3. The two main categories for depressions of mild to moderate severity recognized by DSM-IV are dysthymia and adjustment disorder with depressed mood. Place the name of each disorder next to its clinical description. (p. 192; p. 194)

a. _____ Symptoms essentially similar to major depression, but the nonpsychotic levels of depression last two years or more with intermittent normal moods lasting from a few days to no more than a few weeks.

b. _____ Also characterized by nonpsychotic levels of depression developing within three months of an identifiable psychosocial stressor and lasting no longer than six months.

4. Anger is very common in the _____ phase of grieving. (p. 193)

5. Grief is a psychological process experienced following the death of a loved one. Clayton (1982) suggests that the process of grieving following bereavement is normally completed within _____. (p. 193)

6. To be diagnosed as suffering from major depressive disorder, an individual must experience either depressed mood or loss of interest in pleasurable activities. In addition, at least four symptoms must have been present all day and nearly every day during two consecutive _____. (p. 195)

7. The form of major depressive disorder with the poorest long-term prognosis is severe major depressive episode with _____ features. (p. 196)

8. The individual with a major depressive disorder may have a loss of contact with reality. Ordinarily, any delusions or hallucinations present are _____; that is, they seem in some sense "appropriate" to serious depression. (p. 196)

9. The term major depression of the _____ type may be used for the individual who develops a major depression that includes lost capacity for pleasure and whose other symptoms are likely to include depression being worse in the morning, awakening early in the morning, marked psychomotor retardation or agitation, significant loss of appetite and weight, and excessive guilt. (p. 196)

10. In the dominant theoretical approach to understanding the overlap between anxiety and depression, known as the tripartite model, the overlap between anxiety and depression is attributable to the broad mood and personality dimension of _____ _____; depressed individuals only are characterized by low levels of a second dimension of mood and personality known as _____ _____; and anxious but not depressed individuals show high levels of yet another mood dimension known as _____ _____. (Highlight 6.2, p. 197)

11. Post-partum depression is best understood as a(n) _____ disorder, because it tends to be relatively mild and is resolved quickly. (p. 198)

12. Major depression may coexist with dysthymia in some individuals; this condition is termed _____ _____. (p. 198)

13. The average duration of an untreated episode of major depression is about _____ months, according to DSM-IV. (p. 198)

14. _____ refers to the return of symptoms within a fairly short period of time and probably reflects the fact that the underlying episode of depression has not yet run its course. (p. 198)

15. Based on an extensive review of studies done between 1970 and 1993, Piccinelli and Wilkinson estimated that ____% of patients experienced a recurrence of major depression within one year of recovery and ____% experienced a recurrence within ten years of recovery. (p. 198)

16. Family and twin studies have converged to suggest that there may be a _____ genetic contribution to unipolar depression, except for milder forms of unipolar depression, such as _____. (p. 199)

17. Depression has been hypothesized to be due at least sometimes to an absolute or relative depletion of one or more of three neurotransmitters (norepinephrine, dopamine, and serotonin) at important receptor sites in the brain. This hypothesis is called the _____ hypothesis and has been challenged by more recent findings of net *increases* in norepinephrine activity in depressed patients. (p. 200)

18. Studies using brain imaging techniques such as PET suggest that severely depressed patients show _____ metabolism in the _____ regions of the cerebral hemispheres, especially on the _____ side. (pp. 200-201)

19. Depressed patients, especially those with _____ features, show a variety of sleep problems, including early morning awakening, poor sleep maintenance, and sometimes difficulty falling asleep. (p. 201)

20. Patients diagnosed with _____ _____ _____ are responsive to the total quantity of available light in the environment. (p. 202)

21. Determining whether stressful life events cause depression is complicated by the fact that depressed individuals sometimes _____ stressful life events, in part as a by-product of their depressed state. (p. 202)

22. Brown and Harris (1978) estimated that stressful life events played a causal role in the depression of about ____% of their female subjects. (p. 203)

23. Women at genetic risk are _____ times more likely than those not at genetic risk to respond to severely stressful life events with depression, according to Kendler and colleagues. (p. 203)

24. Whybrow (1997) suggested that psychosocial stressors may play a role in the development of mood disorders by causing long-term changes in _____ functioning. (p. 203)

25. Researchers have concluded that there is good evidence that _____ is the primary personality variable that serves as a vulnerability factor for depression. (p. 204)

26. Gotlib and Hammen (1992) concluded that it seems that the contradictory findings regarding the effects of early parental loss on depression in adulthood can be resolved if one considers the _____ of _____ _____ following the loss. (p. 204)

27. Perhaps the most important contribution of the psychodynamic approaches to depression has been to note the importance of _____ (both real, and symbolic or imagined) to the onset of depression and the striking similarities between the symptoms of _____ and the symptoms of depression. (p. 205)

28. Lewinsohn and colleagues proposed that depression can be elicited when a person's behavior no longer brings the accustomed _____ (as, for example, when employment is terminated). (p. 205)

29. According to Beck, _____ _____, when activated by current stressors, produce a pattern of _____ _____ _____, which then produce depressive symptoms. (pp. 206-207)

30. A "negative cognitive triad" consists of negative thoughts about the self, world, and _____. (p. 206)

31. The cognitive biases in depression postulated by Beck have been shown to exist in research suggesting that depressed individuals show better recall for _____ information, while nondepressed individuals tend to remember _____ information better. (p. 207)

32. A depressogenic or pessimistic attribution for a negative event, such as receiving a low grade on an exam, would be a(n) _____, _____, and _____ one. According to the hopelessness theory, this pessimistic attributional style in conjunction with one or more negative life events should lead to depression if and only if a state of hopelessness was earlier experienced. (p. 208)

33. Women are more likely than men to _____ when they become depressed, a finding possibly at least partially accounting for the sex difference in unipolar depression. (Highlight 6.3, p. 209)

34. People who lack _____ _____ are more vulnerable to becoming depressed. Depressed individuals also have _____ and less supportive social networks, and, to make matters worse, they elicit _____ _____ in others. (p. 210)

35. According to Murray and Cooper (1997), depressed mothers show more _____ and have less _____, mutually rewarding interactions with their children. (p. 211)

36. Roberts, Gotlib, and Kassell (1996) demonstrated what appears to be a causal relationship between _____ _____ and the emergence of depressive symptoms. (Highlight 6.4, p. 212)

37. Individuals in societies that take on the ways of _____ _____ appear to become more prone to developing mood disorders as conceptualized by DSM-IV. (p. 213)

Bipolar disorders

38. Non-disabling, cyclical mood alterations between depression and hypomania are indicative of _____, a milder form of bipolar disorder. (p. 214)

39. Bipolar mood disorder is distinguished from major depression by at least one episode of _____. (p. 215)

40. A variant of bipolar disorder in which hypomania (but not mania) is present is called _____ _____ _____. This disorder usually evolves into bipolar disorder. (p. 215)

41. The diagnosis of schizoaffective disorder is controversial. Some clinicians believe that these individuals are basically _____; others believe that they have primarily psychotic _____ disorders; and still others consider this disorder a distinct entity. (p. 218)

42. The early monoamine hypothesis for unipolar mood disorder was extended to bipolar disorder, suggesting that mania might be caused by excesses of norepinephrine and/or serotonin. Although there is some support for increased _____ activity during manic episodes, _____ activity appears to be low in both depressive and manic phases. (p. 218)

43. Bipolar patients, at least when depressed, show evidence of dysregulation of the _____ axis at about the same rate as do unipolar patients. (p. 219)

44. Stressful life events may act to _____ critical biological rhythms; these rhythms are strongly implicated in biological accounts of the etiology of bipolar disorder. (p. 220)

45. Bipolar disorder is _____ common in the higher than in the lower socioeconomic classes, the opposite of what has been found for unipolar mood disorder. Furthermore, bipolar disorder (and to a lesser extent unipolar mood disorder) occurs with alarming frequency among _____, _____, _____, and _____. (pp. 220-221)

Treatments and outcomes for mood disorders

46. Because of unpleasant side effects of the tricyclics, physicians are increasingly prescribing one of the new _____ _____ _____ _____ or SSRIs, such as Prozac (fluoxetine). (pp. 222-223)

47. Early studies indicated that lithium carbonate was considered an effective preventative for approximately ____% of patients suffering repeated bipolar attacks, but other large and more recent studies found only slightly over _____% of patients remaining free of an episode over a five-year follow-up period. Another category of drugs, known as the _____, may be useful in the treatment of bipolar disorder. (p. 223)

48. Electroconvulsive therapy (ECT) is often used with severely depressed, suicidal patients because antidepressant drugs often take ___ to ___ weeks to produce significant improvement. ECT is also used with patients who have not responded to other forms of _____ treatment. When selection criteria are carefully observed, a complete remission of symptoms occurs after about ___ to ___ treatments. (p. 224)

49. What is the verdict regarding the relative effectiveness in treating unipolar mood disorder of cognitive-behavioral therapy (CBT) and interpersonal therapy (IPT), according to the carefully designed, multi-site study sponsored by the National Institute of Mental Health? Circle the correct statement from among the choices listed. (p. 225)
    1. IPT is more effective than CBT.
    2. CBT is more effective than IPT.
    3. IPT and CBT are equally effective.
    4. IPT and CBT are equally effective, but antidepressant drugs are yet more effective.

Suicide

50. Women are about three to four times as likely as men to attempt suicide, but three to four times more men than women die by suicide each year in the United States. True or False? (p. 227)

51. For individuals between the ages of 15 and 19, the rate of successful suicides _____ between the mid-1950s and the mid-1980s. (p. 228)

52. _____ people use methods for a suicide attempt that are often dangerous but moderately slow-acting, such as drug ingestion. (p. 231)

53. The primary objective of crisis intervention therapy is to help suicidal individuals regain their ability to cope with their immediate problems, and to do so as quickly as possible. Complete the following list of the five main objectives in crisis intervention: (p. 234)

    a. Maintaining contact with a suicidal individual for one to six contacts

    b.

    c.

    d.

    e. Helping the suicidal individual see that the present distress will not be endless

---

◊ CRITICAL THINKING ABOUT DIFFICULT TOPICS

1. Milder versions of traditional diagnostic categories are quite common. For example, dysthymia is a milder version of unipolar mood disorder, and cyclothymia is a milder version of bipolar disorder. What does the existence of less severe variants of traditional diagnostic categories imply about the categorical approach to diagnosis, in which a disorder is viewed as either present or absent?

2. Women are twice as likely as men to become clinically depressed. A number of theories have been proposed in order to account for this finding (see Highlight 6.3, p. 209). Consider some facts about the sex difference in unipolar depression. First, it is true across cultures. Second, it emerges in adolescence and reaches its most dramatic peak between 15 and 18 years old. Now propose a program of research that you think might effectively support one or another of these theories to the exclusion of others.

3. The popularity of the antidepressant drug Prozac has raised questions about the ethics of "prescribing drugs to essentially healthy people simply because those drugs make them feel more energetic, outgoing, and productive" (p. 223). Consider under what conditions it would be legitimate to prescribe a psychoactive drug for many years. Think about the following issues: (a) whether there are negative side effects of the drug to be prescribed; (b) whether the drug is obtained "on the street" or by prescription; and (c) to what degree an individual on medication is responsible for his or her actions.

4. In the pharmacological treatment of depression, "discontinuing the drugs when symptoms have remitted may result in relapse . . . because the underlying depressive episode [is] actually still present and only [its] symptomatic expression [has] been suppressed" (p. 223). A common criticism of pharmacological treatment is that psychological symptoms are treated, but the underlying "episode" is not eliminated, and the drug is not expected to reduce the risk of future episodes once discontinued. Do you think about psychological treatments in the same way, or do you expect them to be of long-term benefit? Think about the processes involved in psychotherapy. Might these processes confer continued benefits after therapy is discontinued?

5. There are abundant ethical issues involved in the concept of the "right to suicide" (p. 233). If you are like many people who feel some sympathy for the desire to commit suicide in the case of terminal debilitating and painful illnesses, think through your own position with respect to what restrictions you would place on this right to suicide. What about a young person who is obviously depressed over some recent perceived failure or rejection? What about a person recently diagnosed as having Alzheimer's disease or schizophrenia, or a person who has become paralyzed from the waist down? Try to articulate the concepts involved in granting or denying the right to suicide in each of these cases.

◊ CHAPTER 6 QUIZ

Circle the best of the four answers provided and check them according to answers provided at the back of this study guide. Be sure you understand why each answer is correct.

1. The lifetime prevalence rate of major depression among men is 13%. Among women it is: (p. 191)
   a. 4%.
   c. 21%.
   b. 14%.
   d. 27%.

2. Infants may experience a form of depression that is called: (p. 191)
   a. melancholic depression.
   c. anaclitic depression.
   b. psychotic depression.
   d. endogenous depression.

3. All of the following is true of dysthymia EXCEPT: (p. 192; p. 194; p. 199)
   a. Symptoms must be present for at least two years in order for the diagnosis to be made.
   b. Dysthmics show fewer symptoms, on average, than do major depressives.
   c. Any genetic contribution to dysthymia is likely to be very modest, at best.
   d. Normal moods may briefly intercede, but last at most from a few days to a few weeks.

4. Which of the following is *not* one of Bowlby's four phases of response to the loss of a spouse or close family member? (p. 193)
   a. numbing and disbelief
   b. denial and rejection of the dead person
   c. disorganization and despair
   d. some level of reorganization

5. According to the tripartite model, depressed individuals are best described as being: (p. 197)
   a. low in positive affect and low in negative affect.
   b. low in positive affect and high in negative affect.
   c. high in positive affect and low in anxious hyperarousal.
   d. low in positive affect, negative affect, and anxious hyperarousal.

6. Return of the symptoms of a disorder within a fairly short period of time is known as: (p. 198)
   a. relapse.
   c. symptom substitution.
   b. recurrence.
   d. chronicity.

7. In the original monoamine hypothesis, depression was attributed to: (p. 200)
   a. an increase in norepinephrine and/or dopamine.
   b. an increase in acetylcholine.
   c. a depletion of norepinephrine and/or serotonin.
   d. a depletion of acetylcholine and/or GABA.

8. All of the following is true of stressful life events and unipolar mood disorder EXCEPT: (pp. 202-203)
   a. Depressed individuals sometimes generate stressful life events.
   b. The relationship between stressful life events and depression is stronger in those who have had one or more previous episodes of depression than in those having their first onset of depression.
   c. Chronic stressors are associated with increases in both depressive symptoms and in major depressive disorder.
   d. Women at genetic risk for depression have been shown to experience more stressful events and to be more sensitive to them.

9. Behaviorists such as Lewinsohn assert that depression results when: (p. 205)
   a. angry responses are inhibited by aversive conditioning.
   b. conditioned grief responses are reactivated.
   c. negative reinforcers overwhelm positive reinforcers.
   d. response-contingent positive reinforcement is no longer available.

10. Believing that "If I can't get it 100% right, there's no point in doing it at all" is an example of: (p. 206)
    a. dichotomous reasoning.
    b. selective abstraction.
    c. overgeneralization.
    d. an internal, unstable, and global attribution.

11. The original learned helplessness theory refers to the depressed patient's perception that: (p. 208)
    a. accustomed reinforcement is no longer forthcoming.
    b. there is no control over aversive events.
    c. reinforcement is inadequate.
    d. the world is a negative place.

12. Blaming your bad grade on an exam to the fact that your professor writes very difficult exams is an example of which kind of attribution? (p. 208)
    a. internal, global, and stable
    b. external, specific, and stable
    c. internal, global, and unstable
    d. external, global, and stable

13. Unipolar mood disorders are most likely caused by: (p. 202)
   a. biological factors.
   b. psychosocial factors.
   c. sociocultural factors.
   d. some combination of biological, psychosocial, and sociocultural factors.

14. A disorder involving mood swings between subclinical levels of depression and hypomania is: (p. 214)
   a. bipolar disorder.
   b. bipolar II disorder.
   c. dysthymia.
   d. cyclothymia.

15. Bipolar mood disorder is distinguished from major depression by: (p. 215)
   a. at least one episode of mania.
   b. the disturbance of circadian rhythms.
   c. evidence of earlier cyclothymia.
   d. evidence of earlier dysthymia.

16. All of the following are symptoms of the manic phase of bipolar disorder EXCEPT: (pp. 215-217)
   a. notable increase in activity.
   b. euphoria.
   c. high levels of verbal output.
   d. deflated self-esteem.

17. All of the following have been suggested as biological causes of bipolar disorder EXCEPT: (pp. 218-219)
   a. abnormalities of the hypothalamic-pituitary-thyroid axis.
   b. hereditary factors.
   c. disturbances in biological rhythms.
   d. norepinephrine depletion.

18. All of the following are true of cognitive-behavioral therapy (CBT) for depression EXCEPT: (p. 225)
   a. It is at least as effective as pharmacotherapy.
   b. It may have a special advantage in preventing relapse.
   c. It is effective with unipolar depressed outpatients and inpatients.
   d. It is ineffective for the treatment of depression of the melancholic type.

19. Marital therapy is _____ effective _____ cognitive-behavioral therapy (CBT) in reducing unipolar depression for the depressed spouse. (p. 226)
   a. less; than
   b. more; than
   c. as; as
   d. not at all; relative to

20. Even without formal therapy, the great majority of manic and depressed patients recover from a given episode within less than: (p. 226)
   a. two weeks.
   b. one month.
   c. one year.
   d. two years.

21. At least half of the time, suicide is committed during the _____ phase of a depressive episode. (p. 226)
   a. early onset
   b. late onset
   c. peak
   d. recovery

Chapter 7
Somatoform and Dissociative Disorders

◊ OVERVIEW

This chapter contains a detailed description of the clinical picture, causal pattern, and treatment of somatoform and dissociative disorders. In somatoform disorders, the hallmark feature is the report of physical complaints or disabilities that occur in the absence of accompanying physical pathology. These disorders are hypothesized to be expressions of psychological distress converted into physical form. The dissociative disorders, in contrast, are conditions that involve disruption, or dissociation, in one's sense of personal identity. What these two types of disorders share is the purpose they serve to reduce or avoid anxiety in the face of stress that might otherwise overwhelm the sufferer's typical coping mechanisms. In somatoform disorders, physical complaints or disabilities function to mask psychological ones. In dissociative disorders, pathological dissociation (escape from one's own autobiographical memory or personal identity) serves to mask psychological distress. Both kinds of disorders appear to allow the sufferer to avoid psychological stress while denying personal responsibility for doing so. A psychosocial causal factor important in both disorders is having experienced physical and/or sexual abuse during childhood. Somatoform and dissociative disorders are unusual, and they will probably seem less comprehensible to you than disorders like depression and anxiety, which are simply exaggerated forms of everyday psychological phenomena.

◊ CHAPTER OUTLINE

I.   Somatoform Disorders
    A. Somatization Disorder
    B. Hypochondriasis
        1. Major Characteristics
        2. More Than Meets the Eye?
    C. Pain Disorder
        1. The Subjectivity of Pain

D. Conversion Disorder
   1. Escape and Secondary Gain
   2. Decreasing Incidence
   3. Sensory Symptoms
   4. Motor Symptoms
   5. Visceral Symptoms
   6. Diagnosis of Conversion Disorder
   7. Precipitating Circumstances
   8. Distinguishing Conversion Disorder from Malingering/Factitious Disorder
E. Causal Factors in Somatoform Disorders
   1. Biological Causal Factors
   2. Psychosocial Causal Factors
   3. Sociocultural Causal Factors
F. Treatment and Outcomes in Somatoform Disorders

II. Dissociative Disorders
   A. Dissociative Amnesia and Fugue
      1. Types of Dissociative Amnesia
      2. Typical Symptoms
      3. Fugue States
   B. Dissociative Identity Disorder (DID)
      1. The Nature of Alters
      2. Incidence and Prevalence – Why Are They Increasing?
      3. The DID Diagnosis: Continuing Controversy
   C. Depersonalization Disorder
   D. Causal Factors in Dissociative Disorders
      1. Biological Causal Factors
      2. Psychosocial Causal Factors
      3. Sociocultural Causal Factors
   E. Treatment and Outcomes in Dissociative Disorders

III. Unresolved Issues: DID and Childhood Trauma

IV. Summary

After studying this chapter, you should be able to:

1. Describe the major symptoms and causal factors of somatoform disorders. (pp. 238-247)

2. Identify the similarities and differences between somatization disorder and hypochondriasis. (pp. 238-241)

3. Describe the symptoms of conversion disorder and summarize its development. (pp. 243-246)

4. Discuss the effectiveness of various treatments for somatoform disorders. (pp. 247-248)

5. Describe the major symptoms and causal factors of dissociative disorder, and differentiate among dissociative amnesia and fugue, dissociative identity disorder, and depersonalization disorder. (pp. 248-256)

6. Identify the most appropriate treatments for the dissociative disorders, and list the limitations of biological and psychological treatments. (pp. 256-257)

◊ **TERMS YOU SHOULD KNOW**

somatoform disorders (p. 238)

dissociative disorders (p. 238)

somatization disorder (pp. 238-239)

hypochondriasis (pp. 240)

malingering (p. 240)

pain disorder (p. 242)

conversion disorder (p. 243)

secondary gain (p. 243)

factitious disorder (pp. 245-246)

implicit memory (p. 248)

implicit perception (p. 248)

amnesia (p. 248)

psychogenic (dissociative) amnesia (p. 249)

fugue (pp. 249-250)

dissociative identity disorder (DID) (pp. 250-253)

host personality (p. 250)

alter identities (p. 251)

depersonalization disorder (pp. 252-253)

derealization (p. 253)

◊ NAMES YOU SHOULD KNOW

J. Kihlstrom (p. 248)

C. A. Ross (p. 254)

◊ CONCEPTS TO MASTER

---

1. Compare and contrast somatoform disorders with dissociative disorders. (pp. 238-241)

2. List the four types and levels of symptoms that must be present to justify a DSM-IV diagnosis of somatization disorder. (p. 239)

3. Explain why hypochondriasis may be viewed as a type of needful interpersonal communication. (p. 241)

4. Describe the symptoms of pain disorder and explain what is meant by the statement that people with psychogenic pain disorders may adopt an invalid life style. (p. 242)

5. Describe the major manifestations of conversion disorder and describe some sensory, motor, and visceral symptoms that often appear. (pp. 243-245)

6. What are the four criteria that help clinicians distinguish between conversion disorders and true organic disturbances? (p. 245)

7. How can a therapist distinguish between an individual with conversion symptoms and a malingerer (one who is consciously faking an illness)? (pp. 245-246)

8. Explain the psychosocial contributions of neuroticism and childhood abuse to somatoform disorders. (p. 247)

9. Describe the similarities and differences in the psychological functions of somatoform disorders and dissociative disorders. (p. 248)

10. Compare and contrast the four types of dissociative amnesia and explain why fugue is grouped with dissociative amnesia. (pp. 248-250)

11. Discuss fugue, and explain why the Case Study of Burt Tate illustrates the disorder. (pp. 249-250)

12. Explain how dissociative amnesia and conversion symptoms are similar. (p. 250)

13. Describe the symptoms of dissociative identity disorder (formerly multiple personality disorder) and explain the complexities inherent in determining whether some cases of DID are genuine and others fraudulent. (pp. 250-252)

14. Explain the nature of alter identities and list some common alter "roles." Is the Case Study of Mary consistent with such alter identities? (pp. 250-252)

15. Review the evidence pertaining to the conflict regarding to what extent dissociative identity disorder (DID) is "real." (p. 252; pp. 257-258)

16. Describe the symptoms of depersonalization. (pp. 252-253)

17. List and explain Ross's (1997) four causal pathways for DID. (p. 254)

18. Review psychosocial and sociocultural causal factors for DID. (pp. 254-256)

19. Describe Kluft's (1993) three-stage model for the treatment of DID. (pp. 256-257)

20. Discuss the unresolved issue of "recovered memories." (pp. 257-258)

Somatoform disorders

1. Somatic symptoms that are thought to represent an expression of psychological difficulties and for which no organic basis can be found are diagnosed as _____ disorders. (p. 238)

2. Complete the following list of four distinct somatoform patterns: (p. 238)
   a. Somatization disorder
   b.
   c.
   d.

3. _____ _____ is characterized by multiple complaints of physical ailments that extend over a long period, beginning before age _____, that cannot be attributed to illness or injury. (pp. 238-239)

4. Somatization disorder is relatively common among _____ in primary _____ _____ _____ around the world. (p. 239)

5. Somatization disorder is _____ times more common among women than among men. There is also evidence of a familial linkage with _____ _____ disorder. (p. 239)

6. Describe the typical attitude among hypochondriacal patients toward their illnesses. (p. 240)

7. Hypochondriasis can be viewed as an interpersonal strategy that results when an individual has learned to view illness as way to obtain special consideration and avoid responsibility. Complete the following statements typical of hypochondriacal adults: (p. 241)

   a. I deserve more of your attention and concern.
   b.

8. In approaching the phenomenon of pain, it is important to underscore that it is always a _____ experience. (p. 242)

9. The experienced intensity of pain is a function of the level of _____ a patient is undergoing. (p. 242)

10. In contrast to Freudian views about conversion disorder, the symptoms of this disorder are now usually seen as serving a defensive function, enabling the individual to _____ or _____ an intolerably stressful situation without having to take _____ for doing so. (p. 243)

11. The term _____ _____ is used to refer to any "external" circumstances such as attention from loved ones or financial compensation that would tend to reinforce the maintenance of conversion disorder. (p. 243)

12. Over time, conversion disorder is being diagnosed less. True or False? (p. 243)

13. What is the reason for this change in the incidence of conversion disorder? (p. 243)

14. Ironside and Batchelor (1945) studied hysterical visual symptoms among airmen in World War II. They found that the symptoms of each airman were closely related to his _____ _____. (p. 244)

15. Motor symptoms of conversion disorder, such as paralysis, are usually confined to a single limb. True or False? (p. 244)

16. Mutism is one of the two most common speech-related conversion disturbances. True or False? (pp. 244-245)

17. One criterion used for distinguishing between conversion disorder and true organic disturbances is the presence of _____ _____ _____, which occurs when the patient describes what is wrong in a rather matter-of-fact way, with little anxiety and fear. Other criteria include the failure of the dysfunction to conform clearly to the symptoms of the particular disease or disorder simulated, the _____ nature of the dysfunction, and the fact that under _____ or _____, the symptoms can usually be removed, shifted, or re-induced. (p. 245)

18. Patients feigning symptoms, referred to as malingerers, can be distinguished from those with conversion disorder by their inclination to be _____, _____, and _____. (p. 246)

19. Bishop, Mobley, and Farr (1978) reported the observation that somatoform disorders involving _____ _____ and _____ symptoms showed a pronounced tendency to be located on the _____ side of the body. (p. 246)

20. _____ and a reported history of _____ _____ are two major psychosocial causal factors for somatoform disorders. (p. 247)

21. Cultures in which frank expression of emotional distress is considered unacceptable should show a relatively lower prevalence of somatoform disorders. True or False? (p. 247)

22. In many instances, the best treatment for somatoform disorders turns out to be _____ _____ _____ _____, but rather the provision of support and reassurance. With the exception of conversion and pain disorders, the prognosis for full recovery from somatoform disorders is _____ _____. (pp. 247-248)

Dissociative disorders

23. Dissociative disorders, like somatoform disorders, are ways of avoiding anxiety and stress in a manner that permits the person to deny personal _____ for his or her "unacceptable" wishes or behaviors. (p. 248)

24. Amnesia is partial or total inability to recall or identify past experience. If it is due to brain disorder, the amnesia usually involves an actual failure of retention. In such cases, the memories are permanently lost. In _____ amnesia, the forgotten material is still there beneath the level of consciousness and can sometimes be recalled under hypnosis or narcosis. (pp. 248-249)

25. Label the following descriptions of four forms of dissociative amnesia using the following terms: localized amnesia, selective amnesia, generalized amnesia, or continuous amnesia. (p. 249)

Forms of Psychogenic Amnesia	Definition
_____	In this form of amnesia, an individual forgets some but not all of what happened during a given period.
_____	In this form of amnesia, an individual remembers nothing that happened during a specific period (usually the first few hours following some traumatic event).
_____	In this form of amnesia, an individual remembers nothing beyond a certain point in the past.
_____	In this form of amnesia, an individual forgets his or her entire life history.

26. Dissociative amnesia is highly selective. _____ or _____ memory is likely to suffer, while semantic, _____, perceptual representation, and _____-_____ storage almost always remain intact. (p. 249)

27. Defending against stress by fleeing from one's surroundings is called _____. (p. 249)

28. Dissociative identity disorder is a dramatic dissociative pattern, usually due to stress, in which an individual manifests two or more complete _____ _____ _____. (p. 250)

29. Alters are usually strikingly similar to the host personality in DID. True or False? (p. 250)

30. The diagnosed occurrence of DID has increased enormously in recent years, in part due to the increased _____ of the diagnosis by clinicians. Considerable controversy remains about the _____ of the DID diagnosis. (p. 252)

31. Depersonalization, or the loss of the sense of self, is often precipitated by _____ _____ resulting from an infectious illness, an accident, or some other traumatic event. (p. 253)

32. Simeon and colleagues (1997) noted a widespread occurrence of _____ _____ _____ among 30 cases of depersonalization disorder. (p. 253)

33. Ross's (1997) causal pathways possibly leading to the emergence of DID are the _____ _____ pathway, the childhood neglect pathway, the _____ pathway, and the _____ pathway. (p. 254)

35. The interesting and impressive study of 12 convicted murderers diagnosed as having DID is unfortunately flawed by the lack of inclusion of a control group of _____ not evidencing _____ symptomatology. (p. 254)

36. Kluft (1993) offered a three-stage model for the treatment of DID. These three stages are: (pp. 256-257)
    a.
    b.
    c. Post-integration therapy

Unresolved issues: DID and childhood trauma

37. In the controversy over the link between childhood abuse (especially sexual) and DID, skeptics about "recovered memories" argue that human memory is _____ and highly subject to _____ or _____ based on experiences or events happening after an original memory trace is established. (p. 257)

◊ CRITICAL THINKING ABOUT DIFFICULT TOPICS

1. To what extent do you think lack of information about basic medical processes contributes to somatoform disorders? Consider that "a high level of medical sophistication does not necessarily rule out a person's developing hypochondriasis" (pp. 240-241).

2. "We all dissociate when we start the car while thinking about all we have to do that day, or wash the dishes while talking on the phone, with little or no conscious attention to the task in which we're engaged" (p. 248). These are called automatisms. Is it possible that the compulsions seen in individuals with obsessive-compulsive disorder might involve a failure to engage in automatisms, or a failure to dissociate? What research might you conduct to test this hypothesis? Use the Dissociative Experiences Scale (p. 256) in your research.

3. A number of Freud's female patients reported childhood sexual abuse. Yet in disseminating this finding, Freud received a cold reception from his colleagues, in part because high rates of childhood sexual abuse were unthinkable in the Vienna of his time. He eventually concluded that most such reports by patients were mere libidinal fantasies. Do you think cultural factors make the incidence and prevalence of childhood sexual abuse vastly higher today than in Freud's Vienna? Or is it possible that the incidence and prevalence of childhood sexual abuse has not changed from Freud's Vienna to today, but that it is simply over-diagnosed today, in part because of the "recovered memories" climate (pp. 257-258), while under-diagnosed in the past? Which of these possibilities is more likely, and why?

4. There are several points of overlap between somatoform and dissociative disorders. For example, Kihlstrom (1994) has suggested that conversion disorder, categorized as a somatoform disorder, is in fact a dissociative disorder (p. 248). If somatoform and dissociative disorders share enough features, it might be unwise to assign them to distinct categories simply because of their somatic versus non-somatic manifestations. Are there good reasons for categorizing somatoform and dissociative disorders separately? Or do you think that the somatoform and dissociative categories should be integrated, using the somatic versus non-somatic variable as a subtype categorization? Justify your answer.

◊ CHAPTER 7 QUIZ

Circle the best of the four answers provided and check them according to answers provided at the back of this study guide. Be sure you understand why each answer is correct.

1. Which of the following is characterized by multiple complaints of physical ailments that extend over a long period and that are inadequately explained by independent findings of physical illness? (pp. 238-239)
   a. somatization disorder
   b. hypochondriasis
   c. pain disorder
   d. conversion disorder

2. Somatization disorder appears be familially linked with: (p. 239)
   a. hypochondriasis.
   b. generalized anxiety disorder.
   c. avoidant personality disorder.
   d. antisocial personality disorder.

3. A hidden message in the complaints of the hypochondriacal adult is: (p. 241)
   a. "I am terribly anxious about dying."
   b. "I can do things as well as you even though I'm sick."
   c. "I deserve more of your attention and concern."
   d. "You make me sick."

4. The experienced intensity of pain is a function of: (p. 242)
   a. overall psychological health.
   b. level of neuroticism.
   c. current level of stress.
   d. number of pain receptors.

5. Aphonia is: (pp. 244-245)
   a. inability to speak.
   b. ability to talk only in a whisper.
   c. a grotesque, disorganized walk.
   d. pseudopregnancy.

6. *La belle indifférence* would be expected in cases of: (p. 245)
   a. malingering.
   b. hypochondriasis.
   c. conversion disorder.
   d. psychogenic pain disorder.

7. All of the following are part of a chain of events in the development of a conversion disorder EXCEPT: (p. 245)
   a. a conscious plan to use illness as an escape.
   b. a desire to escape from some unpleasant situation.
   c. a fleeting wish to be sick in order to avoid the situation.
   d. the appearance of the symptoms of some physical ailment.

8. All of the following were mentioned as psychosocial causal factors for somatoform disorders EXCEPT: (p. 247)
   a. reported history of childhood abuse.
   b. level of neuroticism.
   c. prolonged physical illness of a parent.
   d. inability to communicate personal distress in other than somatic language.

9. Dissociative disorders serve the purpose of avoiding stress by allowing: (p. 248)
   a. escape from one's personal identity.
   b. projection of blame for one's "sins" on others.
   c. retreat into physical symptoms.
   d. withdrawal from stressful situations.

10. In _____ amnesia, an individual forgets his or her entire life history. (p. 249)
    a. localized   c. generalized
    b. selective   d. continuous

11. Fugue refers to: (p. 249)
    a. selective paralysis.   c. switching of alters.
    b. generalized amnesia.   d. defense by actual flight.

12. Alter identities would be expected in cases of: (p. 251)
    a. psychogenic pain disorder.   c. conversion disorder.
    b. hypochondriasis.   d. dissociative identity disorder.

13. In two major studies, the number of alter identities in DID patients averaged: (p. 251)
    a. 2.   c. 10.
    b. 5.   d. 15.

14. The diagnosed occurrence of DID has _____ in recent years. (p. 252)
    a. decreased   c. not fluctuated
    b. increased   d. stabilized

15. _____ commonly accompanies depersonalization disorder. (pp. 252-253)
    a. Fugue   c. Localized amnesia
    b. Derealization   d. Psychosis

16. All of the following personality disorders were shown by Simeon and colleagues (1997) to be comorbid with depersonalization disorder EXCEPT: (p. 253)
   a. avoidant personality disorder.   c. borderline personality disorder.
   b. antisocial personality disorder. d. obsessive-compulsive personality disorder.

17. The strongest evidence implicates _____ as a risk factor for dissociative identity disorder. (p. 254)
   a. death of a parent during childhood
   b. traumatic childhood abuse
   c. low self-esteem developed during childhood
   d. parental use of strict discipline with excessive punishment

| **Chapter 8** |
| *Psychological Compromises of Physical Health* |
| *and Eating Disorders* |

◊ **OVERVIEW**

This chapter opens with a discussion of the role of psychological factors in physical health and illness. In particular, the effect of psychosocial stress on immune functioning is considered in detail. The focus then narrows to allow an examination of psychological factors in one specific disease process known as cardiovascular disease. Next, biological, psychosocial, and sociocultural causal factors for psychogenic (psychologically induced or maintained) illness are reviewed, along with treatments and outcomes for psychogenic illness. Finally, the chapter closes with a review of the clinical presentations, causes, and treatments of eating disorders. These disorders, sometimes life-threatening, have generated much attention in recent years.

◊ **CHAPTER OUTLINE**

I.   General Psychological Factors in Health and Disease
    A. Attitudes, Coping Styles, and Health
    B. Psychological Stress and Autonomic Arousal
    C. Psychosocial Factors and the Immune System
        1. Elements of the Human Immune System
        2. Psychosocial Compromise of the Immune Response
        3. Psychoneuroimmunology
        4. Determining the Pathway for Brain Mediation
            a) The Hypothalamic-Pituitary-Adrenocortical Axis
            b) Other Neurochemicals and Immune Function
            c) Conditioned Immunosuppression
            d) Immune Feedback
        5. Stressor Toxicity
    D. Lifestyle as a Factor in Health Endangerment

II. Psychological Factors and Cardiovascular Disease
    A. Essential Hypertension
    B. Coronary Heart Disease and the Type A Behavior Pattern
        1. Characteristics of Type A Personalities
    C. Depression, Anxiety, and Coronary Heart Disease

III. General Causal Factors in Physical Disease
    A. Biological Causal Factors
        1. Genetic Factors
        2. Differences in Autonomic Reactivity and Somatic Weakness
        3. Disruption of Physiological Equilibrium
    B. Psychosocial Causal Factors
        1. Personality Characteristics
        2. Interpersonal Relationships as Sources of Protection
        3. The Learning of Illnesses
    C. Sociocultural Causal Factors

IV. Treatments and Outcomes for Psychogenic Illnesses
    A. Biological Measures
    B. Psychosocial Measures
        1. Traditional Psychotherapy
        2. Biofeedback
        3. Behavioral Therapy
        4. Cognitive-Behavioral Therapy
    C. Sociocultural Measures

V. Eating Disorders
    A. Clinical Picture in Eating Disorders
        1. Anorexia Nervosa
        2. Bulimia Nervosa
        3. Other Eating Disorders
    B. Distinguishing Among Diagnoses
    C. Prevalence of Eating Disorders
    D. Generalized Risk and Causal Factors in Eating Disorders
        1. Self-Ideal Body Image Discordance
        2. Biological Considerations
        3. Psychopathologic Vulnerability
        4. Dysfunctional Cognitive Styles
    E. Specific Risk and Causal Factors in Anorexia and Bulimia Nervosa
        1. Personality Characteristics
        2. Family Patterns
    F. Treatment of Eating Disorders
        1. Treatment of Anorexia Nervosa
        2. Treatment of Bulimia Nervosa

VI. Summary

◊ LEARNING OBJECTIVES

After studying this chapter, you should be able to:

1. Discuss the influence of general health, attitudes, and coping styles on the risk of physical illness. (pp. 261-264)

2. Describe the focus of the field of psychoneuroimmunology and explain how stress affects the immune system. (pp. 264-268)

3. Discuss the relationship between hypertension and coronary heart disease and how both are affected by Type A behavior and other psychological factors. (pp. 268-271)

4. Summarize the biological, psychosocial, and sociocultural factors contributing to psychogenic illness. (pp. 271-275)

5. Describe several treatment approaches for psychogenic diseases. (pp. 275-278)

6. Compare and contrast the symptoms and diagnostic criteria for anorexia nervosa, bulimia nervosa, and binge eating disorder. (pp. 278-282)

7. Describe the typical personality patterns, cognitive styles, and family dynamics of anorexic and bulimic patients. (pp. 285-287)

◊ TERMS YOU SHOULD KNOW

---

behavioral medicine (p. 261)

psychogenic illness (p. 261)

health psychology (p. 261)

placebo effect (p. 263)

psychoneuroimmunology (pp. 266-267)

essential hypertension (p. 269)

Type A behavior pattern (pp. 270-271)

anorexia nervosa (p. 278)

bulimia nervosa (p. 278)

Binge Eating Disorder (BED) (pp. 280-281)

◊ NAMES YOU SHOULD KNOW

Walter Cannon (p. 264)

Meyer Friedman and Ray Rosenman (pp. 270-271)

Hilde Bruch (p. 287)

◊ CONCEPTS TO MASTER

---

1. List the six problem areas targeted by the behavioral medicine approach and define the relationship between behavioral medicine and health psychology. (pp. 261-262)

2. Describe how optimism can serve as a buffer against disease (or hinder a person's ability to cope with illness). Discuss how a *deficit* in optimism affects health outcomes. (p. 263)

3. How does a person's attitude and outlook on life affect health maintenance and deterioration? (pp. 263-264)

4. What physiological mechanisms are involved in autonomic nervous system arousal? (p. 264)

5. List and describe the component parts of the two main branches (humoral and cellular) of the immune system and explain the functions of each of the component parts. (pp. 265-266)

6. Summarize the research findings that point to psychosocial effects on the immune system, describing the recent evidence that the relationship between stress and compromised immune function is causal. (pp. 265-266)

7. Explain the field of psychoneuroimmunology and summarize the evidence supporting its major premise. (pp. 266-268)

8. List several aspects of the way we live that may produce severe physical problems and explain why healthy individuals find it difficult to change their habits. (p. 268)

9. Define essential hypertension, list some physical diseases that it causes, and explain the suppressed-rage hypotheses about the cause of essential hypertension. (p. 269)

10. Describe the chief clinical manifestations of coronary heart disease (CHD) and list several potential risk factors for CHD. (pp. 269-270)

11. What is meant by the Type A personality? Summarize the evidence linking it to coronary heart disease (CHD). (pp. 270-271)

12. Explain the problem of specificity in the etiology of psychogenic illnesses. (p. 272)

13. What are three possible genetic contributions to diseases. (p. 272)

14. How will genetic mapping help to unravel genetic contributions to diseases? (p. 272)

15. What personality characteristics appear to be associated with disease resistance? (pp. 273-274)

16. What theoretical explanation for the high rate of heart disease in industrialized societies is offered in the book *The Broken Heart*? (p. 274)

17. What is a heart attack? (Highlight 8.3, p. 274)

18. How important is a good social support system to health maintenance? Cite relevant research supporting your answer. (p. 274)

19. Explain how learning might be involved in the development of psychogenic illness. (pp. 274-275)

20. Compare and contrast the effectiveness of various psychosocial measures for treating psychogenic disorders. (pp. 276-278)

21. Indicate the major objectives of sociocultural measures aimed at psychogenic diseases. (p. 278)

22. Define the three major adult eating disorders, including mortality rates, rate of onset, and gender orientation. (pp. 278-279)

23. Distinguish between the restricting and the binge-eating/purging subtypes of anorexia nervosa and characterize the behavioral patterns of the two subtypes. (p. 279)

24. Describe bulimia nervosa, including the criteria that DSM-IV emphasizes. (pp. 279-280)

25. Differentiate between bulimia nervosa and binge-eating disorder (BED). (pp. 280-281)

26. Explain the difficulty in accurate diagnosis of the eating disorders, noting problems of overlap and comorbidity. (p. 281)

27. How do the prevalence rates for eating disorders vary according to socioeconomic status, gender, sexual orientation, and nationality? (p. 282)

28. Discuss self-ideal body image discordance as a generalized risk and causal factor for eating disorders. Refer to Figure 8.1 in your discussion. (pp. 282-284)

29. Explain the dysfunctional cognitive styles and psychopathologic vulnerability of anorexia and bulimia nervosa patients. Describe set-point theory as a biological causal factor for the eating disorders. (pp. 284-285)

30. What are the major specific risk and causal factors in anorexia and bulimia nervosa? (pp. 285-287)

31. Compare the effectiveness of treatments for anorexia and bulimia nervosa. Describe how cognitive-behavioral therapy is applied to these disorders. (pp. 287-288)

General psychological factors in health and disease

1. The interdisciplinary approach to the treatment of physical disorders thought to have psychosocial factors as major aspects in their causation and/or maintenance is known as _____ _____. Psychologists who are interested in psychological factors that contribute to the diagnosis, treatment, and prevention of physical dysfunction specialize in _____ _____. (p. 261)

2. Why are some surgeons reluctant to operate unless the patient has a reasonably optimistic attitude about the outcome? (p. 263)

3. A patient who believes a treatment is going to be effective has a much better chance of showing improvement than does one who is neutral or pessimistic, even when the treatment is subsequently shown to have no direct or relevant physiological effects. This is called the _____ effect. (p. 263)

4. The fight-or-flight response is mediated by the _____ division of the _____ nervous system. (p. 264)

5. An organism has been invaded by an antigen (a substance recognized as foreign). Once this foreign substance has been detected, _____ and _____ become activated and multiply rapidly, deploying the various forms of counterattack mediated by each type of cell. (p. 265)

6. B-cell functioning is involved chiefly with protection against the more common varieties of _____ infection; T-cells mediate immune reactions that, while slower, are far more _____ and more _____ in character and protect against _____ and neoplasms, as opposed to bacteria. (p. 265)

7. Research suggests that behavioral interventions, such as _____ exercise, had positive psychological and _____ effects among groups of uninfected high-risk and early-stage infected gay men. (p. 266)

8. More recently, Kemeny and colleagues (1994) presented evidence that a _____ mood was associated with enhanced HIV-1 activity among infected gay men, confirming in this group the more general point that psychological _____ compromises _____ _____. (p. 266)

9. Until recently, researchers were convinced that the _____ _____ _____ axis was the pathway through which stress affects immune response. However, recent research has turned up a number of competing paths. We now know that a number of other hormones, including growth hormone, _____, and _____, respond to stress and also affect immune competence. The same is true of a variety of neurochemicals, including _____. There may even be direct neural control of immunologic agents, as suggested by the discovery of _____ _____ in the thymus, spleen, and lymph nodes. (p. 267)

10. In a surprising result, it was found that immunosuppression can be _____ _____ (that is, it can come to be elicited as an acquired response to previously neutral stimuli). (p. 267)

11. Lifestyle factors (habits or behavior patterns presumably under our own control) play a major role in three of the leading causes of death in this country: _____ _____ _____; _____ accidents; and _____-_____ deaths. (p. 268)

Psychological factors and cardiovascular disease

12. Hypertension is estimated to afflict more than _____ million Americans, and it is a major predisposing factor for coronary heart disease (CHD). Its incidence among African-Americans is about _____ as high as among white Americans. (p. 269)

13. Essential hypertension is often _____ until its effects become manifest in medical complications. (p. 269)

14. The "suppressed rage" hypotheses of hypertension suggest either that affected people inhibit the expression of certain _____ _____. (p. 270)

15. The clinical picture of coronary heart disease (CHD) includes (1) _____ _____, which is severe chest pain signaling that insufficient blood is getting to the heart muscle; (2) _____ _____, which is complete blockage of a section of the coronary arterial system, resulting in death of heart muscle tissue; and (3) disturbance of the heart's _____ conduction consequent to arterial blockage, resulting in disruption or interruption of the heart's pumping action, often leading to death. (p. 269)

16. Friedman's and Rosenman's (1959) Type A behavior pattern includes excessive _____ drive, even when it is unnecessary, impatience or _____ _____, and _____. More recent work has shown that only the _____ component, perhaps in association with status insecurity, correlates strongly with demonstrable coronary artery deterioration. (pp. 270-271)

17. List the warning signs of heart attack. (Highlight 8.3, p. 274)

    a.

    b.

    c.

    d.

18. Two mechanisms have been proposed to explain the association between depression and CHD. First, depressed people may engage in more _____ known to put people at risk for CHD. Second, it may be that depression is linked to CHD through _____ mechanisms. (p. 271)

General causal factors in physical disease

19. The three general biological causal factors involved in all disease are genetic factors, differences in _____ reactivity and _____ weakness, and disruption of _____ equilibrium. (pp. 272-273)

20. In the autonomic reactivity/somatic weakness theory, presumably the _____ _____ in the chain of visceral organs will be the organ affected. (p. 272)

21. What are the three major psychosocial factors that play a prominent role in causing many diseases? (pp. 273-275)

    a.

    b.

    c.

22. Not only can autonomic reactivity be conditioned involuntarily via the classical Pavlovian model, but _____ conditioning of the autonomic nervous system can also take place. (pp. 274-275)

23. In Bleeker's 1968 study, 19 of 40 volunteer asthmatic subjects developed asthma symptoms after breathing the mist of a salt solution that they were falsely told contained allergens, such as dust or pollen. This study clearly shows the effect of _____ on an autonomically mediated response. (p. 275)

24. As nonindustrialized societies are exposed to social change, psychogenic illnesses become more prevalent. True or False? (p. 275)

Treatments and outcomes for psychogenic illnesses

25. The following are the biological treatments used for psychogenic illnesses. Briefly indicate what each treatment accomplishes. (p. 276)
    a. Tranquilizers

    b. Antidepressant medication

    c. Other drugs (e.g., nicotine-delivering skin patch)

26. In the treatment of psychogenic illnesses, verbally oriented psychotherapies have been relatively ineffective. On the other hand, _____ _____ by writing expressively about life problems under a systematic regimen, does seem to be an effective therapy for those with psychogenic illnesses. (p. 276)

27. _____ treatment for psychogenic diseases had until recently generally failed to live up to the enthusiasm it generated when first introduced more than 30 years ago. That situation may be changing, although it is still not entirely clear that _____ is anything more than an elaborate means to teach patients to _____. There have been increasingly favorable reports regarding efficacy for _____ in the control of musculoskeletal pain. (pp. 276-277)

28. On what assumption is behavioral therapy for psychogenic disorders based? (p. 277)

29. Relaxation techniques have been successfully used to treat _____ _____ _____. (p. 277)

30. Kobasa (1985) and others have experimented with cognitive-behavioral methods to increase _____, which is defined as the ability to withstand stressful circumstances and remain healthy despite them. (p. 278)

Eating disorders

31. The central features of anorexia nervosa are: (a) intense fear of _____ _____ coupled with refusal to maintain adequate _____, usually associated with an obviously erroneous complaint of being "fat"; (b) loss of original body weight at least to a level of ____% of that expected on the basis of height/weight norms; (c) disturbance of _____ _____ or undue influence of the latter in determining self-evaluation; (d) absence of at least _____ consecutive menstrual periods. Subtypes of anorexia nervosa include _____ or _____. (p. 279)

32. The central features of bulimia nervosa are: (a) the frequent occurrence of binge-eating episodes accompanied by a sense of loss of _____ of the over-eating process; (b) recurrent inappropriate behavior intended to prevent weight gain. _____ and _____ subtypes of bulimia nervosa are recognized. (p. 280)

33. The anorexia nervosa diagnosis of binge-eating/purging subtype _____ the bulimia nervosa diagnosis. (p. 280)

34. What problems are typically associated with the purging subtype of bulimia nervosa? (p. 280)

35. The individual with binge-eating disorder binges at a level comparable to bulimia nervosa patients but does not regularly engage in any form of _____ _____ _____ to limit weight gain. (pp. 280-281)

36. The point prevalences of the full syndromes among adolescent and young adult women in the United States are estimated to be between _____% and ____% for anorexia nervosa, and between ____% and ___% for bulimia. (p. 282)

37. Figure 8.1 illustrates the self-ideal _____ _____ _____ to which some women are susceptible. (pp. 282-283)

38. How do changes in the average body weight of American young women compare with changes in the average weight of cultural icons of attractiveness over time? (p. 284)

39. What is set-point theory, and how is it relevant to eating disorders? (pp. 284-285)

40. People with eating disorders, like those with depression, routinely engage in _____ (all-or-none) thinking. (p. 285)

41. Bulimia nervosa patients, like patients with anorexia nervosa, show a long-standing pattern of excessive _____, which appears to manifest itself in widespread negative _____-_____. (p. 286)

42. Family patterns among anorexics and bulimics are similar. The parents of those with eating disorders have been found to be _____, despite their overt intentions to be helpful or generous. These families are described as having limited tolerance for _____ affect. However, it is important to remember that the eating disorder itself has an impact on family dynamics. (pp. 286-287)

43. What are the treatments of choice for anorexia nervosa, bulimia nervosa, and binge-eating disorder? (pp. 287-288)

◊ **CRITICAL THINKING ABOUT DIFFICULT TOPICS**

1. As with the anxiety disorders, the depressive disorders, the somatic disorders, and the dissociative disorders, neuroticism or negative affect is a key personality vulnerability factor for eating disorders (p. 285). Why does this trait promote susceptibility to so many psychological disorders? Do you believe that neuroticism is a cause or consequence of a disorder? Are the pathways involved the same for each of the disorders just mentioned?

2. As you have seen in previous chapters, unequivocal demonstrations of the contribution of stress to psychopathology are difficult to produce. In contrast, the present chapter offers undeniable evidence of the role of stress in physical illness. What accounts for this difference? In thinking about your answer, consider that many components of the immune system's response to stress can be measured (e.g., p. 266), which allows more definitive conclusions about causal relationships. Can you think of any similar underlying processes in anxiety and depression that might help researchers document causal effects of stress?

3. The methodologies of family, twin, and (more rarely) adoption studies together provide clear evidence for the role of genetic factors in psychopathology and physical illnesses. This conclusion tells us nothing, however, about *what* is inherited, leaving unanswered many of the most interesting questions. Regarding genetic contributions to psychogenic disease, for example, it is difficult to determine whether a genetic contribution acts through "an underlying physical vulnerability for acquiring the disease in question" or "the psychological makeup of the individual and his or her stress tolerance" (p. 272). In the first case, there might be an "organ weakness," by which, for example, the cardiovascular system is prone to develop atherosclerosis (see Highlight 8.3, p. 274). In the second case, the person may be anxiety-prone or unduly sensitive to stress, as a result of which the person responds with a stress response to many minor irritations, thereby straining the cardiovascular system. Can you apply this train of thought to psychopathology? Given that we have evidence for a strong genetic contribution to schizophrenia and to bipolar disorder and for a moderate genetic contribution to depression and anxiety, what underlying processes might be inherited?

4. Some of the best-established risk factors are not easy to alter, "even in cases where virtual proof of causation exists" (p. 268). Why is it so difficult to change human behavior? Note the implications for the efficacy of psychological interventions. Psychological interventions must attack and conquer resistance to change that is often so strong that individuals readily risk death rather than change their habits. Does this explain the huge popularity of biological treatments?

5. There are documented patterns of interaction unique to the families of individuals with anorexia nervosa and bulimia nervosa (pp. 286-287). Yet determining the direction of causation of these patterns is problematic (p. 286). There are "starvation symptoms" of these disorders, such as irritability and anger, that are likely highly aversive to family members. Is it more likely that families develop poor communication patterns because of one member's disorder and its consequences, or that dysfunctional families contribute to the onset of anorexia or bulimia nervosa in one member? Plan a program of research that might help untangle these pathways of causation.

◊ CHAPTER 8 QUIZ

Circle the best of the four answers provided and check them according to answers provided at the back of this study guide. Be sure you understand why each answer is correct.

1. Which of the following is a broad interdisciplinary approach to the treatment of physical disorders thought to have psychosocial factors as major aspects in their causation and/or maintenance? (p. 261)
   a. health psychology
   b. behavioral medicine
   c. biobehavioral psychology
   d. physiological psychology

2. Optimism can: (p. 263)
   a. be a buffer against disease.
   b. be problematic when defensive.
   c. produce a placebo effect.
   d. a, b, and c are all true.

3. All of the following are features of the fight-or-flight response EXCEPT: (p. 264)
   a. increased muscle tone.
   b. decreased sweating.
   c. increased heart rate.
   d. pupillary dilation.

4. The immune system is divided into two branches, which are: (p. 265)
   a. blood-related and lymph-related.
   b. glandular and nervous.
   c. humoral and cellular.
   d. red cell-mediated and white cell-mediated.

5. Compared to B-cells, T-cells mediate _____ immune reactions. (p. 265)
   a. faster
   b. more extensive
   c. indirect
   d. bacterially caused

6. Psychosocial factors were originally thought to play little or no role in the pervasive immune breakdown characteristic of AIDS (HIV-1). More recent research suggests that behavioral interventions, such as _____, had positive psychological and immunocompetence effects among groups of uninfected high-risk and early-stage infected gay men. (p. 266)
   a. aerobic exercise
   b. treatment of depression
   c. relaxation training
   d. group therapy

7. The discovery of nerve endings in the thymus suggests that: (p. 267)
   a. the thymus is centrally involved in the General Adaptation Syndrome.
   b. the HPA axis is the pathway for brain mediation of the effect of stress on immune response.
   c. there exists direct neural control of immunological agents.
   d. the placebo effect is mediated by the pons.

8. Which of the following is the least likely cause of hypertension? (p. 269)
   a. kidney dysfunction   c. excessive sodium intake
   b. unremitting stress   d. poor metabolic retention of sodium

9. According to Friedman and Rosenman (1959), all of the following are characteristics of Type A personalities EXCEPT: (p. 270)
   a. excessive competitive drive.   c. impatience or time urgency.
   b. hostility.   d. decelerated speech and motor activity.

10. Lynch (1977) suggests that the relatively high incidence of heart disease in industrialized societies is caused in part by: (p. 274)
    a. the absence of positive human relationships.
    b. depression and/or anxiety.
    c. poor lifestyle choices.
    d. environmental contaminants.

11. In Bleeker's 1968 study, 19 of 40 volunteer asthmatic subjects developed asthma symptoms after breathing the mist of a salt solution they believed to contain allergens. This study supports the effect of _____ on an autonomically mediated response. (p. 275)
    a. classical conditioning   c. suggestion
    b. operant conditioning   d. sympathetic arousal

12. As a treatment for psychogenic disease, biofeedback: (pp. 276-277)
    a. is the therapy of choice.
    b. involves the teaching of relaxation and a host of other techniques specific to the disease.
    c. has shown modest success in treating headache.
    d. has failed to benefit individuals with musculoskeletal pain.

13. Sociocultural treatment of psychogenic disease is targeted most often toward: (p. 278)
    a. encouraging diseased individuals to seek help.
    b. obtaining social support for recovered individuals after treatment.
    c. preventing pathogenic lifestyle behaviors at the group level.
    d. raising money for research.

14. Which of the following would be the best diagnosis for an individual who meets criteria for anorexia nervosa but who also has binging and purging episodes? (pp. 279-281)
    a. eating disorder not otherwise specified
    b. anorexia nervosa, binge-eating/purging subtype
    c. bulimia nervosa
    d. binge-eating disorder

15. Among patients with bulimia nervosa, _____ personality disorders are the most commonly diagnosed Axis II comorbid personality disorders. (p. 281)
    a. obsessive-compulsive   c. borderline
    b. avoidant   d. antisocial

16. In the study in which women with abnormal and normal eating patterns and men rated their current and ideal figures, as well as the figure thought most attractive by the opposite sex: (p. 283)
    a. only eating-disordered women rated their ideal figure as substantially thinner than the figure thought most attractive by the opposite sex.
    b. men's ratings were comparable to those of women having normal eating patterns.
    c. women's ratings were essentially the same, whether or not they were eating-disordered.
    d. men rated their ideal figure as heavier than their current figure.

17. In which of the following disorders do patients NOT appear to overvalue thinness? (p. 283)
    a. anorexia nervosa
    b. binge-eating disorder
    c. bulimia nervosa
    d. eating disorder not otherwise specified

18. Which of the following, according to Strober (1997), is NOT a premorbid personality characteristic of the individual who develops anorexia nervosa? (p. 285)
    a. lack of conformity and oppositional style
    b. excessive focus on perfectionism
    c. preference for routine, order, and predictable environments
    d. emotional reserve and cognitive inhibition

19. Which of the following is NOT a feature of typical families of patients with anorexia nervosa? (pp. 286-287)
    a. poor conflict resolution skills
    b. encouragement of autonomous strivings
    c. emphasis on propriety and rules
    d. limited tolerance of psychological tension

Chapter 9
Personality Disorders

◊ OVERVIEW

Ideally, personality is organized and developed in concert with societal expectations and demands. Yet some individuals instead show inflexible, maladaptive personality and behavioral patterns—patterns that prevent them from fulfilling societal roles adequately. A personality disorder is defined as an enduring pattern of inner experience and behavior that deviates markedly from the expectations of one's culture. Essential to this definition is that the pattern of experience and behavior is stable and enduring. In this chapter, the categories of personality disorders are described, and case studies are presented that illustrate the descriptions. Biological, psychosocial, and sociocultural causal factors in personality disorders are then discussed. Finally, treatments and outcomes for these disorders are considered. One of the personality disorders, antisocial personality disorder, has engendered more research than any of the other disorders, perhaps because those who suffer from it can do serious societal harm. Thus, the clinical features, causal factors, and treatments of antisocial personality disorder are reviewed in detail at the end of the chapter.

◊ CHAPTER OUTLINE

I. Clinical Features of Personality Disorders
   A. DSM-IV's Criteria
   B. Difficulties in Diagnosing Personality Disorders

II. Categories of Personality Disorders
   A. Paranoid Personality Disorder
   B. Schizoid Personality Disorder
   C. Schizotypal Personality Disorder
   D. Histrionic Personality Disorder
   E. Narcissistic Personality Disorder
   F. Antisocial Personality Disorder
   G. Borderline Personality Disorder
   H. Avoidant Personality Disorder
   I. Dependent Personality Disorder
   J. Obsessive-Compulsive Personality Disorder
   K. An Overview of Personality Disorders

III. Causal Factors in Personality Disorders
    A. Biological Causal Factors
    B. Psychological Causal Factors
        1. Early Learning Experiences
        2. Psychodynamic Views
    C. Sociocultural Causal Factors

IV. Treatments and Outcomes for Personality Disorders
    A. Adapting Therapeutic Techniques to Specific Personality Disorders
    B. Treating Borderline Personality Disorder
        1. Pharmacotherapy
        2. Psychological Treatments
    C. Treating Other Personality Disorders

V. Antisocial Personality and Psychopathy
    A. Psychopathy and ASPD
        1. Two Dimensions of Psychopathy
    B. The Clinical Picture in Antisocial Personality and Psychopathy
        1. Inadequate Conscience Development
        2. Irresponsible and Impulsive Behavior
        3. Ability to Impress and Exploit Others
    C. Causal Factors in Psychopathy and Antisocial Personality
        1. Genetic Influences
        2. Deficient Aversive Emotional Arousal and Conditioning
        3. More General Emotional Deficits
        4. A Developmental Perspective
        5. Sociocultural Causal Factors and Psychopathy
    D. Treating Psychopathy and Antisocial Personality Disorder
        1. Cognitive-Behavioral Treatments

VI. Unresolved Issues: Axis II of DSM-IV

VII. Summary

◊ LEARNING OBJECTIVES

After studying this chapter, you should be able to:

1. List the major symptoms of the various personality disorders and give several reasons why their diagnosis is difficult. (pp. 291-305)

2. Identify the three clusters into which the different personality disorders are grouped. (p. 294)

3. Summarize what is known about the biological, psychological, and sociocultural causal factors of the personality disorders. (pp. 306-308)

4. Discuss the difficulties of treating individuals with personality disorders and describe approaches to treatment. (pp. 308-311)

5. Compare and contrast the symptoms and causal factors for psychopathy and antisocial personality disorder. (pp. 311-318)

6. Explain why it is difficult to treat psychopathy and antisocial personality disorder and describe the most promising of the current treatment approaches. (pp. 318-321)

◊ TERMS YOU SHOULD KNOW

---

personality disorders (pp. 291-292)

paranoid personality disorder (Table 9.1, p. 295; pp. 294-295)

schizoid personality disorder (Table 9.1, p. 295; pp. 295-296)

schizotypal personality disorder (Table 9.1, p. 295; pp. 296-297)

histrionic personality disorder (Table 9.1, p. 295; pp. 297-298)

narcissistic personality disorder (Table 9.1, p. 295; pp. 298-299)

antisocial personality disorder (ASPD) (Table 9.1, p. 295; pp. 299-300; pp. 311-315)

borderline personality disorder (BPD) (Table 9.1, p. 295; pp. 300-301)

avoidant personality disorder (Table 9.1, p. 295; pp. 301-303)

dependent personality disorder (Table 9.1, p. 295; p. 303)

obsessive-compulsive personality disorder (OCPD) (Table 9.1, p. 295; p. 304)

psychopathy (p. 311)

◊ **CONCEPTS TO MASTER**

_____

1. Define personality disorder. (pp. 291-292)

2. What are the general criteria of DSM-IV for diagnosing personality disorders? (p. 292)

3. What are three reasons for the high frequency of misdiagnoses of personality disorders? (pp. 292-293)

4. What are the general characteristics of the three clusters of personality disorders? (p. 294)

Cluster A:

Cluster B:

Cluster C:

5. Describe and differentiate among the following Cluster A personality disorders: paranoid, schizoid, and schizotypal. (Table 9.1, p. 295; pp. 294-297)

6. Describe and differentiate among the following Cluster B personality disorders: histrionic, narcissistic, antisocial, and borderline. (Table 9.1, p. 295; pp. 297-301)

7. Describe and differentiate among the following Cluster C personality disorders: avoidant, dependent, and obsessive-compulsive. (Table 9.1, p. 295; pp. 301-304)

8. Beck and Freeman (1990) argue that personality disorders can be characterized by one set of behavior patterns that are overdeveloped and a second set of behavior patterns that are underdeveloped, as well as by characteristic core dysfunctional beliefs. Use this scheme to compare and contrast the personality disorders. (Table 9.2, p. 305)

9. Explain why we know relatively little about the causal factors in personality disorders and summarize what we do know about the biological, psychological, and sociocultural factors that seem important. (pp. 306-308)

10. Zanarini and colleagues (1997) found that borderline personality disorder patients reported significantly higher rates of abuse than did patients with other personality disorders. Explain the shortcomings of this and many other studies that make these results suggestive rather than definitive. (p. 307)

11. List several reasons why personality disorders are especially resistant to therapy. Under what circumstances do persons with personality disorders generally get involved in psychotherapy? (pp. 308-309)

12. Describe Beck and Freeman's (1990) cognitive-behavioral therapy for personality disorders and Marsha Linehan's dialectical behavior therapy for borderline personality disorder. What is known about the effectiveness of treatments for specific personality disorders? (pp. 309-311)

13. List the three DSM-IV criteria (in addition to being age 18 or older) that must be met before an individual is diagnosed as an antisocial personality. (p. 311)

14. What additional personality traits that define psychopathy are not included in the DSM-IV criteria for antisocial personality disorder? (pp. 311-315)

15. Describe the two dimensions of psychopathy according to the 20-item Psychopathy Checklist, and indicate which dimension is closely related to the DSM-IV diagnosis of antisocial personality disorder. (p. 312)

16. Summarize Fowles' application of Gray's theory to psychopathy, including the roles of the behavioral inhibition system and the behavioral activation system. (pp. 315-316)

17. List two major childhood predictors of psychopathy or antisocial personality disorder. What other diagnosis is often a precursor to psychopathy or antisocial personality disorder? (pp. 316-317)

18. Describe some other psychosocial causal factors for psychopathy or antisocial personality disorder. Refer to Figure 9.1 in your description. (Figure 9.1, p. 318; p. 317)

19. Discuss sociocultural causal factors for psychopathy or antisocial personality disorder. (pp. 317-318)

20. Explain why most individuals with psychopathy or antisocial personality disorder seldom come to the attention of mental hospitals and community clinics, and evaluate the success of treatments for this disorder. (p. 312; pp. 318-321)

21. Discuss ways to prevent psychopathy and antisocial personality disorder. (Highlight 9.1, p. 320)

22. Identify and explain two major problems that make Axis II diagnoses unreliable. (pp. 321-322)

◊ **STUDY QUESTIONS**

Clinical features of personality disorders

1. Personality disorders typically do not stem from debilitating reactions to stress. Rather, they stem largely from the gradual development of _____ and _____ personality and behavioral patterns, which result in persistently _____ ways of perceiving, thinking about, and relating to the world. (p. 291)

2. Weissman's (1993) comprehensive summary of epidemiological studies of all the personality disorders concluded that about ___ to ___ percent of the population meets the criteria for one or more personality disorders at some point in life. (p. 291)

3. In DSM-IV, personality disorders are coded on Axis ___. (p. 291)

4. Personality disorders are difficulty to diagnose for three reasons. First, the personality disorder categories are not as _____ _____ as most Axis I diagnostic categories. Second, the diagnostic categories are not _____ _____. Third, the assumption in DSM-IV is that we can make a clear distinction between the presence and the absence of a personality disorder, but the personality characteristics that define these disorders are all _____ in nature. (pp. 292-293)

Categories of personality disorders

5. List the personality disorders that belong to each cluster: (p. 294)
   a. Cluster A (odd or eccentric individuals)

   b. Cluster B (dramatic, emotional, and erratic individuals)

   c. Cluster C (anxious and fearful individuals)

6. Fill in the clinical description for some of the following personality disorders:

   Personality Disorder   **Clinical Description**

   paranoid (p. 294)   Pervasive suspiciousness and distrust of others

   schizoid (pp. 295-296)

   schizotypal (pp. 296-297)

   histrionic (pp. 297-298)

   narcissistic (pp. 298-299)

   borderline (pp. 300-301)

   avoidant (pp. 301-303)

   dependent (p. 303)

   obsessive-compulsive (p. 304)

7. A genetic and biological association with _____ has been clearly documented for schizotypal personality disorder. (p. 297)

8. Over-diagnosis of _____ personality disorder in women may occur in Western cultures because many of the criteria for this disorder are more likely to be observed in women than in men. (p. 298)

9. Approximately ___ percent of individuals receiving the diagnosis of borderline personality disorder are women. (p. 301)

10. Distinguishing avoidant personality disorder from _____ _____ _____ is difficult. (p. 306)

Causal factors in personality disorders

11. Of possible biological factors, it has been suggested that infants' _____ (high or low vitality, behavioral inhibition, and so on) may predispose them to the development of particular personality disorders. (p. 306)

12. People with borderline personality disorder appear to be characterized by lowered functioning of the neurotransmitter _____, which may be why they show impulsive-aggressive behavior, and perhaps by a hyper-responsive _____ system, which may be related to their hypersensitivity to environmental changes. (p. 306)

13. Although Zanarini and colleagues (1997) found that borderline personality disorder patients reported significantly higher rates of childhood abuse than did patients with other personality disorders, this study relied on _____ self-reports of individuals known for their exaggerated and distorted views of other people. (p. 307)

14. Heinz Kohut, a psychodynamic theorist, argued that narcissistic personality disorder results from parents failing to _____ their infants' grandiosity. In contrast, Theodore Millon has proposed that narcissistic personality disorder comes from parental _____. (pp. 307-308)

Treatment and outcomes for personality disorders

15. Because many people with personality disorders (especially those in Cluster A and B) enter treatment only at someone else's insistence, they often do not believe that they need to _____. (p. 309)

16. Beck and Freeman (1990) highlight the importance of _____ that tend to produce consistently biased judgments, as well as tendencies to make cognitive errors in many types of situations. (p. 309)

17. The use of drugs to treat borderline personality disorder is controversial, because borderline personality disorder is so frequently associated with _____ behavior. (p. 310)

18. Probably the most promising treatment for borderline personality disorder is the recently developed _____ behavior therapy. According to this approach, the inability to tolerate strong states of _____ _____ is central to this disorder. (p. 310)

19. Linehan's dialectical behavior therapy for borderline personality disorder is a problem-focused treatment in which the hierarchy of goals includes: (p. 310)
   a.
   b. decreasing behaviors that interfere with therapy
   c.
   d.
   e. other goals the patient chooses

Antisocial personality and psychopathy

20. There are apparently two related but separate dimensions of psychopathy, the first involving the affective and interpersonal core of the disorder and including traits such as lack of remorse and callousness. The second dimension reflects _____ and is much more closely related to the DSM-IV diagnosis of _____ personality disorder. (p. 312)

21. The diagnosis of psychopathy has been shown to be a better predictor of a variety of important facets of criminal behavior than is the diagnosis of ASPD. For example, a diagnosis of psychopathy appears to be the single best predictor of _____. (p. 312)

22. Fill in the missing information on the following chart that summarizes the personality characteristics of individuals with psychopathy or antisocial personality disorder: (pp. 312-314)

Area of Functioning	Behavior Typical of Psychopaths
Conscience development	
Impulse control	
Ability to exploit others	

23. Results from twin and adoption studies show a _____ heritability for antisocial or criminal behavior and probably for psychopathy. (p. 315)

24. Psychopaths show deficient conditioning of anxiety to signals for punishment, and they have difficulty learning to inhibit responses that may result in punishment. Fowles believes that this is due to a deficient _____ _____ _____. Psychopaths also are very focused on actively avoiding threatened punishment. According to Fowles, this is because psychopaths have a normal or possibly overactive _____ _____ _____. (pp. 315-316)

25. Psychopaths show less significant physiological reactivity to _____ cues. (p. 316)

26. What is the single best predictor of who develops an adult diagnosis of psychopathy or antisocial personality? (p. 316)

27. A childhood history of _____ _____ _____ or of _____/_____ disorder is often a precursor to adult psychopathy or ASPD. (pp. 316-317)

28. List some childhood psychosocial and sociocultural contextual variables that may predispose to adult psychopathy or ASPD. (p. 317)

29. Collectivist societies are less likely than individualistic societies to promote some of the behavioral characteristics that, carried to the extreme, result in psychopathy. True or False? (p. 318)

30. In general, psychodynamic psychotherapies have not proven very effective in treating psychopathy or ASPD. Among the factors inherent in the psychopath's personality that interfere with successful treatment are the inability to _____, to feel as others do, to learn from _____, and to accept _____ for one's actions. (pp. 318-319)

31. Perhaps the most promising treatment for psychopathy or ASPD is _____-_____ therapy. (p. 319)

32. What is meant by a "controlled situation," and why is it necessary in order for treatment of psychopathy or ASPD to succeed? (p. 319)

33. According to Beck and Freeman (1990), the dysfunctional beliefs of psychopaths include: (p. 319)
   a. "Wanting something or wanting to avoid something justifies my actions."
   b.
   c. "The views of others are irrelevant to my decisions, unless they directly control my immediate consequences."
   d.

34. Psychopathy is probably more difficult to treat than ASPD. True or False? (p. 321)

35. Psychopathy and ASPD tend to become more severe after the age of 40. True or False? (p. 321)

Unresolved issues: Axis II of DSM-IV

36. Axis II diagnoses are more unreliable than Axis I diagnoses. Two reasons for this are: (p. 321)
    a. DSM-IV follows a categorical approach to diagnosis, but the classifications on Axis II are
       _____ in nature.
    b. There are enormous _____ in the kinds of symptoms shown by people who nevertheless obtain the same diagnosis.

◊ CRITICAL THINKING ABOUT DIFFICULT TOPICS

1. "Applying categorical diagnostic labels to people who are in some cases functioning reasonably well is always risky; it is especially so when the diagnosis involves judgment about characteristics that are also common in normal people" (p. 293). What do you think about the concept of "personality disorder"? Consider the case studies you have read that illustrate each of the personality disorders. Do you believe that these individuals are in significant psychological distress and/or that their social and occupational functioning is severely compromised? What are some benefits accruing to the individual who has been diagnosed as having a personality disorder? What are some disadvantages of being labeled as having a personality disorder?

2. In the case study of Donald S. (pp. 314-315), the following statements express Donald S.'s view: "Although his behavior is self-defeating in the long run, he considers it to be practical and possessed of good sense. Periodic punishments do nothing to decrease his egotism and confidence in his own abilities" (p. 315). Read his case history again and see whether you can apply Fowles' hypotheses of psychopaths' deficient behavioral inhibition systems and normal or overactive behavioral activation systems (p. 316) to specific instances of Donald S.'s behavior. In other words, which of Donald S.'s actions seem to reflect deficiencies in the conditioning of anxiety, and which actions seem to reflect hyper-activation of behavior in response to cues for reward or cues for active avoidance of threatened punishment?

3. Some of the personality disorders show strong gender differences. For example, 75 percent of individuals receiving the diagnosis of borderline personality disorder are women (p. 301). Obsessive-compulsive personality disorder is diagnosed more frequently in men than in women by a 2:1 ratio (p. 295). Do you think that these gender differences are artifactual? Perhaps clinicians are predisposed to diagnose one or another personality disorder more in one gender because its features seem relatively more "masculine" or more "feminine." Consider how "feminine" some of the characteristics of histrionic personality disorder are (p. 298). Or do you think that these gender differences are real? Plan a program of research that would help you address this issue.

4. How might you incorporate the wealth of research into the causal factors for psychopathy or ASPD (pp. 315-318) into the design of a better treatment for these disorders, given that current treatments are only modestly successful?

◊ CHAPTER 9 QUIZ

Circle the best of the four answers provided and check them according to answers provided at the back of this study guide. Be sure you understand why each answer is correct.

1. Personality disorders are: (p. 291)
   a. reactions to stress.
   b. intrapsychic disturbances.
   c. episodic in nature.
   d. maladaptive ways of perceiving, thinking, and relating.

2. Personality disorders are coded on Axis _____ of DSM-IV. (p. 291)
   a. I   c. III
   b. II   d. IV

3. Which of the following is not one of the three reasons given for the high rate of misdiagnoses of personality disorders? (pp. 292-293)
   a. Too few examples of traits associated with each personality disorder are listed.
   b. The diagnostic categories are not mutually exclusive.
   c. The personality characteristics that define these disorders are all dimensional in nature.
   d. The diagnostic categories are not as sharply defined as most Axis I categories.

4. Individuals with this personality disorder typically show oddities of thought, perception, or speech: (pp. 296-297)
   a. schizoid   c. histrionic
   b. schizotypal   d. antisocial

5. A genetic and biological association with schizophrenia has been clearly documented for _____ personality disorder(s): (p. 297)
   a. schizoid   c. paranoid
   b. schizotypal   d. schizoid and schizotypal

6. The _____ seeks attention, whereas the _____ seeks admiration. (p. 299)
   a. histrionic; narcissistic   c. borderline; narcissistic
   b. narcissistic; histrionic   d. borderline; histrionic

7. Individuals with which personality disorder often engage in self-injurious behavior (e.g., self-mutilation)? (pp. 300-301)
   a. histrionic
   b. antisocial
   c. schizoid
   d. borderline

8. Distinguishing generalized social phobia from which personality disorder is difficult? (p. 302)
   a. dependent
   b. narcissistic
   c. avoidant
   d. obsessive-compulsive

9. Excessive conscientiousness is the hallmark of which personality disorder? (p. 304)
   a. avoidant
   b. obsessive-compulsive
   c. dependent
   d. narcissistic

10. Patients with _____ personality disorder report significantly higher rates of childhood abuse than do patients with other personality disorders. (p. 307)
   a. antisocial
   b. obsessive-compulsive
   c. borderline
   d. schizoid

11. According to Kohut, if parents fail to _____ their infant's grandiosity, narcissistic personality disorder may develop. (pp. 307-308)
   a. mirror
   b. notice
   c. inhibit
   d. eliminate

12. Linehan's dialectical behavior therapy for _____ personality disorder is quite promising. (p. 310)
   a. paranoid
   b. schizotypal
   c. antisocial
   d. borderline

13. Researchers prefer to study the diagnosis of psychopathy as opposed to that of ASPD for all of the following reasons EXCEPT: (p. 312)
   a. DSM-IV diagnostic criteria describe psychopathy better than ASPD.
   b. There is a long and rich tradition of research on psychopathy.
   c. Psychopathy better predicts important facets of criminal behavior than does ASPD.
   d. The diagnosis of ASPD fails to include those who show many of the affective and interpersonal features of psychopathy.

14. All of the following are characteristics typical of psychopaths EXCEPT: (pp. 312-314)
   a. inadequate conscience development.
   b. inability to form friendships.
   c. ability to exploit others.
   d. callous disregard for the rights, needs, and well-being of others.

15. According to Fowles, psychopaths are deficient in: (pp. 315-316)
    a. reactivity of the fight-or-flight response.
    b. reactivity of the behavioral activation system.
    c. active avoidance of threatened punishment.
    d. reactivity of the behavioral inhibition system.

16. The sequence of diagnoses common among those who become psychopaths or antisocial personalities is: (p. 317)
    a. oppositional defiant disorder followed by late-onset conduct disorder.
    b. oppositional defiant disorder followed by early-onset conduct disorder.
    c. early-onset conduct disorder followed by oppositional defiant disorder.
    d. attention-deficit/hyperactivity disorder followed by late-onset conduct disorder.

17. In the Capaldi and Patterson (1994) model, the key factor that mediates the influence of other factors and increases the probability of antisocial behavior in the child is: (p. 318)
    a. parental antisocial behavior.
    b. divorce and other parental transitions.
    c. parental stress and depression.
    d. ineffective parenting, especially discipline and supervision.

18. All of the following are true of the treatment of psychopathy or ASPD EXCEPT: (pp. 318-321)
    a. ASPD is more difficult to treat than psychopathy.
    b. Controlled situations are necessary in order for treatment to succeed.
    c. There have been tentative but promising results using SSRI antidepressants.
    d. Factors inherent in the psychopathic or antisocial personality hinder treatment efforts.

Chapter 10
Substance-Related Disorders

◊ OVERVIEW

Addictive behavior is behavior based on the pathological need for a substance (e.g., nicotine, alcohol, or cocaine) or an activity (e.g., gambling). Addictive disorders are associated with potentially serious psychological and/or physiological consequences for the addict—and often for others as well. Abuse of a substance may devolve into dependence, a more severe disorder involving a strong physiological need for increasing amounts of the substance in order to achieve the desired effects from its use. The clinical picture, causal factors, and treatment of alcohol abuse and dependence are reviewed in detail. There is continuing controversy among those who study the treatment of alcohol abuse and dependence as to whether treatment goals ought to include abstinence from alcohol or merely control over its use. Chapter 10 ends with a briefer discussion of abuse and dependence on drugs other than alcohol (e.g., opium and its derivatives, cocaine and amphetamines, barbiturates, LSD and related drugs, and marijuana).

◊ CHAPTER OUTLINE

I.   Alcohol Abuse and Dependence
    A. The Prevalence, Comorbidity, and Demographics of Alcoholism
    B. The Clinical Picture of Alcohol Abuse and Dependence
        1.   Alcohol's Effects on the Brain
        2.   The Physical Effects of Chronic Alcohol Use
        3.   Psychosocial Effects of Alcohol Abuse and Dependence
        4.   Psychoses Associated with Alcoholism
    C. Biological Causal Factors in Alcohol Abuse and Dependence
        1.   The Neurobiology of Addiction
        2.   Genetic Vulnerability
        3.   Genetic Influences and Learning
    D. Psychosocial Causal Factors in Alcohol Abuse and Dependence
        1.   Failures in Parental Guidance
        2.   Psychological Vulnerability
        3.   Stress, Tension Reduction, and Reinforcement
        4.   Expectations of Social Success
        5.   Marital and Other Intimate Relationships

E. Sociocultural Factors
F. Treatment of Alcoholism
    1. Biological Treatment Approaches
        a) Medications to Block the Desire to Drink
        b) Medications to Lower the Side Effects of Acute Withdrawal
        c) Medications to Treat Co-Occurring Disorders
    2. Psychological Treatment Approaches
        a) Group Therapy
        b) Environmental Intervention
        c) Behavior Therapy
    3. Alcoholics Anonymous
    4. Outcome Studies
    5. Relapse Prevention

II. Drug Abuse and Dependence
A. Opium and Its Derivatives (Narcotics)
    1. Effects of Morphine and Heroin
    2. Causal Factors in Opiate Abuse and Dependence
        a) Neural Bases for Physiological Addiction
        b) Addiction Associated with Psychopathology
        c) Addiction Associated with Sociocultural Factors
    3. Treatments and Outcomes
B. Cocaine and Amphetamines (Stimulants)
    1. Cocaine
    2. Amphetamines
        a) Causes and Effects of Amphetamine Abuse
        b) Treatments and Outcomes
C. Barbiturates (Sedatives)
    1. Effects of Barbiturates
    2. Causal Factors in Barbiturate Abuse and Dependence
    3. Treatments and Outcomes
D. LSD and Related Drugs (Hallucinogens)
    1. LSD
    2. Mescaline and Psilocybin
E. Marijuana
    1. Effects of Marijuana
    2. Treatment of Marijuana Dependence

III. Unresolved Issues: Genetics of Alcoholism

IV. Summary

◊ LEARNING OBJECTIVES

After studying this chapter, you should be able to:

1. Define *addictive behavior*, *psychoactive drug*, and *tolerance*. (pp. 325-327)

2. Distinguish between alcohol abuse and alcohol dependence. (pp. 327)

3. Identify the major biological, psychosocial, and sociocultural causal factors of alcohol abuse and dependence. (pp. 334-339)

4. Evaluate the results of various treatment programs and relapse prevention for alcohol dependency. (pp. 339-344)

5. Summarize the effects, causal factors, and treatments for dependency on or abuse of narcotics, stimulants, sedatives, and hallucinogens. (pp. 344-354)

◊ TERMS YOU SHOULD KNOW

---

addictive behavior (p. 325)

psychoactive drugs (p. 325)

toxicity (p. 325)

psychoactive substance abuse (pp. 325-326)

psychoactive substance dependence (p. 326)

tolerance (p. 326)

withdrawal symptoms (p. 326)

alcoholic (p. 327)

alcoholism (p. 327)

fetal alcohol syndrome (FAS) (pp. 331-332)

mesocorticolimbic dopamine pathway (MCLP) (p. 334; Figure 10.2, p. 334)

binge drinking (p. 337)

opium (p. 345)

morphine (p. 345)

heroin (pp. 346-347)

endorphins (p. 348)

methadone (p. 349; Highlight 10.7, p. 349)

cocaine (p. 350)

amphetamines (p. 351)

barbiturates (p. 352)

hallucinogens (pp. 352-353)

LSD (lysergic acid diethylamide) (pp. 352-353)

flashback (p. 353)

mescaline (pp. 352-353)

psilocybin (pp. 352-353)

phencyclidine (PCP or angel dust) (p. 352)

marijuana (p. 353)

hashish (p. 353)

◊ **NAMES YOU SHOULD KNOW**

Sergei Korsakoff (p. 333)

G. Alan Marlatt (p. 341; p. 343)

1. Describe the major categories of addictive or psychoactive substance-related disorders. Define each class. Include the distinction between abuse and dependence in your answer to part b. (pp. 325-326)

    a. Psychoactive substance-induced organic mental disorders

    b. Psychoactive substance-abuse and -dependence disorders

2. Describe two effects of dependence. (p. 326)

3. Explain why hyperobesity and compulsive gambling may be considered addictive. (Highlight 10.1, p. 326).

4. Describe alcohol's seemingly contradictory effects on the brain. (p. 329)

5. Describe three major physiological effects of alcohol. (p. 330)

6. Describe some physical ailments that can result from chronic alcohol use and explain how these may lead to interpersonal and occupational problems. (pp. 330-332)

7. Alcohol withdrawal delirium is a form of psychosis that may occur following a prolonged drinking spree when the person is in a state of withdrawal. List the symptoms and indicate how long they last and how dangerous they are or are not. (p. 333)

8. Describe the memory deficit that occurs in alcoholic amnestic disorder. (p. 333)

9. Describe the mesocorticolimbic dopamine pathway (MCLP), and indicate how it is involved in the processes of abuse and subsequent dependence. (p. 334; Figure 10.2)

10. How do the physiological patterns of pre-alcoholic men differ from those of non-alcoholic men? (pp. 334-335)

11. Describe five major psychosocial factors that may be partially responsible for the development of alcohol dependence. (pp. 335-338)

12. Discuss the problem of college-based drinking. (Highlight 10.3, p. 338)

13. Describe some sociocultural influences on alcohol abuse and dependence. (pp. 338-339)

14. What are three factors that complicate the treatment of alcohol abuse and dependence? (pp. 339-340)

15. List the three purposes of medications in the treatment of alcohol abuse and dependence, and discuss more specifically the pros and cons of treatment with Antabuse. (p. 340)

16. Describe three psychological interventions (excluding AA) that have been used to treat alcohol-dependent individuals. (pp. 340-341)

17. Discuss the controversy between those advocating the treatment goal of controlled drinking and those advocating that of abstinence. Why should we be hesitant to conclude that AA is effective? (p. 342)

18. Review research on the outcomes of various treatments for alcohol abuse and dependence. Be sure to discuss Project MATCH. (pp. 342-343)

19. What is relapse prevention, and why does it seem to be so important as a component of treatment for alcohol abuse and dependence? What is the abstinence violation effect? (pp. 343-344)

20. Aside from alcohol, what are the five psychoactive drugs most commonly associated with abuse and dependence? (p. 344)

21. Discuss caffeinism and nicotine addiction. (Highlights 10.5 and 10.6, p. 346)

22. Describe the major physical and psychological effects of morphine and heroin use. (pp. 347-348)

23. Explain three major causal factors in the development of opiate dependence. (pp. 348-349)

24. Describe some psychosocial and biological treatments that have been used for opiate dependency, and explain the controversy over using methadone. (pp. 349-350; Highlight 10.7, p. 349))

25. Describe some physical and psychological effects of cocaine and amphetamine abuse, and list some withdrawal symptoms. (pp. 350-351)

26. Describe some of the effects of barbiturate abuse, list some of its causes, and describe typical withdrawal symptoms. (p. 352)

27. Describe the physical and psychological effects of using LSD and specify the treatment used for the acute psychosis sometimes induced by its use. (pp. 352-353)

28. What are the short-term and long-term effects of marijuana use and abuse? (pp. 353-354)

29. Summarize the evidence both for and against genetics as a major cause of alcohol abuse and dependence. (pp. 355-356)

◊ STUDY QUESTIONS

Alcohol abuse and dependence

1. Psychoactive substance dependence is a more severe form of psychoactive substance abuse. True or False? (pp. 325-326)

2. In a large NIMH epidemiological study, lifetime prevalence for alcoholism in the United States was found to be _____ percent. (p. 327)

3. Complete the following statements of some of the ways in which alcoholism harms the individual and harms society at large: (pp. 327-329)

Individual harm:
a. Alcoholism leads to a life span shorter by ___ years than that of the average citizen.
b. Alcohol ranks as the _____ major cause of death in the United States.
c. _____ impairment, including brain shrinkage, occurs in many alcoholics.
d. Alcohol abuse is associated with ___ percent of all suicides.

Harm to society:
a. Alcohol abuse is related to over _____ the deaths and major injuries in auto accidents.
b. Alcohol abuse is related to ___ percent of all murders.
c. Alcohol abuse is related to ___ percent or more of all rapes.
d. Alcohol abuse is related to one out of every _____ arrests.

4. The ratio of male problem drinkers to female problem drinkers is __:1. (p. 329)

5. Alcohol is a depressant. Indicate how alcohol: (pp. 329-330)

a. affects higher brain centers:

b. affects behavior:

6. List and define five early warning signs of drinking problems. (Table 10.2, p. 330)
   a.
   b.
   c.
   d.
   e.

7. When the alcohol content of the bloodstream reaches _____ percent, the individual is considered to be intoxicated, at least with respect to driving a vehicle. (p. 330)

8. Three physiological effects of alcohol are common. First, alcohol _____ sexual inhibition, but at the same time _____ sexual performance. Second, alcohol may trigger _____ (lapses of memory). Finally, alcohol causes _____, the symptoms of which include headache, nausea, and fatigue. (p. 330)

9. Malnutrition may result from alcohol abuse and dependence for two reasons. First, alcohol is high-_____ and may reduce the drinker's _____ for other food. Second, heavy drinking impairs the body's ability to _____ _____. (p. 331)

10. Heavy drinking by a pregnant woman may result in _____ _____ _____ in her child. (p. 331)

11. Two alcoholic psychoses are _____ _____ _____ and _____ _____ _____. (p. 333)

12. Direct stimulation of the _____ _____ _____ produces great pleasure and has strong reinforcing properties. (p. 334)

13. Cloninger and colleagues (1986) found strong evidence for the inheritance of alcoholism. They found the following rates of alcoholism: _____ percent among women with no alcoholic parents; _____ percent among women with one alcoholic parent; and _____ percent among women whose parents were both alcoholics. (p. 334)

14. Pre-alcoholic men tend to feel a greater _____ of _____ with alcohol ingestion than do non-alcoholic men. They also show larger _____ _____ _____ to alcohol cues than those at low risk for alcoholism. (pp. 334-335)

15. Fenna and colleagues (1971) and Wolff (1972) found that Asians and Eskimos showed abnormal physiological reactions to alcohol, a phenomenon referred to as _____ _____ _____. (p. 335)

16. An alcoholic personality has been described as an individual who is impulsive, prefers taking _____ _____, is emotionally _____, has difficulty planning and _____ _____, finds that alcohol is helpful in coping with _____, and who does not experience hangovers. (p. 336)

17. The two psychopathological conditions that have been most frequently linked to addictive disorders are _____ and _____ _____. (p. 336)

18. According to the _____ _____ model, adolescents begin drinking as a result of expectations that alcohol will increase their popularity and acceptance by their peers. (p. 337)

19. Excessive use of alcohol is one of the most frequent causes of _____ in the United States and is often a hidden factor in the two most common causes (financial and sexual problems). (pp. 337-338)

20. Religious _____ and social _____ can determine whether alcohol is one of the coping methods commonly used in a given group or society. (p. 339)

21. List the three reasons that alcohol abuse and dependence are difficult to treat. (p. 339)
    a.
    b.
    c.

22. Treatment program objectives usually include detoxification, physical _____, control over _____-_____ behavior, and development of an individual's realization that he or she can _____ with the problems of _____ and lead a much more rewarding life without alcohol. (pp. 339-340)

23. Medications that block the desire to drink include _____ and _____, whereas drugs such as _____ have largely revolutionized the treatment of withdrawal symptoms. (p. 340)

24. The value of Antabuse is in its ability to _____ the alcoholic cycle for a brief time, during which _____ therapy may be undertaken. (p. 340)

25. _____ _____ is a behavior therapy that involves the presentation of a wide range of noxious stimuli accompanying alcohol consumption in order to suppress drinking behavior. (p. 341)

26. One contemporary procedure for treating alcoholics is the cognitive-behavioral approach recommended by Marlatt (1985). Often referred to as a skills-training procedure, the program is aimed at younger problem drinkers considered to be at risk for developing more severe drinking problems on the basis of their family history of alcoholism or their current heavy consumption. The procedure has four components: (p. 341)
    a. Teaching facts about alcohol

    b.

    c.

    d.

27. Alcoholics Anonymous (AA) is a self-help counseling program. Its philosophy is that the alcoholic simply has a(n) _____ (he or she cannot drink) and that because one is never _____ of alcoholism, _____ is the only plausible treatment goal. Unfortunately, little _____ has been conducted on the efficacy of AA. (p. 342)

28. Controlled drinking is more likely to be successful in individuals with _____ _____ alcohol problems. (p. 342)

29. Under what conditions is treatment for alcohol abuse and dependence likely to be most effective? (p. 344)

30. Describe the results of Project MATCH. (p. 343)

31. Define the following components of a cognitive-behavioral approach to relapse prevention. (pp. 343-344)

   a. Indulgent behaviors

   b. Mini-decisions

   c. Abstinence violation effect

Drug abuse and dependence

32. Complete the following table that summarizes psychoactive drug abuse: (Table 10.4, p. 345)

Classification	Drug	Effect
Sedatives	Alcohol	Reduce tension, facilitate social interaction, blot out feelings or events
Stimulants		
Narcotics		
Psychedelics		
Anti-anxiety		

33. Many Civil War veterans returned to civilian life addicted to morphine, a condition euphemistically referred to as _____ _____. (p. 345)

34. The use of an opium derivative over a period of time usually results in a _____ _____ for the drug. This period of time is typically ___ days. Once dependency has been established, withdrawal symptoms will occur and may include runny nose, tearing eyes, _____, _____, increased respiration rate, and a(n) _____ desire for the drug. (p. 347)

35. Researchers have isolated and studied _____ _____ for narcotic drugs in the brain. (p. 348)

36. A high incidence of _____ _____ has been found among heroin addicts. Yet this may be a _____ rather than a cause of heroin dependence. (p. 348)

37. Apparently, the majority of narcotics addicts participate in the _____ _____. What changes are seen in this group? (pp. 348-349)

38. Psychotherapy increases the effectiveness of _____ treatment for heroin dependence. (p. 349)

39. What are the effects of taking cocaine? Discuss symptoms of cocaine withdrawal in your answer. (p. 350)

40. What are two problems encountered in treatment for cocaine dependency? (pp. 350-351)

41. What are some causes and effects of amphetamine abuse? Describe amphetamine psychosis in your answer. (p. 351)

42. Barbiturates act as _____ to slow down the action of the central nervous system and significantly reduce performance on _____ tasks. Impaired decision-making and _____-_____, sluggishness, slow _____, and sudden mood _____ are also common effects of barbiturates. Those who become dependent on barbiturates tend to be _____-_____ and _____ people who often rely on them as _____ _____ and who do not commonly use other classes of drugs. These individuals are often referred to as _____ _____. (p. 352)

43. Name four hallucinogenic drugs: (p. 352)

    a.
    b.
    c.
    d.

44. LSD causes changes in _____ _____, mood swings, and feelings of _____ and _____. One phenomenon that may occur following the use of LSD is called _____, although this is relatively rare. Users do not develop _____ dependence. Although users claim that LSD enhances _____, there is no evidence that it does. (pp. 352-353)

45. Marijuana is related to a stronger drug, _____. (p. 353)

46. Describe the following effects of marijuana: (p. 354)

    a. Psychological effects:

    b. Physiological effects:

47. Marijuana leads to _____ but not _____ dependence. (p. 354)

48. Mice can be bred to have a(n) _____ or _____ for alcohol. Yet the great majority of children who have alcoholic parents ____ _____ themselves become alcoholics. The role of genetics in the development of alcoholism is important, but _____ also matters. (pp. 355-356)

CRITICAL THINKING ABOUT DIFFICULT TOPICS

1. The World Health Organization defines alcohol dependence syndrome as "a state, psychic and usually also physical, resulting from taking alcohol, characterized by behavioral and other responses that always include a compulsion to take alcohol on a continuous or periodic basis in order to experience its psychic effects, and sometimes to avoid the discomfort of its absence; tolerance may or may not be present" (p. 327). Discuss aspects of this definition that make it psychologically based in addition to being biologically based.

2. Whether to treat alcohol abuse and dependence with the goal of eventual abstinence or controlled drinking is controversial (p. 342). In treating eating disorders (especially bulimia nervosa and binge eating disorder), abstinence is not a feasible goal, but controlled eating is clearly an important and reasonable goal. For many psychological disorders, abstinence from a problem behavior makes little sense; yet for some, it not only makes good sense but seems essential (e.g., pedophilia). Do you think that the attainment of abstinence is an unrealistic and/or unfair goal for alcoholics, or that abstinence is essential in the treatment of alcohol abuse and dependence?

3. Alcoholics Anonymous tries to "ease some personal responsibility" by helping alcoholics to "see themselves not as weak-willed or lacking in moral strength, but rather simply as having an affliction" (p. 342). Discuss where this philosophy falls along the continuum of free will versus determinism.

4. What do you think of the classification of hyper-obesity and pathological gambling as addictive disorders (Highlight 10.1, p. 326)? If one accepts this classification, one would need to argue that these disorders involve addiction to *activities* instead of to substances with chemical properties that induce dependency (p. 326). Compare and contrast hyper-obesity and pathological gambling with the disorders you studied in Chapter 10. Think about likely psychological and/or physiological effects of these two disorders, and likely treatments for them. Do they seem to belong with the other addictions, or would they be better classified elsewhere? Explain your point of view.

CHAPTER 10 QUIZ

Circle the best of the four answers provided and check them according to answers provided at the back of this study guide. Be sure you understand why each answer is correct.

1. An individual who shows tolerance for a drug or withdrawal symptoms when it is unavailable is diagnosed with: (pp. 325-326)
   a. psychoactive substance abuse.
   b. psychoactive substance dependence.
   c. psychoactive substance toxicity.
   d. psychoactive substance-induced organic mental disorder.

2. The life span of the average alcoholic is about ___ years shorter than that of the average citizen. (p. 327)
   a. 3   c. 12
   b. 6   d. 18

3. All of the following are associated with a lower incidence of alcoholism EXCEPT: (p. 329)
   a. being male versus female.
   b. being married versus unmarried.
   c. having higher versus lower levels of education.
   d. being older versus younger.

4. A person is considered intoxicated when the alcohol content of the bloodstream reaches ____ percent. (p. 330)
   a. 0.1   c. 1.0
   b. 0.5   d. 1.5

5. All of the following are physiological effects of alcohol on the brain EXCEPT: (p. 330)
   a. blackouts.
   b. hangovers.
   c. decreased sexual inhibition.
   d. heightened sexual performance.

6. Mr. H. is 75 and has been an alcoholic for 15 years. He has a lot of trouble remembering recent events. In order to avoid embarrassment, he often falsifies events so others won't know he has forgotten these recent events. Mr. H.'s disorder is probably: (p. 333)
   a. alcohol amnestic disorder.
   b. alcohol idiosyncratic intoxication.
   c. alcohol withdrawal delirium.
   d. delirium tremens.

7. Which of the following does *not* differentiate pre-alcoholic men from non-alcoholic men? (pp. 334-335)
   a. reduction of stress after alcohol ingestion
   b. alpha wave patterns on EEG recordings
   c. size of the mesocorticolimbic dopamine pathway (MCLP)
   d. size of conditioned physiological responses to alcohol cues

8. All of the following are psychosocial causal factors in alcohol abuse and dependence EXCEPT: (pp. 335-338; p. 329)
   a. failures in parental guidance.
   b. socioeconomic status.
   c. expectations of social success.
   d. troubled marital and other intimate relationships.

9. A cultural attitude of permissiveness toward drinking, such as exists in France, generally: (p. 338)
   a. is correlated with a low rate of alcoholism and problem drinking.
   b. is a sign that alcoholism has been accepted as a normal behavior pattern.
   c. is associated with the common use of alcohol as a means of coping with stress.
   d. has no significant effect on either alcoholism or drinking behavior.

10. Extinguishing drinking behavior by associating it with nausea is a procedure called: (p. 341)
    a. Antabuse.   c. covert sensitization.
    b. systematic desensitization.   d. aversive conditioning.

11. In their four-year follow-up of a large group of treated alcoholics, Polich and colleagues (1981) found that ____ percent continued to show alcohol-related problems. (pp. 342-343)
    a. 7   c. 36
    b. 18   d. 54

12. According to Marlatt's cognitive-behavioral view, alcoholic relapse is typically based upon: (p. 343)
    a. a sudden "falling off the wagon."
    b. an overpowering psychological craving.
    c. small, apparently irrelevant decisions.
    d. unexpected increases in stressor strength.

13. All of the following is true of opiate addiction EXCEPT: (p. 347)
    a. using an opiate continually for 30 days is enough time to establish a drug habit.
    b. in the United States, young addicts typically move from snorting to mainlining.
    c. many addicts compare the heroin "rush" to a sexual orgasm.
    d. opiate use cannot lead to physiological dependence.

14. The human body produces its own opium-like substances called _____ in the brain and pituitary gland. (p. 348)
    a. antibodies   c. endorphins
    b. antigens   d. phagocytes

15. Which of the following personality disorders has the *highest* incidence among heroin addicts? (p. 348)
    a. antisocial   c. obsessive-compulsive
    b. avoidant   d. dependent

16. All of the following is true of methadone as a treatment for narcotic addiction EXCEPT: (p. 349)
    a. methadone is less physiologically addictive than heroin.
    b. treatment with methadone alone may work only for a small minority of heroin abusers.
    c. some patients can eventually stop taking methadone without relapse to heroin addiction.
    d. psychotherapy along with methadone increases the effectiveness of treatment.

17. Cocaine is classified as a(n): (p. 350)
    a. hallucinogen.   c. sedative.
    b. narcotic.   d. stimulant.

18. Chronic abuse of amphetamines can result in a disorder known as: (p. 351)
    a. delirium tremens.
    b. amphetamine psychosis.
    c. paranoid schizophrenia.
    d. tardive dyskinesia.

19. The individual most likely to become dependent on barbiturates is: (p. 352)
    a. a high school student.
    b. a college student.
    c. a middle-aged homeless person who abuses multiple classes of drugs.
    d. a middle-aged person who abuses barbiturates only at home.

20. Goodwin and colleagues (1974) concluded that which of the following situations put a son at *greatest* risk of becoming an alcoholic? (p. 355)
    a. being born to an alcoholic parent
    b. being born to non-alcoholic parents
    c. being raised by an alcoholic parent
    d. being raised by non-alcoholic parents

Chapter 11
Sexual Variants, Abuse, and Dysfunctions

◊ **OVERVIEW**

Chapter 11 opens with a discussion of the enormous variability within and between cultures with respect to sexual practices and attitudes (in particular, toward homosexuality, which is not viewed as a psychological disorder in DSM-IV). Then the chapter turns to the paraphilias — defined as persistent sexual behavior patterns in which unusual objects, rituals, or situations are required for full sexual satisfaction—and their treatment. Gender identity disorder, defined as the desire to be of the opposite biological sex along with persistent discomfort about one's own biological sex, and transsexualism is discussed. Sexual abuse is then discussed, including childhood sexual abuse, pedophilia, incest, and rape. Finally, sexual dysfunctions, impairments either in the desire for sexual gratification or in the ability to achieve it, are discussed. There are highly effective treatments available for at least some of the sexual dysfunctions.

◊ **CHAPTER OUTLINE**

I.   Sociocultural Influences on Sexual Practices and Standards
    A. Case I: Degeneracy and Abstinence Theory
    B. Case II: Ritualized Homosexuality in Melanesia
    C. Case III: Homosexuality and American Psychiatry
        1. Homosexuality as Sickness

II. Sexual and Gender Variants
    A. The Paraphilias
        1. Fetishism
        2. Transvestic Fetishism
        3. Voyeurism
        4. Exhibitionism
        5. Sadism
        6. Masochism
    B. Causal Factors and Treatments for Paraphilias
        1. Treatments for Paraphilias
    C. Gender Identity Disorders
        1. Gender Identity Disorder of Childhood
            a) Treatment
        2. Transsexualism
            a) Treatment

III. Sexual Abuse
    A. Childhood Sexual Abuse
        1. Prevalence of Childhood Sexual Abuse
        2. Consequences of Childhood Sexual Abuse
        3. Controversies Concerning Childhood Sexual Abuse
            a) Children's Testimony
            b) Recovered Memories of Sexual Abuse
    B. Pedophilia
    C. Incest
    D. Rape
        1. Prevalence of Rape
        2. Is Rape Motivated by Sex or Aggression?
        3. Rape and Its Aftermath
        4. Rapists and Causal Considerations
    E. Treatment and Recidivism of Sex Offenders
        1. Psychotherapies
        2. Biological and Surgical Treatments
        3. Combination of Biological and Psychosocial Treatments
        4. Efficacy of Treatments

IV. Sexual Dysfunctions
    A. Dysfunctions of Sexual Desire
        1. Sexual Desire Disorders
    B. Dysfunctions of Sexual Arousal
        1. Male Erectile Disorder
        2. Female Sexual Arousal Disorder
    C. Orgasmic Disorders
        1. Premature Ejaculation
        2. Male Orgasmic Disorder
        3. Female Orgasmic Disorder
    D. Dysfunctions Involving Sexual Pain
        1. Vaginismus
        2. Dyspareunia

V. Summary

After studying this chapter, you should be able to:

1. Discuss several examples of sociocultural influences on sexual practices and cultural standards and values. (pp. 360-364; Highlight 11.1, pp. 363-364)

2. Define, give examples of, and describe the clinical features of the following paraphilias: fetishism, transvestic fetishism, voyeurism, exhibitionism, sadism, and masochism. (pp. 365-370)

3. Describe the most effective treatments for paraphilias, and summarize their causal factors. (pp. 370-371)

4. Identify the clinical features of and describe the treatments for gender identity disorders (gender identity disorder of childhood and transsexualism). (pp. 371-374)

5. Discuss the controversies surrounding children's testimony regarding sexual abuse and adults' "recovered memories" of childhood sexual abuse. (pp. 376-379; Highlight 11.3, pp. 377-378)

6. Review what is known about the frequency of different kinds of childhood sexual abuse and its perpetrators. (pp. 374-381)

7. List the major sexual dysfunctions, describe their general features, review etiological theories, and summarize the major approaches to treatment. (pp. 386-392)

◊ TERMS YOU SHOULD KNOW

paraphilias (p. 365)

fetishism (p. 365)

transvestic fetishism (p. 366)

voyeurism (p. 367)

exhibitionism (p. 368)

sadism (pp. 368-369)

masochism (p. 369)

gender identity disorder (p. 371)

cross-gender identification (p. 371)

gender dysphoria (p. 371)

transsexualism (pp. 372-374)

autogynephilia (p. 373)

sexual abuse (p. 374)

pedophilia (p. 379)

incest (p. 380)

rape (p. 380)

sexual dysfunction (p. 386)

desire phase (p. 386)

excitement phase (p. 386)

orgasm (p. 386)

resolution (p. 386)

hypoactive sexual desire disorder (p. 386)

sexual aversion disorder (p. 388)

male erectile disorder (p. 388)

female sexual arousal disorder (p. 390)

premature ejaculation (p. 390)

male orgasmic disorder (p. 391)

female orgasmic disorder (p. 391)

vaginismus (p. 392)

dyspareunia (p. 392)

◊ NAMES YOU SHOULD KNOW

Alfred Kinsey (p. 363)

Evelyn Hooker (p. 363)

John Money (p. 365; p. 370; p. 371)

Kurt Freund (p. 370)

Ray Blanchard (p. 370; p. 372; p. 373; p. 374)

Richard Green (p. 372)

Stephen Ceci (p. 377; Highlight 11.3, pp. 377-378)

Barry Maletzky (p. 383; p. 384)

William Masters and Virginia Johnson (p. 386; p. 388; p. 391)

1. Explain how the case histories of (a) degeneracy and abstinence theory and (b) ritualized homosexuality in Melanesia illustrate cultural differences and historical changes in what is considered acceptable and normal sexual behavior. (pp. 360-362)

2. How has the psychiatric view of homosexuality changed over time? Identify a few key historical events that propelled this change. (pp. 362-364)

3. Discuss evidence from Bailey and colleagues' twin studies (1991, 1993) regarding the influence of genetic (and environmental) factors in human sexual orientation. (Highlight 11.1, p. 364)

4. Define *paraphilias* and list the eight examples recognized in DSM-IV. (p. 365)

5. Describe the clinical features of each of the paraphilias listed below: (pp. 365-370)

Paraphilia	Clinical Features
Fetishism	
Transvestic Fetishism	
Voyeurism	
Exhibitionism	
Sadism	
Masochism	

6. Describe Money's (1986) attempt to account for the fact that almost all paraphiliacs are male. (p. 370)

7. What do Freund and Blanchard (1993) mean by "erotic target location"? How does this concept help to account for the fact that people with paraphilias often have more than one paraphilia? (p. 370)

8. What do cognitive-behavioral treatments for paraphilias involve, and how effective are they? (pp. 370-371)

9. What two components characterize gender identity disorder? (p. 371)

10. What are the arguments in favor of and against labeling children with atypical gender identity as disordered? (p. 372)

11. Distinguish the two types of male-to-female transsexuals, and discuss their developmental course. Also discuss female-to-male transsexuals. (pp. 372-374)

12. What are the most effective treatments for childhood gender identity disorder and transsexualism? (p. 372; pp. 373-374)

13. List the short-term consequences of childhood sexual abuse and explain why knowledge about the long-term consequences is more uncertain. (pp. 374-376; Highlight 11.2, p. 375)

14. What are the major issues surrounding children's testimony about sexual abuse and adults' recovered memories of sexual abuse? (pp. 376-379; Highlight 11.3, pp. 377-378)

15. Describe the method and results of the "Sam Stone Study" (Leichtman & Ceci, 1995) and explain the implications for the validity of preschool children's testimony. (Highlight 11.3, pp. 377-378)

16. Define *pedophilia* and describe the clinical features of its perpetrators, including the results of studies investigating the sexual responses of pedophiles. (pp. 379-380)

17. What do we know about the incidence and prevalence patterns of incest and rape? Why are these rates difficult to estimate, and what factors contribute to the variability in the estimates? (pp. 380-381)

18. What are the major clinical features of the perpetrators of incest and rape? (pp. 380-381)

19. Is rape motivated by sex or aggression, or both? Explain. (p. 381)

20. Discuss some causal factors in rape. (pp. 382-383)

21. Identify the main goals of treatment of sex offenders, and describe the different treatment approaches. (pp. 383-386)

22. Discuss the pros and cons of Megan's Law. (Highlight 11.4, p. 385)

23. Compare and contrast the symptoms of the dysfunctions of sexual desire, arousal, and orgasm in men and women. (pp. 386-392)

24. Summarize research on the role of anxiety and other potential causal factors in male erectile disorder. (pp. 388-389)

25. List the most effective treatments for male erectile disorder and female sexual arousal disorder. (pp. 389-390)

26. Summarize the most effective treatments for and the etiological theories of the orgasmic disorders (i.e., premature ejaculation, male orgasmic disorder, and female orgasmic disorder). (pp. 390-392)

27.Why is it understandable that dyspareunia is often associated with vaginismus in women? (p. 392)

◊ STUDY QUESTIONS

Sociocultural influences on sexual practices and standards

1. Tissot's degeneracy theory concerned the importance of _____ for physical and sexual vigor in men. (p. 360)

2. A descendant of degeneracy theory, called _____ theory, was advocated by the Rev. Sylvester Graham, who emphasized the importance of healthy food, physical fitness, and _____ _____. (p. 360)

3. Kellogg's corn flakes were invented, almost literally, as _____-_____ food. (p. 361)

4. Many used to believe that masturbation caused _____. (p. 361)

5. Two beliefs related to Sambian sexual practices are semen _____ and female _____. Consequently, homosexual behavior is encouraged among young Sambian males. Homosexual behavior stops after the _____ of a man's _____ _____. (p. 361)

6. Freud's attitude toward homosexuality was _____ _____. (p. 362)

7. Evelyn Hooker demonstrated that trained psychologists could not distinguish the _____ _____ _____ of homosexual and heterosexual subjects. (p. 363)

8. In _____, homosexuality was removed from DSM-II. (p. 363)

9. Bailey and Pillard (1991) found that concordance rates for homosexuality were _____% for male monozygotic twins, compared with _____% for male dizygotic twins. These findings are consistent with a substantial causal role for _____. (Highlight 11.1, p. 364)

Sexual and gender variants

10. Paraphilias are a group of persistent sexual behavior patterns in which unusual objects, _____, or _____ are required for full sexual satisfaction. (p. 365)

11. In fetishism, sexual interest typically centers on some _____ object, such as an article of clothing, or some _____ part of the body. (p. 365)

12. Fetishes can be acquired through _____ conditioning, although this is not a sufficient causal factor for fetishism. It is also likely that those high in _____ _____ are especially prone to developing one or more fetishes. (pp. 365-366)

13. The vast majority of transvestites are _____. (p. 366)

14. Voyeurism refers to obtaining sexual pleasure by clandestine peeping. Voyeurism occurs as a sexual offense primarily among _____ _____. (p. 367)

15. Voyeuristic activities often provide important _____ feelings of power and secret domination over an unsuspecting victim, which may contribute to the _____ of this pattern. (p. 367)

16. The intentional exposure of the genitals to others (generally strangers) in inappropriate circumstances and without their consent is called _____. According to some estimates, as many as _____% of women may have been the target of either exhibitionism or voyeurism. Some research indicates that there may be a subclass of exhibitionists who may best be considered as having _____ _____ _____. (p. 368)

17. On what does the arousal of sadistic individuals depend? (p. 368)

18. It is important to distinguish transient or occasional interest in sadomasochistic practices from sadism as a _____. (p. 368)

19. According to Warren, Dietz, and Hazelwood (1996), what is the typical clinical profile of a sexually sadistic serial killer? (pp. 368-369)

20. Masochism (achieving sexual stimulation and gratification from the experience of pain and degradation in relating to a lover) appears to be much _____ common than sadism. (p. 369)

21. One highly dangerous form of masochism is called _____ _____. (p. 369)

22. Two facts about paraphilias are likely to be etiologically important: (p. 370)
    a. Almost all paraphiliacs are _____.
    b. People with paraphilias often have _____ _____ _____.

23. According to Money (1986), men's vulnerability to paraphilias is closely linked to their greater dependency on _____ _____ _____. (p. 370)

24. Freund and Blanchard (1993) suggested that some men (those who have more than one paraphilia) may be especially vulnerable to errors in _____ _____ _____. (p. 370)

25. Success has recently been achieved in the treatment of paraphilias by using the technique of _____ _____ _____, which involves having the patient imagine a deviant arousal scene. At the point where arousal is high, the patient imagines _____ consequences, and a foul odor is introduced via an open vial or an automated odor pump to help condition a real aversion to these deviant scenes. In treating paraphilias, restructuring of cognitive _____ that may be helping to maintain the deviant sexual arousal and behavior patterns is also important. (p. 371)

26. Gender identity disorder is characterized by two components: (p. 371)
    a.
    b.

27. Boys with gender identity disorder are often ostracized as _____ by their peers, while young girls with gender identity disorder are treated more normally by their peers, because cross-gender behavior in girls is better tolerated. (p. 371)

28. The most common adult outcome of boys with gender identity disorder, who outnumber girls with this disorder by five to one, appears to be _____. (p. 372)

29. How do autogynephilic transsexuals differ from homosexual transsexuals? (pp. 372-273)

30. The only treatment shown to be effective for transsexualism is _____ _____ _____. (p. 373)

31. Describe the procedures involved in the following surgical sex reassignments: (pp. 373-374)
    a. male-to-female

    b. female-to-male

32. According to Green and Fleming (1990), ____% of 220 male-to-female transsexuals had satisfactory outcomes, and ____% of 130 female-to-male transsexuals had such outcomes. (p. 374)

Sexual abuse

33. List at least three possible causal pathways between childhood sexual abuse and borderline personality disorder. (Highlight 11.2, p. 375)

34. In children's testimony concerning sexual abuse, the use of anatomically correct dolls _____ _____ improve the accuracy of the children's reports of where (or even if) they were touched. (p. 377)

35. Stephen Ceci has found that preschoolers are deficient in distinguishing between _____ versus _____ acts. (Highlight 11.3, p. 377)

36. When professionals were asked to rate the children for the accuracy of their testimony in the "Sam Stone Study" (Leichtman & Ceci, 1995), the videotape of the child who was least accurate was rated as being _____ credible. (Highlight 11.3, p. 378)

37. Nearly all pedophiles are men. About two-thirds of their victims are _____, typically between the ages of _____ and _____. (p. 379)

38. Respond to the following questions: (p. 379)
    a. Do most pedophiles use physical force or violence?

    b. Do most pedophiles show sexual arousal only to children?

    c. What motivates most pedophiles?

39. Culturally prohibited sexual relations between family members, such as a brother and sister or a parent and child, are known as _____. (p. 380)

40. _____-_____ is clearly the most common form of incest. (p. 380)

234

41. Incestuous fathers tend to be of lower _____ than other fathers, but they do not typically evidence serious _____. Indeed, they are often _____ and _____. Most incestuous offenders are not _____. (p. 380)

42. Estimates of how frequently rape occurs are biased by the precise _____ of rape used in a particular study and by the _____ in which the information is gathered. (pp. 380-381)

43. Respond to the following questions: (pp. 381-382)
    a. Is rape motivated by sex or aggression?

    b. Is rape a repetitive activity?

    c. Are most rapes planned?

    d. Do a third or more of rapes involve more than one offender?

    e. Does a close relationship between victim and offender mean the victim is more or less likely to be brutally beaten?

    f. How old is the typical rapist?

44. Distinguish the profile of a date rapist from that of an incarcerated rapist. (p. 382)

45. The case can be made that some rapists have a _____. (p. 382)

46. Rapists show some deficits in their _____ appraisals of women's feelings and _____. (p. 382)

47. Aversion therapy as a treatment for sex offenders should include not only the reduction of deviant sexual arousal patterns, but also the learning of arousal to _____ _____. (p. 383)

48. The most controversial biological treatment for sex offenders involves _____. Recidivism rates of castrated offenders are typically less than ____%, compared with greater than ____% of uncastrated offenders. However, many feel that the treatment is _____ and _____. (p. 384)

49. The term *sexual dysfunction* refers to impairment either in the desire for sexual gratification or in the ability to achieve it. Dysfunctions can occur in any of the first three phases of the human sexual response: the _____ phase, the _____ phase, or _____. (p. 386)

50. There are two types of sexual desire disorders: _____ sexual desire disorder, and _____ _____ disorder, a more extreme version of the former. _____ may contribute to some cases of sexual desire disorders. The most common female sexual dysfunction appears to be _____ _____ disorder. (p. 386; p. 388).

51. Two theories have been proposed in order to account for the etiology of male erectile disorder. According to Masters and Johnson (1975), the important causal factor is _____ about sexual performance. Barlow and colleagues have instead suggested that _____ _____ frequently associated with anxiety seem to interfere with sexual arousal in dysfunctional people. (p. 388)

52. Circle the correct term. Prolonged or permanent erectile disorder before the age of 60 is relatively: Common or Rare? (pp. 388-389)

53. What is priapism, and what are three of its causes? (p. 389)

54. Viagra promotes erection only if _____ _____ is present. (p. 389)

55. Female sexual arousal disorder is in many ways the female counterpart of _____ _____ in men. List three causes of female sexual arousal disorder: (p. 390)

56. _____ _____ is the most prevalent male sexual dysfunction. (p. 390)

57. The _____-_____-_____ technique is a behavioral therapy for premature ejaculation, which at first was thought to be 90% effective. More recent studies suggest that it is not nearly that effective. (p. 391)

58. Which is more difficult to treat: lifelong or situational female orgasmic dysfunction? Explain why, according to Beck (1992), this is so. (p. 392)

59. An involuntary spasm of the muscles at the entrance to the vagina that prevents penetration and sexual intercourse is called _____. Often associated with this dysfunction is _____, or painful sexual intercourse. (p. 392)

◆━━━━━━━━━━━━━━━━━◆━━━━━━━━━━━━━━━━━

◊ CRITICAL THINKING ABOUT DIFFICULT TOPICS

1. Freund and Blanchard's (1993) concept of *erotic target location* assumes that men are not born with a heterosexual orientation, but rather that they "must learn . . . which stimuli together constitute a female sex partner, who is their target stimulus" (p. 370). Yet evidence from the genetics of human sexual orientation (Highlight 11.1, p. 364) appears to conflict with Freund and Blanchard's theory. How might you reconcile these two theories?

2. Although sexual advances toward prepubertal children are viewed as a psychiatric disorder and diagnosed as pedophilia in DSM-IV, rape and incest (including advances directed at postpubertal children) are not. The reason for this is thought to be "the seriousness with which society views these offenses and its preference for treating coercive sex offenders as criminals rather than as individuals having a mental disorder" (p. 374). On what basis would you decide whether sexual advances directed at postpubertal children should be seen as reflecting psychopathology or as simple criminal behavior, or perhaps both? What implications do you think your choice would have for treatment?

3. Do you think that castration is indeed "brutal and dehumanizing" (p. 385)? Explain your position regarding castration. Address the following issues in your answer: (1) whether the idea of castration is less intolerable to you if the incarcerated sex offender requests it; (2) whether castration is intolerable (if it is) because it is a *biological* treatment or for some other reason; (3) whether the proven efficacy of castration (e.g., recidivism rates of castrated offenders are typically less than 3%, compared with more than 50% of uncastrated offenders; p. 384) affects your position.

4. Do you think that Megan's Law (Highlight 11.4, p. 385) is just, or do you think it unfairly assumes that once a sex offender, always a sex offender? Justify your answer using research on (1) recidivism rates of sex offenders; and (2) the effectiveness of Megan's Law to date.

Circle the best of the four answers provided and check them according to answers provided at the back of this study guide. Be sure you understand why each answer is correct.

1. A form of paraphilia in which there usually is not a "victim" is: (p. 366)
   a. voyeurism.
   b. exhibitionism.
   c. sadism.
   d. transvestic fetishism.

2. Which of the following persons is most likely to engage in voyeurism? (p. 367)
   a. a married woman who has female orgasmic disorder
   b. a homosexual man who is "in between" lovers
   c. an adolescent male who is shy and feels inadequate in his relations with women
   d. an elderly man who lives by himself

3. The most common sexual offense reported to the police in the United States, Canada, and Europe is: (p. 368)
   a. voyeurism.
   b. exhibitionism.
   c. masochism.
   d. transvestic fetishism.

4. In Maletzky's (1998) treatment outcome study of nearly 1500 paraphiliac offenders, the *lowest* rates of success were found for: (p. 371)
   a. exhibitionism.
   b. fetishism.
   c. voyeurism.
   d. transvestic fetishism.

5. The most common adult outcome of boys with gender identity disorder appears to be: (p. 372)
   a. homosexuality.
   b. heterosexuality.
   c. homosexual transsexualism.
   d. autogynephilic transsexualism.

6. Most transsexuals who are sexually attracted to men and who recall being extremely feminine in childhood are: (p. 372)
   a. female-to-male transsexuals.
   b. homosexual male-to-female transsexuals.
   c. autogynephilic male-to-female transsexuals.
   d. heterosexual transsexuals.

7. Autogynephilic transsexuals usually report a history of: (p. 373)
   a. exhibitionism.
   b. voyeurism.
   c. transvestic fetishism.
   d. masochism.

8. In the "Sam Stone Study," Leichtman and Ceci (1995) found that ____ percent of children given a prior stereotype and asked leading questions during the four interviews continued to give inaccurate testimony after being gently challenged, compared with only ____ percent among control children. (Highlight 11.3, pp. 377-378)
   a. 14; 4.5
   b. 5; 1
   c. 44; 2.5
   d. 23; 8

9. All of the following is true of false memories EXCEPT: (p. 378)
   a. they can be highly vivid.
   b. they can be induced.
   c. their validity is heatedly debated.
   d. trained professionals can easily distinguish them from normal "unrepressed" memories.

10. In studies investigating the sexual responses of pedophiles: (p. 379)
   a. pedophiles show sexual arousal only to nude or partially clad girls.
   b. pedophiles show sexual arousal equally to boys and girls.
   c. pedophiles show sexual arousal to girls, but also to adult women.
   d. pedophiles show sexual arousal to girls, but also to adult men.

11. In Williams and Finkelhor's (1990) study, incestuous fathers tended to be _____ _____ than other fathers. (p. 380)
   a. of lower intelligence
   b. more impulsive
   c. more psychopathic
   d. less religious

12. Knight and Prentky (1990) found that rapists: (p. 381)
   a. have only sexual motives.
   b. have only aggressive motives.
   c. have both aggressive and sexual motives.
   d. have both aggressive and sexual motives, but to varying degrees.

13. All of the following is true of rape EXCEPT: (pp. 381-382)
   a. most rapists are young men.
   b. most rapists rape only once.
   c. most rapists are strangers to their victims.
   d. rapists show deficits in their cognitive appraisals of women's intentions.

14. Which of the following best distinguishes incarcerated rapists from date rapists? (p. 382)
   a. hostile masculinity
   b. impulsive, antisocial behavior
   c. emotionally detached, predatory personalities
   d. promiscuity

15. Recidivism rates of castrated offenders are typically less than ____%, compared with greater than ____% of uncastrated offenders. (p. 384)
   a. 3; 50
   b. 12; 40
   c. 36; 60
   d. 51; 75

16. All of the following are phases of the human sexual response EXCEPT: (p. 386)
   a. excitement.
   c. plateau.
   b. desire.
   d. orgasm.

17. According to the findings of Diokno, Brown, and Herzog (1990), more than _____ of married men over age 70 had some erectile difficulties. (p. 389)
   a. one-fourth
   c. two-thirds
   b. one-half
   d. three-fourths

18. Which of the following is the most common male sexual dysfunction? (p. 390)
   a. male erectile disorder
   c. male orgasmic disorder
   b. premature ejaculation
   d. sexual desire disorder

Chapter 12
The Schizophrenias

◊ OVERVIEW

The schizophrenias are perhaps the most severe of the mental disorders. Although schizophrenia is quite likely the end product of a group of disorders with differing etiologies, courses, and outcomes, the schizophrenias do all share a hallmark feature: psychosis, or significant loss of contact with reality. Chapter 12 opens with background information, including a brief history, prevalence rates, and onset estimates.

Although there is no one clinical profile for schizophrenia, many affected individuals show disturbances of thought, perception, emotion, self, and/or motor behavior. Subtyping an individual's schizophrenia depends in part on the symptom pattern exhibited. The undifferentiated, catatonic, disorganized, and paranoid types of schizophrenia are discussed. Like many other mental disorders, schizophrenia is likely caused by an interaction of biological, psychosocial, and sociocultural factors unique to each sufferer.

Chapter 12 continues with a review of treatments and outcomes for the schizophrenias. Because anti-psychotic drugs were so revolutionary when first introduced in the 1950s, psychosocial approaches to treatment fell by the wayside. This was at some cost, because while anti-psychotic drugs may reduce symptoms, they do nothing to promote social recovery, the ability to manage independently as an economically effective and interpersonally connected member of one's society. Chapter 12 closes with a call for mental health professionals to reintegrate psychosocial therapies into their treatment plans.

◊ CHAPTER OUTLINE

I. The Schizophrenias
    A. Origins of the Schizophrenia Concept
    B. Prevalence and Onset

II. The Clinical Picture in Schizophrenia
    A. Disturbance of Associative Linking
    B. Disturbance of Thought Content
    C. Disruption of Perception
    D. Emotional Dysfunction

E. Confused Sense of Self
F. Disrupted Volition
G. Retreat to an Inner World
H. Disturbed Motor Behavior
I. Continuing Problems in Defining Schizophrenia

III. The Classic Subtypes of Schizophrenia
    A. Undifferentiated Type
    B. Catatonic Type
    C. Disorganized Type
    D. Paranoid Type
    E. Other Schizophrenic and Psychotic Patterns

IV. Causal Factors in Schizophrenia
    A. Biological Factors in Schizophrenia
        1. Genetic Influences
        2. Twin Studies
        3. Adoption Studies
        4. Biochemical Factors
        5. Neurophysiological Factors
        6. Neuroanatomical Factors
            a) Brain Mass Anomalies
            b) Deficit Localization
        7. Neurodevelopmental Issues
        8. Interpreting the Biological Evidence: Diathesis and Stress
    B. Psychosocial Factors in Schizophrenia
        1. Damaging Parent-Child and Family Interactions
            a) Destructive Parental Interactions
            b) Faulty Communication
        2. The Role of Excessive Life Stress and Expressed Emotion
    C. Sociocultural Factors in Schizophrenia

V. Treatments and Outcomes for Schizophrenia
    A. The Effects of Antipsychotic Medication
    B. Psychosocial Approaches in Treating Schizophrenia
        1. Family Therapy
        2. Individual Psychotherapy
        3. Social-Skills Training and Community Treatment
        4. A Problem: Overcoming Inertia

VI. Unresolved Issues: The Overlooked Value of Psychosocial Intervention in the Schizophrenias

VII. Summary

◊ LEARNING OBJECTIVES

After studying this chapter, you should be able to:

1. Summarize the history of the concept of schizophrenia. (pp. 397-398)

2. Discuss the prevalence rates and age of onset of schizophrenia in terms of gender and sociocultural differences. (pp. 398-399)

3. Describe the major symptoms of schizophrenia. (pp. 399-403)

4. List the DSM-IV criteria for the diagnosis of schizophrenia. (Table 12.2, p. 401)

5. Compare and contrast the subtypes of schizophrenia. (pp. 403-410)

6. Summarize the biological, psychosocial, and sociocultural causal factors in schizophrenia. (pp. 410-425)

7. Describe and evaluate the major biological and psychosocial treatments for schizophrenia. (pp. 425-429)

◊ TERMS YOU SHOULD KNOW

---

the schizophrenias (p. 396)

psychosis (p. 396)

delusional disorder (p. 396)

shared psychotic disorder (p. 397)

brief psychotic disorder (p. 397)

positive-syndrome schizophrenia (p. 399; Table 12.1, p. 400)

Type I schizophrenia (p. 399; Table 12.1, p. 400)

negative-syndrome schizophrenia (p. 399; Table 12.1, p. 400)

Type II schizophrenia (p. 399; Table 12.1, p. 400)

delusions (p. 401)

hallucinations (p. 402)

schizophrenia, residual type (p. 403; Table 12.3, p. 404)

schizophrenia, undifferentiated type (pp. 404-405; Table 12.3, p. 404)

schizophrenia, catatonic type (pp. 406-407; Table 12.3, p. 404)

schizophrenia, disorganized type (pp. 407-408; Table 12.3, p. 404)

schizophrenia, paranoid type (pp. 408-410; Table 12.3, p. 404)

schizoaffective disorder (p. 410)

schizophreniform disorder (p. 410)

expressed emotion (EE) (p. 424)

social recovery (p. 426)

assertive community treatment (ACT) (p.428)

intensive case management (ICM) (p. 428)

◊ NAMES YOU SHOULD KNOW

Eugen Bleuler (p. 398)

Paul Meehl (p. 400; p. 422)

Irving Gottesman (p. 414; p. 415)

E. Fuller Torrey (p. 414)

Pekka Tienari (p. 415)

Timothy Crow (p. 419)

Elaine Walker (p. 421)

Theodore Lidz (p. 422)

Gregory Bateson (p. 423)

◊ CONCEPTS TO MASTER

---

1. The original term for the schizophrenias was *dementia praecox*. In light of current knowledge, this term is misleading, because there is no convincing evidence that schizophrenia leads to permanent mental deterioration. Later, Bleuler introduced the term *schizophrenia* (split mind). By this he did not mean "multiple personality;" what *did* he mean? (p. 398)

2. What are some of the difficulties in determining the prevalence of the schizophrenias? (p. 398)

3. When does initial onset of schizophrenia usually occur, and how does it vary by gender? (p. 398; Figure 12.1, p. 399)

4. What are the main features distinguishing positive-syndrome schizophrenia from negative-syndrome schizophrenia? (pp. 399-400; Table 12.1, p. 400)

5. List the DSM-IV criteria for the diagnosis of schizophrenia. (Table 12.2, p. 401)

6. Briefly describe the eight symptom domains that are relevant to the construct of schizophrenia. (pp. 400-403)

Disturbance of Associative Linkage:

Disturbance of Thought Control:

Disturbance of Perception:

Emotional Dysfunction:

Confused Sense of Self:

Disrupted Volition:

Retreat to an Inner World:

Disturbed Motor Behavior:

7. What kinds of delusions and hallucinations are common in the schizophrenias? (pp. 401-402)

8. Describe the five major subtypes of schizophrenia listed in DSM-IV. (pp. 403-410; Table 12.3, p. 404)

9. Compare and contrast the time of onset, symptoms, and prognosis of each of the major subtypes of schizophrenia. (pp. 404-410)

10. What distinguishes schizophreniform disorder from other schizophrenic disorders? (p. 410)

11. Review the evidence from twin studies that supports a genetic contribution to schizophrenia. (pp. 414-415)

12. How do studies of the Genain quadruplets show that psychosocial factors interact with genetics in the development and outcome of schizophrenia. (Highlight 12.1, pp. 412-413)

13. List the major findings from the following studies: (pp. 415-416)
    a) the follow-up study of 47 adoptees born to schizophrenic mothers in a state mental hospital

    b) the Danish adoption studies

    c) Tienari and colleagues' Finnish Adoption Study

14. What is the dopamine hypothesis? Explain the current status of this explanation for schizophrenia. (pp. 416-417)

15. Describe the deficiencies in smooth pursuit eye movement (SPEM) that have been observed in schizophrenics and in some of their close relatives and discuss the implications of these findings. (p. 417)

16. In addition to SPEM deficiencies, what other abnormal neurophysiological processes have been found to be associated with increased risk for schizophrenia? (pp. 417-418)

17. What neuroanatomical anomalies differentiate people with schizophrenia from people who do not suffer from the disorder? (pp. 418-419)

18. Are these anomalies neurodegenerative, neurodevelopmental, or both? (pp. 418-419)

19. Explain what is meant by hypofrontality, summarize the evidence in support of this concept, and note the authors' cautionary statement about these findings. Also discuss how temporolimbic structures are thought to be involved in schizophrenia. (p. 419)

20. What is the season of birth effect in schizophrenia, and what evidence supports its neurodevelopmental framework? (pp. 420-421)

21. Describe Walker and colleagues' methodology and summarize their findings regarding early childhood deficits in facial/emotional expressions and motor competence among pre-schizophrenic children. How might such deficits increase the risk of developing schizophrenia? Incorporate the diathesis-stress model into your answer. (p. 421)

22. Describe theories of pathogenic parent-child and family interactions, as well as some caveats regarding this type of research. (pp. 422-423)

23. What is expressed emotion (EE)? Describe the findings suggesting EE's genuinely causal role in precipitating relapse into schizophrenia following remission. (pp. 423-424)

24. Summarize the sociocultural factors that may contribute to the development of schizophrenia. (pp. 424-425)

25. How did the introduction in the mid-1950s of pharmacotherapy with phenothiazines transform the environment of mental hospitals? (pp. 425-426)

26. What is the importance of social recovery in the prognosis of a person with schizophrenia? Is social recovery addressed by treatment with anti-psychotic drugs? (pp. 426-427; p. 429)

27. Describe the major psychosocial approaches to treating schizophrenia, including assertive community treatment (ACT) and intensive case management (ICM). (pp. 427-428)

◊ STUDY QUESTIONS

The schizophrenias

1. The "final common pathway" in the schizophrenias is a significant loss of _____ with _____, often referred to as _____. (p. 396)

2. A disorder in which the sufferer's behavior does not show the gross disorganization and performance deficiencies characteristic of schizophrenia is _____ _____. When two or more people, usually in the same family, develop persistent, interlocking delusional ideas, the disorder is called _____ _____ _____. (pp. 396-397)

3. The term _____ _____ was adopted by the German psychiatrist Emil Kraepelin to refer to a group of conditions that all seemed to have the feature of mental deterioration beginning early in life. Later, a Swiss psychiatrist, Eugen _____, more accurately termed these conditions _____. (pp. 397-398)

4. Allen (1997) noted that schizophrenia appears to be more common in traditional, small-scale societies than it is in modern, well-developed societies. True or False? (p. 398)

5. During any given year, approximately ____ % of adult U.S. citizens (over ___ million persons) meet diagnostic criteria for schizophrenia. (p. 398)

6. The median age of initial onset for schizophrenic disorders is in the mid-_____. (p. 398)

7. Which gender has an earlier onset of schizophrenia? Which gender has a late-onset pattern of schizophrenia? (p. 398)

The clinical picture in schizophrenia

8. Fill in the following chart comparing and contrasting positive-syndrome to negative-syndrome schizophrenia, and Type I to Type II schizophrenia: (pp. 399-400; Table 12.1, p. 400)

Positive-syndrome
Hallucinations

_____

Derailment of _____
Bizarre behavior
Minimal _____ impairment
_____ onset
_____ course

Type I: (the above, plus...)
_____ response to drugs
_____ _____ abnormalities
_____ brain ventricles

Negative-syndrome
Emotional flattening
_____ of speech
Asociality
_____
Significant _____ impairment
_____ onset
_____ course

Type II: (the above, plus...)
_____ response to drugs
_____ _____ abnormalities
_____ brain ventricles

9. The DSM-IV diagnostic criteria for schizophrenia are very specific. Complete the following list of symptoms, at least two of which must be present to qualify for a diagnosis of schizophrenia: (Table 12.2, p. 401)
   a. Delusions
   b. Hallucinations
   c.
   d.
   e.

10. Eight domains of disturbed behavior appear relevant to the construct of schizophrenia. These domains are listed in the following chart. Fill in the empty spaces by writing a short description of the characteristic or providing a clinical example chosen from the text to illustrate the characteristic, as appropriate. (pp. 400-403)

Characteristics of Schizophrenia		
Characteristic	**Brief Description**	**Example**
Disturbance of Associative Linking		Patient says, "I cannot be a nincompoop in a physical sense (unless Society would feed me chemicals for my picture in the nincompoop book)."
Disturbance of Thought Content	Many types of delusions may be seen.	
Disruption of Perception	Breakdown in perceptual selectivity occurs; hallucinations may be seen.	
Emotional Dysfunction	a) b)	a) Patient can't find joy or pleasure in any life events. b) Patient may laugh wildly at news of a parent's death.
Confused Sense of Self		Patient feels tied up with universal powers.
Disrupted Volition	A disruption of goal-directed activity occurs	
Retreat to an Inner World		Patient develops fantasy world, including the creation of strange beings who interact with the person in various self-directed dramas.

Disturbed Motor Behavior		Patient is in a stupor with rigid posture or shows ritualistic mannerisms and bizarre grimacing.

11. Dolphus and colleagues (1996) have suggested that there are at least four discriminable patterns of schizophrenia signs: _____, _____, _____, and _____. However, because most patients display a(n) _____ picture, especially over time, it is not clear that this proposal adds much to our understanding. (p. 403)

12. It must be kept in mind that the schizophrenias remain a _____ construct, one whose definition has evolved and changed over time. (p. 403)

The classic subtypes of schizophrenia

13. Match the following types of schizophrenia with the appropriate definition: (pp. 403-410; Table 12.3, p. 404)

a. Undifferentiated type	__	Those persons who are in remission following a schizophrenic episode and show only mild indications of schizophrenia.
b. Paranoid type	__	A form of schizophrenia that occurs at an early age and includes blunting, inappropriate mannerisms, and bizarre behavior.
c. Catatonic type	__	A person in whom symptoms of schizophrenia have existed for less than six months.
d. Disorganized type	__	A person who shows absurd, illogical, and changeable delusions, as well as frequent and vivid hallucinations.
e. Residual type	__	A form of schizophrenia in which all the primary indicators of schizophrenia are seen in a rapidly changing mixture.
f. Schizoaffective disorder	__	A person who shows some schizophrenic signs as well as obvious depression or elation.
g. Schizophreniform disorder	__	A type of schizophrenia characterized by alternating periods of extreme excitement and extreme withdrawal.

14. What are *echolalia* and *echopraxia*, and in what subtype of schizophrenia are they seen? (p. 406)

15. What has happened to the relative frequency of paranoid schizophrenia and undifferentiated schizophrenia in recent years, and what reasons are given for these changes? (p. 408)

16. Under what circumstances might a paranoid schizophrenic become violent? (p. 409)

Causal factors in schizophrenia

17. What does the story of the Genain quadruplets tell us about the etiology of schizophrenia? (Highlight 12.1, pp. 412-413)

18. According to Torrey and colleagues (1994), the overall pairwise concordance rates for schizophrenia are _____ % in MZ twins and _____ % in DZ twins. Thus, a reduction in shared genes from 100% to 50% reduces the risk of schizophrenia nearly _____%. (p. 414)

19. If schizophrenia were *exclusively* a genetic disorder, the concordance rate for identical twins would be _____ %. (p. 414)

20. Torrey and colleagues' (1994) study of discordant schizophrenia outcomes among 27 pairs of MZ twins strongly implicates _____ _____ as often playing a role in the causal pattern of schizophrenia. (pp. 414-415)

21. Researchers conducting the Danish adoption studies found a preponderance of schizophrenia and "schizophrenia spectrum" problems in the _____ relatives, but not the _____ relatives, of schizophrenic adoptees. However, these studies did not include independent assessments of the _____-_____ _____ of the adoptive families into which index and control youngsters had been placed. (p. 415)

22. The results of Tienari and colleagues' Finnish Adoption Study show a(n) _____ genetic effect. However, _____ _____ and disturbed _____ have a substantial impact on outcome for both index and control cases. Further, the findings indicate a strong interaction between genetic vulnerability and a(n) _____ _____ environment in the causal pathway leading to schizophrenia. The Finnish Adoption Study provides strong support for the _____-_____ model of the origins of schizophrenia. (pp. 415-416)

23. All of the early anti-schizophrenic drugs had the common property of blocking _____-mediated neural transmission. This fact led to the popular _____ hypothesis of schizophrenia. However, evidence against this hypothesis is that (1) the neuroleptics are not _____ for schizophrenia; and (2) the receptor-blocking effect is accomplished too _____ to be consistent with the clinical picture of a gradual improvement following initiation of neuroleptic drug therapy in schizophrenia. (p. 416)

24. Specific attention difficulties in schizophrenia include deficiencies in _____ _____ _____ _____, the ability to track a moving target visually. (p. 417)

25. In a minority of cases of schizophrenia, particularly among those of chronic, negative-symptom course, there is an abnormal enlargement of the brain's _____, as well as enlarged _____. Both findings imply a loss of _____ _____ _____, possibly some type of _____ or degeneration. (p. 418)

26. In a review of neuro-imaging studies in schizophrenia, Gur and Pearlson (1993) concluded that the evidence implicates primarily three brain regions: the _____, the _____, and the _____ _____. However, few of these findings are _____ for schizophrenia. (p. 419)

27. Dysfunctional frontal lobes (i.e., hypofrontality) are believed to be especially important in accounting for _____ signs and symptoms, and perhaps also attentional-cognitive deficits. (p. 419)

28. Recent neurodevelopmental thinking about schizophrenia has led to the suspicion that early, even prenatal, _____ to the brain later also interferes with normal brain _____ development during a period of intensive reorganization, occurring for most people during adolescence or early adulthood. (p. 419)

29. The observation that people who become schizophrenic are more likely than people in general to have been born in the winter and early spring months is known as the _____ _____ _____ _____. Bradbury and Miller (1985) hypothesized that this effect was due to some type of _____ process or _____ complications, or both. (pp. 420-421)

30. Much of the available psychosocial research in schizophrenia is seriously _____. Much of it is also of _____ quality. (p. 422)

31. What have several researchers (e.g., Mishler & Waxler, 1968; Liem, 1974) noted about the impact of schizophrenic children's behavior on their parents? (p. 422)

32. In a study of 14 families with schizophrenic offspring, Lidz and colleagues (1965) failed to find a single family that functioned in a reasonably effective and well-integrated manner. Eight of the 14 couples lived in a state of severe _____ _____ in which the continuation of the marriage was constantly threatened. In the other 6 families, family members had entered into a _____ in which the seriously disturbed behavior of a family member was redefined as normal. (p. 422)

33. Bateson (1959, 1960) coined the term _____-_____ _____ to describe the conflicting and confusing nature of communications among members of schizophrenic families. Give an example of this. (p. 423)

34. Singer and Wynne (1963, 1965) linked the thought disorders in schizophrenia to two styles of thinking and communication in the family: _____ and _____. In their later research, they referred to these styles as _____ _____. (p. 423)

35. Relapse into schizophrenia following remission is often associated with a pattern of negative communication called expressed emotion (EE). What two components appear critical in the pathogenic effects of EE? (p. 424)
a.
b.

36. The _____ the socioeconomic status, the _____ the prevalence of schizophrenia. While the conditions of lower-class existence may cause stress and help to precipitate schizophrenia, it is also true that lower-class membership can be a(n) _____ of schizophrenia. (p. 424)

Treatments and outcomes for schizophrenia

37. A person with schizophrenia who enters a mental hospital or other facility as a first-time inpatient today has a(n) ____% to ____% chance of being discharged within a matter of weeks or, at most, months. (p. 426)

38. After attending a meeting of Schizophrenics Anonymous, Roger Brown, a Harvard social psychologist, concluded that there is something about schizophrenia that the anti-psychotic drugs _____ _____ _____ or even always _____ on a long-term basis. Attendees of the meeting had not shown what mental health professionals call _____ _____ (i.e., the ability to manage independently as an economically effective and interpersonally connected member of one's society). (p. 426)

39. Hegarty and colleagues (1994) did a quantitative analysis of worldwide clinical outcomes for patients treated for schizophrenia on a decade-by-decade basis from 1895 through 1991. Although there was an increase in social recoveries following the introduction of anti-psychotic medication, that increase was a quite _____ one, going roughly from ____% to ____% socially recovered. (p. 426)

40. Psychosocial approaches to the treatment of schizophrenia include _____ therapy, which ought to be especially effective against the _____ hazards of familial expressed emotion (EE). (p. 427-428)

41. What is involved in assertive community treatment (ACT) and intensive case management (ICM)? (p. 428)

42. Despite such difficulties, what economic losses does society incur when treatment is limited to pharmacotherapy alone? (pp. 428-429)

Unresolved issues

43. The difficulties in expanding psychosocial intervention attempts appear two-fold. What are these difficulties? (p. 429)
>   a)
>   b)

◊ **CRITICAL THINKING ABOUT DIFFICULT TOPICS**

1. Heston (1966) found that the adopted-away children of schizophrenic mothers were more likely than controls to be diagnosed as schizophrenic, but also as mentally retarded, neurotic, and psychopathic (p. 415). These findings suggest that "any genetic liability [to schizophrenia] conveyed by the mothers is not specific to schizophrenia but also includes a liability for other forms of psychopathology" (p. 415). While it is true that what is inherited is broader than the DSM-IV diagnosis of schizophrenia, including mental retardation, anxiety, and psychopathy in the schizophrenia spectrum makes little sense. Can you think of other explanations? Consider two. First, it has been suggested that the fathers may have contributed genes increasing the risk of psychopathy. Second, nonspecific genetic liability to schizophrenia might involve low intelligence and anxiety-proneness. If you accept this argument, note how difficult it is to identify the forms of psychopathology that are *specifically* related to schizophrenia, because other genetic influences will affect the pathology seen among the relatives of schizophrenic index cases.

2. You have already learned that the mesocorticolimbic dopamine pathway is strongly involved in the brain reward system, also called the "pleasure pathway." In Chapter 12, you learned that the majority of anti-psychotic drugs may exert their effect by blocking dopamine-mediated neural transmission (p. 416). Can you offer any explanation for why blocking the reward system would be therapeutic for a disorder already characterized by anhedonia and disruption of (rewarded) goal-directed activity? If you have trouble doing so, you are in good company. This apparent contradiction is difficult to explain. Undoubtedly, you will have noticed that this paradox underscores the complexity of schizophrenia, because it is difficult to fathom why blocking dopaminergic activity would be beneficial in some respects but not others.

3. There has been a good deal of malleability over time and across cultures in the prevalence rates of the subtypes of schizophrenia. Catatonic schizophrenia, although at one time common in Europe and North America, is less so now (p. 406). Meanwhile, in recent years, paranoid schizophrenia has decreased in frequency of diagnosis, and undifferentiated schizophrenia has increased in frequency of diagnosis (p. 408). One possibility, suggested in your text, is that newly-diagnosed schizophrenic patients are put on anti-psychotic medication, which strongly suppresses positive symptoms, such as paranoid delusions (p. 408). What else do you think might be going on here? Does it strike you as odd that a disorder with a marked genetic etiology could fluctuate so over time and across cultures in its clinical presentation? Do you believe that it might be possible that all schizophrenic patients have the capability of expressing the symptoms of every subtype but that certain factors (e.g., the quality of their environments) suppress some of these symptoms? Consider the catatonic subtype of schizophrenia. Do you suppose that long-term confinement in a mental hospital might be more conducive to the expression of this subtype than other subtypes? Why or why not? Does this suggest that symptom expression might to a limited extent be under voluntary control?

4. Do you think that the goal of social recovery for schizophrenic patients (p. 426) is realistic? Or do you think that it might be possible that this disorder is so debilitating as to leave permanent psychosocial scars that interfere with the goal of social recovery? Explain your position.

Circle the best of the four answers provided and check them according to answers provided at the back of this study guide. Be sure you understand why each answer is correct.

1. In the United States, the estimated incidence of schizophrenia is as high as _____ percent of the population per year. (p. 398)
   a. 0.2
   b. 0.5
   c. 0.6
   d. 1.0

2. The median age of onset for schizophrenia is: (p. 398)
   a. below 15.
   b. approximately 35.
   c. higher in men than in women.
   d. higher in women than in men.

3. A schizophrenic's statement that he is "growing his father's hair" is an example of: (p. 400)
   a. anhedonia.
   b. autism.
   c. echolalia.
   d. cognitive slippage.

4. Which of the following is defined as "false beliefs"? (p. 401)
   a. hallucinations
   b. alogia
   c. delusions
   d. echolalia

5. A schizophrenic who has feelings of being intimately tied up with universal powers (often associated with ideas of external control) is said to be experiencing: (p. 402)
   a. disrupted volition.
   b. confused sense of self.
   c. disruption of perception.
   d. retreat to an inner world.

6. Many people who are in the acute, early phases of a schizophrenic breakdown exhibit _____ symptoms. (p. 404)
   a. undifferentiated
   b. paranoid
   c. catatonic
   d. disorganized

7. The central feature of _____ schizophrenia is pronounced motor signs. (p. 406)
   a. undifferentiated
   b. catatonic
   c. disorganized
   d. paranoid

8. The prognosis for a(n) _____ schizophrenic is particularly poor. (p. 408)
   a. disorganized
   b. undifferentiated
   c. paranoid
   d. catatonic

9. Paranoid schizophrenics commonly have delusions with themes of what content? (p. 408)
   a. persecution
   b. grandeur
   c. obscenity
   d. both persecution and grandeur

10. A person in whom symptoms of schizophrenia have been present for less than six months would be diagnosed as having: (p. 410)
    a. schizophrenia, undifferentiated type.
    b. schizophrenia, catatonic type.
    c. schizoaffective disorder.
    d. schizophreniform disorder.

11. The results of twin studies of hereditary factors in the development of schizophrenia show: (p. 414)
    a. equal concordance rates for identical and fraternal twins.
    b. higher concordance rates for fraternal twins.
    c. higher concordance rates for identical twins.
    d. a higher incidence of schizophrenia among ordinary siblings than among twins.

12. Tienari's Finnish Adoption Study stresses the importance of what variable or variables in the development of *schizophrenia* among index and control adopted-away children? (pp. 415-416)
    a. genetic vulnerability
    b. parental inadequacy
    c. expressed emotion
    d. genetic vulnerability and parental inadequacy

13. Which of the following findings did *not* contribute to the demise of the dopamine hypothesis as the cause of schizophrenia? (p. 416)
    a. Dopamine-blocking drugs also reduce psychotic symptoms associated with other disorders.
    b. The receptor-blocking effect of neuroleptics is accomplished too quickly.
    c. Dopamine-blocking drugs effectively treat drug-induced "bad trips."
    d. Dopamine-stimulating drugs cause hallucinations.

14. The main reason that the schizophrenic deficit in smooth pursuit eye movement (SPEM) is problematic as a specific neurophysiologic risk factor is that: (p. 417)
    a. close relatives of schizophrenics do not share this SPEM deficit.
    b. SPEM is not relevant to any of the symptoms of schizophrenia.
    c. SPEM involves the participation of numerous widely disseminated brain processes.
    d. SPEM deficiency is a disorder of nonvoluntary attention.

15. Because the brain normally occupies the skull fully, the enlarged ventricles of some schizophrenics imply a(n): (p. 418)
    a. decreased pressure on the brain.
    b. loss of brain tissue mass.
    c. increased amount of spinal fluid.
    d. predisposition to hydrocephaly.

16. Which brain region(s) is (are) believed to be especially important in accounting for the *negative* signs and symptoms of schizophrenia? (p. 419)
    a. frontal and prefrontal regions
    b. temporolimbic regions
    c. parietal regions
    d. the corpus callosum

17. Which of the following was not a deficit found by Walker and colleagues in their videotape studies of pre-schizophrenic children? (p. 421)
    a. little positive emotion   c. cognitive slippage
    b. poor motor skills   d. neuromotor abnormalities

18. Gregory Bateson (1959, 1960) coined which term in order to emphasize the conflicting and confusing nature of communications among families with a schizophrenic member? (p. 423)
    a. double-bind communication   c. expressed emotion
    b. amorphous style of thinking   d. communication deviance

19. All of the following is true of expressed emotion (EE) EXCEPT: (p. 424)
    a. The association between EE and relapse is strongest in schizophrenics with a chronic course.
    b. EE may be especially intense when family members believe that schizophrenic symptoms are involuntary.
    c. EE involves both emotional over-involvement with the ex-patient and excessive criticism of him or her.
    d. Attempts to reduce EE in family members have been very impressive in terms of relapse prevention.

20. What percent of schizophrenics continue to be resistant to drug (or any other) treatment and undergo an irreversible negative-syndrome and/or disorganized deterioration? (p. 426)
    a. 10   c. 50
    b. 25   d. 60

Chapter 13
Brain Disorders and Other Cognitive Impairments

◊ OVERVIEW

The first half of this chapter concerns neuropsychological disorders and brain damage. These disorders are behavioral and mental impairments resulting from brain injury. The clinical features of neuropsychological disorders are described. Then, specific neuropsychological symptom syndromes are discussed, including delirium, dementia, the amnestic syndrome, the neuropsychological delusional syndrome, neuropsychological mood syndrome, and neuropsychological personality syndromes. Finally, three longer-term disorders, in which an individual's emotional, motivational, and behavioral reactions to brain pathology are critically important, are reviewed in detail. These disorders are HIV-1 infection of the brain, dementia of the Alzheimer's type, and disorders involving traumatic head injury.

Chapter 13 closes with a discussion of mental retardation, defined as compromised brain functioning that is either congenital or that arises in the earliest phases of psychological development. Treatments for and outcomes of mental retardation are reviewed. Finally, efforts aimed at preventing mental retardation are described.

◊ CHAPTER OUTLINE

I. Neuropsychological Disorders and Brain Damage
    A. General Clinical Features of Neuropsychological Disorders
        1. The Nature and Location of Neural Damage
        2. Diagnostic Issues in Neuropsychological Disorders
    B. Neuropsychological Symptom Syndromes
        1. Delirium
        2. Dementia
        3. The Amnestic Syndrome
        4. The Neuropsychological Delusional Syndrome
        5. Neuropsychological Mood Syndrome
        6. Neuropsychological Personality Syndromes
    C. Neuropsychological Disorder with HIV-1 Infection
        1. Prominent Features
        2. Prevalence Studies
        3. Treatment

After studying this chapter, you should be able to:

1. Describe the general clinical features and symptom patterns of neuropsychological disorders. (pp. 432-436)

2. List and characterize the major neuropsychological symptom syndromes. (pp. 436-439)

3. Differentiate between the two neuropsychological disorders associated with HIV-1 infection: AIDS dementia complex (ADC) and AIDS-related complex (ARC). (pp. 439-440)

4. Describe the clinical features of dementia of the Alzheimer's type (DAT), and summarize what is known about its causes and treatment. (pp. 440-445)

5. Compare and contrast vascular dementia (VAD) and DAT. (pp. 445-446)

6. Identify the ways in which traumatic brain injury can affect neuropsychological functioning, as well as the factors that determine prognosis. (pp. 446-449)

7. Explain what is meant by cultural-familial retardation, and review the major causal factors that have been suggested. (pp. 457-458)

8. Identify some problems in assessment of mental retardation, and describe various approaches to treatment and prevention. (pp. 459-461)

◊ TERMS YOU SHOULD KNOW

neuropsychological disorders (p. 432)

organic mental disorders (p. 432)

delirium (p. 436)

dementia (p. 437)

amnestic syndrome (pp. 437-438)

neuropsychological delusional syndrome (p. 438)

neuropsychological mood syndromes (pp. 438-439)

neuropsychological personality syndromes (p. 439)

AIDS dementia complex (ADC) (pp. 439-440)

AIDS-related complex (ARC) (p. 440)

dementia of the Alzheimer's type (DAT) (p. 440)

senile dementias (p. 440)

presenile dementias (p. 440)

vascular dementia (VAD) (pp. 445-446)

traumatic brain injury (TBI) (p. 446)

mental retardation (pp. 449-461)

Down syndrome (pp. 453-456)

phenylketonuria (PKU) (p. 456)

macrocephaly (p. 456)

microcephaly (pp. 456-457)

hydrocephalus (p. 457)

cultural-familial retardation (pp. 457-458)

mainstreaming (p. 460)

---

1. Define neuropsychological disorders and list nine symptoms generally associated with these disorders. (pp. 432-434)

2. Compare and contrast the concepts of "hardware" and "software" as the authors apply them to the brain and mental processes. (Highlight 13.1, p. 433)

3. How is the location of brain damage related to a patient's neuropsychological symptoms? Describe the general functions attributed to the right and left hemispheres of the brain. (pp. 434-436)

4. Define neuropsychological symptom syndrome. Complete the table comparing the six types of syndromes that are typical of individuals with brain pathology. (pp. 436-439)

TYPE	CHARACTERISTICS
Delirium	
Dementia	
Amnestic Syndrome	
Neuropsychological Delusional Syndrome	
Neuropsychological Mood Syndrome	
Neuropsychological Personality Syndrome	

5. Describe the neuropsychological features of AIDS and the neuropathology of the AIDS dementia complex (ADC). (p. 439)

6. What is the typical neuropsychological and neuropathological course of Alzheimer's disease? (pp. 440-442)

7. Discuss both neuropathological and genetic causal factors in dementia of the Alzheimer's type (DAT). (pp. 443-444)

8. Compare and contrast DAT and vascular dementia (VAD). (pp. 445-446)

9. Review the physiological and neuropsychological after-effects of traumatic brain injury (TBI). What are the typical stages from impact to recovery? (pp. 446-447)

10. Describe treatments for and outcomes of TBI. (pp. 448-449)

11. Define mental retardation and describe how it is classified in DSM-IV. (pp. 449-450)

12. Describe mild, moderate, severe, and profound mental retardation. How does the AAMR system differ from that of the APA? (pp. 450-452)

13. Describe five biological conditions that may lead to mental retardation. (pp. 452-453)

14. Describe some of the physical characteristics of children born with Down syndrome. What are some intellectual deficits in Down syndrome? (p. 453; p. 455)

15. Discuss possible causes of Down syndrome. (pp. 455-456)

16. Describe the etiology of and preventive treatment for phenylketonuria (PKU). (p. 456)

17. List three types of cranial anomalies and describe the clinical picture of each, as well as any treatments mentioned. (pp. 456-457)

18. Describe how Table 13.4 supports the existence of cultural-familial mental retardation. (pp. 457-458)

19. Describe some forms of care for the mentally retarded that are alternatives to institutionalization, according to Tyor and Bell (1984). (p. 460)

20. Discuss the pros and cons of the "mainstreaming" approach to the education of mildly retarded children. What is a reasonable conclusion about mainstreaming at this point? (p. 460)

21. Describe Project Head Start and discuss the strengths, weaknesses, frustrations, and potential benefits of this approach to preventing mental retardation. (pp. 460-461)

_____

Neuropsychological disorders and brain damage

1. Most people who have a neuropsychological disorder develop psychopathological symptoms, such as panic attacks, dissociative episodes, or delusions. True or False? (p. 432)

2. The destruction of brain tissue may involve only limited behavioral deficits or a wide range of psychological impairments, depending on four variables. Complete the following list: (p. 433)
   a.
   b.
   c. the individual's total life situation
   d.

3. In recent years, the concept of _____ _____ _____ has been employed increasingly to account for the fact that intelligent, well-educated, mentally active people have enhanced resistance to mental and behavioral deterioration following significant brain injury. (p. 433)

4. Sometimes referred to as loss of "executive" function, impairment in the _____ of behavior is one of the clinical features of neuropsychological disorders. Others include apathy or emotional _____, impairment of _____ and _____ communication, and impairment of _____, in which an individual is unable to locate himself or herself accurately, especially in time but also in space or in relation to the personal identities of self or others. (pp. 433-434)

5. The right hemisphere is generally specialized for configurational or _____ processing. Functions that are dependent on _____ (i.e., _____) processing of familiar information, such as using language or solving mathematical equations, take place mostly in the left hemisphere for nearly everyone. (p. 434)

6. It is possible to make generalizations about the likely effects of damage to particular parts of the brain. Complete the following chart that summarizes these. (p. 435)

Area of the Brain Damaged	Probable Clinical Picture
Frontal areas	either passivity and apathy or impulsiveness and distractibility
Right parietal area	
Left parietal area	
Temporal area	
Occipital area	

7. Match the following: (pp. 436-437)

a. Delirium	___ Caused by degenerative processes of old age, repeated strokes, infections, tumors, severe or repeated head injuries, and dietary deficiencies.
b. Dementia	___ Caused by head injury, toxic or metabolic disturbances, insufficient blood to brain, withdrawal from alcohol or other drugs, and oxygen deprivation.

8. Which of the following would a person with amnestic syndrome have the most problem remembering? (pp. 437-438)
   a. The name of the doctor who just introduced himself or herself one second ago.
   b. What he or she had for breakfast.
   c. Details of his or her childhood, which took place 40-50 years ago.

9. In contrast to the dementia syndrome, overall cognitive functioning in the amnestic syndrome may _____ _____ _____. (p. 438)

10. In the most common forms of amnestic syndrome, those associated with alcohol or barbiturate addiction, the disorder may be irreversible. True or False? (p. 438)

11. A common organic feature in the neuropsychological personality syndromes may be damage to the _____ _____. (p. 439)

12. AIDS dementia complex (ADC) appears to be associated with a disruption of brain function at the _____ level; the most reliably reported (neuropsychological) finding is that of notably _____ _____ _____. (p. 439)

13. Why is the diagnosis of dementia of the Alzheimer's type (DAT) often difficult and uncertain? (p. 440)

14. Describe the onset and subsequent course of Alzheimer's disease. (p. 441)

15. Approximately ____% of all DAT patients display a course of simple deterioration (that is, they gradually lose various mental capacities). (p. 441)

16. The neuropathology associated with Alzheimer's disease includes the widespread appearance of _____ _____, small areas of dark-colored matter that are in part the debris of damaged nerve terminals; the tangling of the normally regular patterning of _____, strand-like protein filaments, within neuronal cell bodies; and the abnormal appearance of small holes in neuronal tissue, called _____, which derive from cell degeneration. (p. 443)

17. Another notable alteration in DAT concerns the neurotransmitter _____, which is known to be important in the mediation of _____. This fact has given rise to the _____ depletion theory of DAT etiology. (p. 443)

18. Studies of the composition of the senile plaques in DAT reveal that their cores consist of a sticky protein substance called _____ _____, which also appears in abnormal quantities in other parts of DAT patients' brains. (p. 443)

19. There is a genetic connection between DAT and _____ _____. (p. 444)

20. Differing forms (genetic alleles) of a blood protein called _____-____ differentially predict risk for late-onset DAT, although many people inheriting the most risky form of _____ do not succumb to DAT. (p. 444)

21. The fact that substantial numbers of _____ _____ are _____ for DAT suggests that DAT is not determined solely by genetic factors. (p. 444)

22. Several of the common problematic behaviors that are associated with DAT (e.g., _____ _____ and _____) can be somewhat controlled using _____ approaches. (p. 444)

23. Treatment research has been focused on the consistent findings of _____ depletion in DAT, although success in this area has been limited. (p. 444)

24. Why has so much attention been paid to the caregivers of individuals with DAT? (p. 445)

25. When a series of small strokes results in dementia, the condition is known as _____ dementia, the underlying cause of ____% of all dementia cases. (p. 446)

26. The clinical features of VAD and DAT are similar, but the decline in VAD is less smooth because of the discrete character of each _____ event; variations over time in the volume of blood delivered by a seriously clogged _____; and a tendency for VAD to be associated with more severe _____ _____, such as violence. (p. 446)

27. Most traumatic brain injuries (TBIs) are the result of _____ _____ _____. If the TBI results in unconsciousness, the individual often experiences both _____ and _____ amnesia. (p. 446)

28. Some degree of bleeding, or _____ _____, can occur with even relatively low-impact head injuries. When hemorrhaging involves small spots of bleeding, the condition is referred to as _____ _____. In severe injuries, enough blood may accumulate within the rigid confines of the skull to cause _____ _____. (p. 447)

29. Perhaps the most famous historical example of TBI is the case of _____ _____, a foreman excavating rock in the 1800s. (p. 447)

30. The great majority of people suffering from mild concussions improve to a _____ _____ _____ within a short time. In severe brain injury cases, the prognosis is _____ _____. (p. 448)

278

31. What four factors influence the likelihood that children with TBI will be adversely affected? (p. 449)

   a.

   b.

   c.

   d.

32. List five factors in the following short example suggesting that the TBI patient has an unfavorable prognosis. (p. 449)

   "An 18-year-old male who had several run-ins with the law during high school received a serious head injury in a motorcycle accident. He was in a coma for almost a month. The patient is currently suffering some paralysis and is very angry and depressed. He refuses to cooperate with his physical therapist. His parents, who live in a remote rural area where no rehabilitation facilities are available, will take him back home but are rather unenthusiastic about the prospect."

   a.

   b.

   c.

   d.

   e.

Mental retardation

33. The DSM-IV defines mental retardation as "significantly sub-average general intellectual functioning . . . that is accompanied by significant limitations in adaptive functioning" in certain skill areas and that is manifested before age 18. Mental retardation is coded on Axis ____ of DSM-IV, along with the _____ _____. (pp. 449-450)

34. Explain why initial diagnoses of mental retardation seem to occur very frequently at ages 5 to 6, to peak at age 15, and to drop off sharply after that. (p. 450)

35. Fill in the following chart that summarizes the educational potential, level of care required, and the degree of physical deformity characteristic of each level of retardation: (pp. 450-451)

Level of Retardation	Description
Mild	Persons in this group are considered "educable." They can master simple academic and occupational skills and can become self-supporting. Physically, these individuals are _____.
Moderate	Persons in this group are considered _____. Most can achieve partial independence in daily _____-_____, acceptable behavior, and work within the family or other sheltered environment. Physically, these individuals usually appear _____ and ungainly.
Severe	Persons in this group are called "dependent retarded." They can develop limited levels of _____ _____ and _____-_____ skills. Physical handicaps are common.
Profound	Persons in this group are considered _____-_____ retarded. They are capable of only the simplest tasks, and speech usually does not develop. They must remain in custodial care all their lives. Serious physical deformities are _____.

36. Of the mild, moderate, severe, and profound mental retardation levels, at which level does the largest proportion of mentally retarded individuals fall? (p. 450)

37. In 1992, the AAMR (American Association on Mental Retardation) adopted an IQ of ____ as the cutoff point for the diagnosis of mental retardation. (p. 451)

38. Mental retardation is associated with known organic brain pathology in approximately ____% of cases. (p. 452)

39. Five biological conditions that may lead to mental retardation are discussed. These are presented below. Complete the requested information. (pp. 452-453)

   a. **Genetic-Chromosomal Factors**
     Mental retardation tends to run in families, but _____ and _____
     _____ also tend to run in families. In some relatively infrequent but more severe types of mental retardation such as _____ _____ and _____
     ___, genetic factors play a much clearer causal role.

   b. **Infections and Toxic Agents**
     Illnesses in a pregnant woman that can cause mental retardation in her offspring include _____, _____, and German measles. After birth, viral _____ in the newborn may lead to mental retardation. Environmental toxins that may cause mental retardation in fetuses or children are _____ _____ and lead. Similarly, an excess of _____ taken by a pregnant woman may lead to congenital malformations.

   c. **Prematurity and Trauma (Physical Injury)**
     Premature children weighing less than about _____ pounds at birth show a high incidence of neurological disorders and often mental retardation. Physical injury at birth can also lead to mental retardation, as can _____, or lack of sufficient oxygen to the brain.

   d. **Ionizing Radiation**
     The list of sources of harmful radiation includes diagnostic X-rays, leakages at _____ _____ _____, and nuclear weapons testing.

   e. **Malnutrition and Other Biological Factors**
     The negative impact of malnutrition on mental development may be more _____, by altering a child's responsiveness, curiosity, and motivation to learn. In this case, the malnutrition-associated intellectual deficit is a special case of _____ deprivation.

40. Down syndrome is the best known of the clinical conditions associated with _____ and _____ mental retardation. It occurs in 1 in every _____ babies born in the United States. (p. 453)

41. List at least two of the physical features often found among children with Down syndrome: (p. 453)

42. Complete the following list of disorders sometimes associated with mental retardation. (Table 13.3, p. 454)
   a. No. 18 trisomy syndrome
   b.
   c.
   d.
   e. Bilirubin encephalopathy
   f.

43. Which intellectual capacities tend to remain relatively intact in children with Down syndrome, and which are most affected by the disorder? (p. 455)

44. The reason for the trisomy of chromosome 21 is not clear, but the defect seems definitely related to _____ _____ _____ _____ . (pp. 455-456)

45. In phenylketonuria (PKU), a baby appears normal at birth but lacks a liver enzyme needed to break down _____, an amino acid found in many foods. (p. 456)

46. PKU can be detected early by the use of a simple test. What is this test, and what procedures can be used to prevent PKU? (p. 456)

47. For a baby to inherit PKU, it appears that both parents must carry the _____ genes. (p. 456)

48. The most obvious characteristic of microcephaly is the _____ _____. Causal factors include _____ _____ and _____ _____ during the mother's early months of pregnancy. Treatment is _____ once faulty development has occurred. (pp. 456-457)

49. Hydrocephalus is a relatively _____ condition in which the accumulation of an abnormal amount of cerebrospinal fluid within the cranium causes damage to the brain tissues and _____ of the skull. A good deal of attention has been directed to the surgical treatment of hydrocephalus, in which _____ devices are inserted to drain cerebrospinal fluid. (p. 457)

50. Most mental retardation is of the _____-_____ type. (p. 457)

51. Whatever the specific etiology, children whose retardation is cultural-familial in origin are usually _____ _____ retarded. (p. 458)

52. Children who are institutionalized today fall into two groups: (p. 459)
    a.

    b.

53. List at least three alternate forms of care for the mentally retarded: (p. 460)

54. Many mildly retarded children fare better by attending regular classes for at least much of the day. This type of approach is called _____. It is not the _____-_____ _____ for retarded children. List at least two reasons why: (p. 460)

55. The best known of the programs geared toward preventing mental retardation is called _____ _____ _____. When well managed, this type of program has a very creditable record in launching children on the path to educational and occupational accomplishment. (pp. 460-461)

◊ CRITICAL THINKING ABOUT DIFFICULT TOPICS

1. Among the elderly, distinguishing depression from dementia (whether DAT or VAD) is sometimes extremely difficult. Furthermore, an elderly individual might be both depressed and demented. Determining whether depression or dementia is present, or whether both are present, has significant implications for treatment. If an elderly individual is depressed but assumed to be demented, he or she may not be given medication and/or cognitive-behavioral therapy that might reduce depressive symptoms substantially. Using the information you have been given about the symptoms of depression and DAT/VAD, describe how you might sort out whether a given elderly individual is demented, depressed, or both.

2. The topic of mental retardation provides a clear illustration of phenomena that do (and do not) fit the categorical approach to diagnosis and classification. Down syndrome and PKU (pp. 453-456) largely are either present or absent and thus meet the demands of a categorical system. Furthermore, children with Down syndrome have more in common with each other than with those who do not have Down syndrome, another hallmark of a categorical system. In contrast, cultural-familial retardation (pp. 457-458) applies to those who simply fall at the low end of the normal curve distribution of IQ. When a cutoff of IQ = 70 is applied to this continuous distribution, isn't it arbitrary to adopt the categorical view that someone with an IQ of 69 is retarded, but someone with an IQ of 71 is not? The individual with IQ = 69 has much more in common with someone whose IQ is 71 than with another "retarded" individual with an IQ of 45. Similarly, the "normal" person with IQ = 71 has more in common with the "retarded" person whose IQ is 69 than with another "normal" person whose IQ is 110. So is a categorical approach completely inappropriate for diagnosing cultural-familial mental retardation?

3. Some people oppose the study of genetic influences on behavior and psychopathology because they are threatened by the belief that there is nothing that can be done about "genetic disorders." There is hardly a better example of a genetic disorder than that of PKU (p. 456), which is inherited as a simple Mendelian recessive disorder (i.e., the affected child receives a recessive gene for PKU from both parents). PKU results in mental retardation in almost all affected children who consume a normal diet (i.e., the gene is highly penetrant). Does the PKU example support the fear that nothing can be done about genetic disorders? Treatment involves a special diet that does not contain the amino acid phenylalanine. Under these dietary conditions, "intellectual functioning may range from borderline to normal" (p. 456) in spite of damage done by exposure to phenylalanine in utero and post-natally before diagnosis. A "genetic" disorder inevitably expressed under one set of environmental conditions may not develop under another set of environmental conditions. What does it mean, then, to say that something is a genetic disorder?

◊ CHAPTER 13 QUIZ

Circle the best of the four answers provided and check them according to answers provided at the back of this study guide. Be sure you understand why each answer is correct.

1. All of the following are common clinical features of neuropsychological disorders EXCEPT: (pp. 432-434)
   a. psychopathological symptoms, such as panic attacks or dissociative episodes
   b. apathy or emotional blunting
   c. impairment in the initiation of behavior
   d. impairment of emotional control or modulation

2. Damage to which of the following brain areas is associated with visual impairments and visual association deficits? (p. 435)
   a. frontal   c. occipital
   b. temporal   d. parietal

3. In DSM-IV, physical or medical disorders are coded on Axis: (p. 436)
   a. I.   c. III.
   b. II.   d. IV.

4. The relatively rapid onset of widespread disorganization of the higher mental processes caused by a generalized disturbance in brain metabolism is called: (p. 436)
   a. amnestic syndrome.   c. dementia.
   b. neuropsychological delusional syndrome.   d. delirium.

5. The essential feature of the amnestic syndrome is a deficit in: (pp. 437-438)
   a. memory for words and concepts.
   b. immediate memory.
   c. memory for the recent past.
   d. memory for the remote past.

6. In comparison with the dementia syndrome, overall cognitive functioning in the amnestic syndrome: (p. 438)
   a. is greatly compromised.   c. is variable over time.
   b. remains relatively intact.   d. declines subtly but noticeably over time.

7. In one study, almost ___ percent of AIDS patients met DSM criteria for dementia. (pp. 439-440)
   a. 10   c. 40
   b. 20   d. 60

8. Which of the following is the most common behavioral manifestation of dementia of the Alzheimer's type (DAT)? (pp. 441-442)
   a. simple deterioration
   b. jealousy delusions
   c. paranoid delusions
   d. psychopathological symptoms

9. One in every __ people over age 65 in the United States is considered clinically demented. (p. 443)
   a. 2
   b. 3
   c. 6
   d. 10

10. All of the following are neuropathological changes in DAT EXCEPT: (p. 443)
    a. the appearance of senile plaques.
    b. the tangling of neurofibrils.
    c. the depletion of the neurotransmitter norepinephrine.
    d. the abnormal appearance of granulovacuoles.

11. Vascular dementia (VAD) involves a(n): (p. 446)
    a. proliferation of senile plaques.
    b. series of circumscribed cerebral infarcts.
    c. increase in neurofibrillary tangles.
    d. loss of neurons in the basal forebrain.

12. If a head injury is sufficiently severe to result in unconsciousness, the person may experience retrograde amnesia, or inability to recall: (p. 446)
    a. events immediately following the injury.
    b. events immediately preceding and following the injury.
    c. events immediately preceding the injury.
    d. names or faces of friends and relatives.

13. Phineas Gage showed significant personality changes after his injury. Most notable was his post-accident inability to control his emotions. This suggests that he suffered damage to which brain area? (p. 448)
    a. frontal
    b. temporal
    c. occipital
    d. parietal

14. All of the following make children with traumatic brain injuries (TBIs) more likely to be adversely affected EXCEPT: (p. 449)
    a. being relatively older at the time of injury.
    b. having fewer language and fine motor skills.
    c. suffering a relatively severe TBI.
    d. returning to a relatively more difficult environment post-injury.

15. Any functional equivalent of mental retardation that has its onset after age 17 must be considered a(n) _____ rather than mental retardation. (p. 450)
   a. pervasive developmental disorder   c. learning disorder
   b. dementia   d. organic syndrome

16. When a retarded individual is referred to as "dependent retarded," he or she is considered: (p. 451)
   a. mildly retarded.   c. severely retarded.
   b. moderately retarded.   d. profoundly retarded.

17. Which of the following levels of mental retardation is by far the most common? (p. 450)
   a. mild   c. severe
   b. moderate   d. profound

18. As opposed to the APA, the AAMR (American Association on Mental Retardation) has adopted an IQ score of ___ as the cutoff point for the diagnosis of mental retardation. (p. 451)
   a. 65   c. 75
   b. 70   d. 80

19. A condition in which excessive cerebrospinal fluid accumulates within the cranium and causes damage to brain tissues and enlargement of the skull is called: (pp. 456-457)
   a. microcephaly.   c. hydrocephalus.
   b. macrocephaly.   d. bilirubin encephalopathy.

20. All of the following were mentioned as reasons that "mainstreaming" has not worked EXCEPT: (p. 460)
   a. insufficient economic contributions from the community.
   b. entrenched teacher attitudes.
   c. difficulty in launching and maintaining mainstreaming programs.
   d. deficits in the self-esteem of mentally retarded children as a result of interacting with cognitively advantaged peers.

Chapter 14
Disorders of Childhood and Adolescence

◊ OVERVIEW

Psychopathology in childhood was long assumed to be merely an immature version of adult psychopathology, an assumption that failed children in a number of ways. For example, children had a unique set of problems, such as those generated by developmental changes that occur for all children (and adolescents). More recently, clinicians have begun to recognize the unique problems children face and to provide treatments more appropriate to children's needs.

Chapter 14 begins with a consideration of some general characteristics of maladaptive behavior unique to children and adolescents. Then, several disorders of childhood are reviewed in detail, including attention-deficit/hyperactivity disorder, conduct disorder and oppositional defiant disorder, anxiety disorders of childhood and adolescence, childhood depression, and specific symptom disorders, including sleepwalking and tics, among others. Finally, the pervasive developmental disorder of autism is considered separately, because this disorder is so perplexing and devastating.

Chapter 14 closes with a discussion of the treatment of disorders of childhood and adolescence. Treatment tailored to the special needs of children and adolescents is advocated. Play therapy as a technique for resolving psychological problems among children is described.

◊ CHAPTER OUTLINE

I. Maladaptive Behavior in Different Life Periods
    A. Varying Clinical Pictures
    B. Special Vulnerabilities of Young Children

II. Disorders of Childhood
    A. Attention-Deficit/Hyperactivity Disorder (ADHD)
        1. Causal Factors in Attention-Deficit/Hyperactivity Disorder
        2. Treatments and Outcomes
        3. ADHD Beyond Adolescence

IV. Planning Better Programs To Help Children and Adolescents
   A. Special Factors Associated with Treatment for Children and Adolescents
       1. The Child's Inability to Seek Assistance
       2. Vulnerabilities Placing Children at Risk for Developing Emotional   Problems
       3. Need for Treating Parents as Well as Children
       4. Possibilities of Using Parents as Change Agents
       5. Problem of Placing a Child Outside the Family
       6. Value of Intervening Before Problems Become Acute
   B. Using Play Therapy to Resolve Children's Psychological Problems
   C. Child Abuse
       1. Sexual Abuse
       2. Causal Factors in Child Abuse
       3. Treatment and Prevention of Child Abuse

V. Summary

◊ LEARNING OBJECTIVES

After studying this chapter, you should be able to:

1. Discuss how disorders of childhood and adolescence differ from adult disorders and identify some reasons why children are especially vulnerable to developing psychological problems. (pp. 464-466)

2. Describe the clinical features, causal factors, and treatment approaches for attention-deficit/hyperactivity disorder, conduct disorder and oppositional defiant disorder, anxiety disorders of childhood and adolescence, and childhood depression. (pp. 466-479)

3. Identify several symptom disorders that are common in children. (pp. 479-482)

4. Describe the clinical features, causal factors, and treatment of autism. (pp. 482-487)

5. List and explain the special factors that must be considered in treating mental health problems in children and adolescents. (pp. 487-490)

6. Discuss the use of play therapy in treating children with psychological problems. (p. 490)

7. Describe the consequences of child abuse for development of the child. (pp. 491-493)

◊ TERMS YOU SHOULD KNOW

developmental psychopathology (p. 465)

attention-deficit/hyperactivity disorder or *hyperactivity* (pp. 466-469)

Ritalin (p. 468)

Pemoline (p. 468)

conduct disorder (p. 471)

oppositional defiant disorder (p. 471)

juvenile delinquency (p. 471)

separation anxiety disorder (p. 475)

selective mutism (p. 475)

enuresis (pp. 479-480)

encopresis (p. 480)

sleepwalking disorder (somnambulism) (pp. 480-481)

tic (p. 481)

Tourette's syndrome (p. 482)

pervasive developmental disorders (PDD) (pp. 482-483)

Asberger's disorder (pp. 482-483)

autism (p. 483)

echolalia (p. 484)

◊ NAMES YOU SHOULD KNOW

William Pelham (p. 468)

Terrie Moffitt (p. 472)

Stephen Hinshaw (p. 479)

Peter Lewinsohn (p. 477)

Ivar Lovaas (p. 486)

◊ CONCEPTS TO MASTER

1. Define developmental psychopathology. (pp. 464-465)

2. Why is it important to view children's behavior in reference to normal childhood development? (pp. 464-465)

3. What are several of the special psychological vulnerabilities of children? (pp. 465-466)

4. Define attention-deficit/hyperactivity disorder and describe its clinical picture. (pp. 466-467)

5. Which causal factors for ADHD have been supported by research, and which have been discredited? (pp. 467-468)

6. What are the key differences between the pharmacological and behavioral treatments of ADHD? (pp. 468-469)

7. Summarize the long-term outcomes for individuals diagnosed as ADHD in childhood. (pp. 468-469)

8. Summarize and discuss the controversy surrounding the use of drug treatment for ADHD. (Highlight 14.1, p. 469)

9. Distinguish among conduct disorder, oppositional defiant disorder, and juvenile delinquency. (pp. 469-472)

10. Describe several causal factors in conduct disorders. (pp. 472-474)

11. Compare and contrast the cohesive family model and behavioral techniques as means of treating oppositional defiant disorder and conduct disorder. (p. 474)

12. Describe two common anxiety disorders found in children and adolescents. (pp. 475-476)

13. Discuss six causal factors that have been emphasized in explanations of childhood anxiety disorders and summarize what is known about the treatment and outcomes of childhood anxiety disorders. (pp. 476-477)

14. Discuss the symptoms associated with childhood depression and their relation to those seen in adult depression. (p. 477)

15. Summarize the biological and learning factors that appear to contribute to the development of childhood depression. (pp. 477-479)

16. Identify four common symptom disorders that can arise in childhood and specify the treatment(s) of choice for each. (pp. 479-482)

17. Describe the clinical picture, etiology, and treatment of Tourette's syndrome. (p. 482)

18. Explain why autistic disorder is classified as a pervasive developmental disorder and describe its clinical features. (pp. 482-485)

19. Summarize what is known about the causes and treatments of autistic disorder. (pp. 485-487)

20. List and explain six special factors that must be considered in providing treatment for children and adolescents. (pp. 487-490)

21. Why is therapeutic intervention a more complicated process with children than with adults? Describe how play therapy works. (p. 490)

22. What has been learned about parents at high risk for child abuse? (pp. 491-493)

---

1. Multi-site studies in several countries have provided estimates of childhood disorder that range from ___ to ___ percent. In most studies, maladjustment is found _____ _____ among boys than girls. (p. 464)

Maladaptive behavior in different life periods

2. Young children do not have as _____ and realistic a view of themselves and their world. Immediately perceived threats are tempered less by considerations of the _____ or _____ and thus tend to be seen as disproportionately important. As a result, children often have more difficulty in coping with _____ _____ than do adults. Children's limited perspectives, as might be expected, lead them to use _____ _____ to explain events. (pp. 465-466)

3. On the other hand, although their inexperience and lack of self-sufficiency make them easily upset by problems that seem minor to the average adult, children typically _____ more _____ from their hurts. (p. 466)

Disorders of childhood

4. Attention-deficit/hyperactivity disorder, often referred to as hyperactivity, is characterized by difficulties that interfere with effective _____-_____ behavior in children – particularly _____, excessive or exaggerated _____ _____, and difficulties in sustaining _____. (p. 466)

5. ADHD is thought to occur in about ___ to ___ percent of school-aged children. The disorder is ___ to ___ times more prevalent among boys than girls. (p. 467)

6. Complete the following summary of current thinking regarding the possible causes of ADHD: (pp. 467-468)

   a. Biological basis: Likely, but how strong an influence is still unclear.

   b. Diet:

   c. Parental personality problems:

7. Cerebral stimulants, such as amphetamines, have a(n) _____ effect on hyperactive children—just the opposite of what we would expect from their effect on adults. (p. 468)

8. Although stimulant drugs do not _____ hyperactivity, they have reduced the behavioral symptoms in about _____-_____ to _____-_____ of the cases in which medication appears warranted. (p. 468)

9. The long-term pharmacological effects of stimulants on the symptoms of hyperactive children are _____ _____ _____. (p. 468)

10. Behavior therapy is another effective approach to treating hyperactive children. What behavioral techniques are used in treating ADHD? Give an example. (p. 468)

11. Pelham and colleagues (1993) found that both behavior modification and medication therapy significantly reduced ADHD. _____, however, appeared to be the more effective element in the treatment. (p. 468)

12. What criticism has been made about the way children are selected to receive drug treatment? What criticism has been made about the purposes for which drugs are used in children? (Highlight 14.1, p. 469)

13. Oppositional defiant disorder is usually apparent by about age ___, while conduct disorder tends to be seen by age ___. (p. 471)

14. The essential symptomatic behavior in conduct disorder involves a persistent, repetitive _____ _____ _____ and a disregard for the _____ of _____. (p. 471)

15. List at least five characteristics of conduct-disordered children. (p. 472)
    a.
    b.
    c.
    d.
    e.

16. Reconstruct the self-perpetuating cycle of a preschooler who starts with difficulties in understanding language and ends up with conduct disorder. (p. 472)

17. Although only about ____ to ____ percent of cases of early-onset conduct disorder go on to develop adult antisocial personality disorder, over 80 percent of boys with early-onset conduct disorder do continue to have multiple problems of _____ dysfunction. By contrast, most adolescents who develop conduct disorder do not go on to become adult psychopaths or antisocial personalities. (p. 472)

18. There are a number of proposed environmental causal factors for conduct disorder. Kazdin (1995) suggested that having a confused "idea" or relationship with the primary caregiver can result in disorganized _____ _____. Children who are aggressive and socially unskilled are often rejected by their peers, and such rejection can lead to a(n) _____ _____ of social interactions with peers that exacerbates the tendency toward antisocial behavior. (p. 473)

19. Investigators generally seem to agree that the family setting of a conduct-disordered child is typically characterized by ineffective _____, rejection, harsh and inconsistent _____, and often parental _____. (p. 473)

20. One interesting and often effective treatment strategy with conduct disorder is the _____ _____ _____. In this family-group-oriented approach, parents of conduct-disordered children are viewed as lacking in parenting skills and as behaving in inconsistent ways, thereby reinforcing inappropriate behavior and failing to socialize the children. (p. 474)

21. How is behavior therapy used to assist the parents of conduct-disordered children? (p. 474)

22. Separation anxiety disorder is the most common of the childhood anxiety disorders, reportedly occurring with a prevalence of _____ percent of children in a population health study. (p. 475)

23. Children with separation anxiety disorder are characterized by _____ fears, over-sensitivity, self-consciousness, nightmares, and chronic anxiety. They lack self-confidence, are apprehensive in _____ _____, and tend to be immature for their age. (p. 475)

24. Separation anxiety disorder is more common in boys than in girls. True or False? (p. 475)

25. A child whose education is disrupted because he or she fails to speak during the first month of school qualifies for selective mutism. True or False? (p. 475)

26. Selective mutism tends to occur more frequently in families in which _____ behavior is prominent (Steinhausen & Adamek, 1997). It is most commonly associated with _____ _____ (Black & Uhde, 1995). (p. 475)

27. Six general causal factors of childhood anxiety disorders are discussed: (p. 476)
    a. Anxious children often manifest an unusual _____ _____ that makes them easily conditionable by aversive stimuli.
    b. The child can become anxious because of early _____, accidents, or _____ that involved pain and discomfort.
    c. Overanxious children often have the _____ effect of an overanxious and protective parent who sensitizes a child to the dangers and threats of the outside world.
    d. Detached or _____ parents also foster anxiety in their children.
    e. Cultures that favor _____, _____, and obedience appear to increase the levels of fear reported.
    f. Exposure to _____ is associated with a reduced sense of security and psychological well-being.

28. Behavior therapy procedures, sometimes used in school settings, often help anxious children. Such procedures include _____ training, to provide help with mastering essential competencies, and _____, to reduce anxious behavior. Desensitization must be explicitly tailored to a child's particular problem, and _____ methods (using real-life situations graded in terms of the anxiety they arouse) tend to be more effective than having the child "imagine" situations. (pp. 476-477)

29. Currently, childhood depression is classified according to the _____ DSM-IV diagnostic criteria used for _____, with the only modification being that _____ is often found as a major symptom and can be substituted for depressed mood. (p. 477)

30. The lifetime prevalence for major depressive disorders in adolescence is between ____ and ____ percent. Before adolescence, rates of depression are somewhat higher in _____, but depression occurs at about _____ the rate for adolescent _____ as for adolescent _____. (p. 477)

31. A controlled study of family history and onset of depression found that children from mood-disordered families had significantly higher rates of depression than those from non-disordered families. This suggests a potential _____ component to childhood depression, but _____ could also be the causal factor. (p. 478)

32. Extensive research supports the view that patterns of mother-infant behavior are critical to the development of _____ in a child and that depression in the mother can adversely affect the infant. Describe some specific research findings that support this statement: (p. 478)

33. Considerable evidence has accumulated that depressive symptoms are positively correlated with the tendency to attribute negative events to _____, _____, and _____ causes. (p. 479)

34. Research on the effectiveness of antidepressant medications with children is _____ at best. (p. 479)

35. Controlled studies of psychological treatment with depressed adolescents have shown significantly reduced symptoms with _____-_____ _____ derived from Beck's approach. (p. 479)

36. Between the ages of ___ and ___, enuresis (defined as the habitual involuntary discharge of _____, usually at _____, after the expected age of continence) is about two to three times more common among _____ than among _____. The percentages for _____ also diminish at a slower rate. (p. 479)

37. Complete the requested information in the following list of the causes of enuresis: (p. 480)

Causal Factor	Description
1. Faulty learning	Results in the failure to acquire _____ of reflexive bladder emptying.
2. _____ _____	Associated with or stemming from emotional problems.
3. Disturbed family interactions	Particularly situations that lead to sustained _____, _____, or both.
4. Stressful events	A child may _____ to bedwetting in response to a stressful event, such as a new baby entering the family and becoming the center of attention.

38. _____ procedures have proved to be the most effective treatment of enuresis. Houts and colleagues (1994) concluded that the use of learning-based procedures like these was _____ effective in reducing bedwetting than were medications. (p. 480)

39. Encopresis describes a symptom disorder of children who have not learned appropriate toileting for bowel movements after age ___. (p. 480)

40. Respond TRUE or FALSE to the following statements about encopresis: (p. 480)
    a. About one-third of encopretic children are also enuretic.   True or False?
    b. Six times more boys than girls are encopretic.   True or False?
    c. A common time for encopresis is after school.   True or False?
    d. Most encopretic children know they need to
       have a bowel movement.   True or False?
    e. Many encopretic children suffer from constipation.   True or False?

41. The onset of sleepwalking disorder is usually between the ages of ___ and ___. (p. 480)

42. During sleepwalking, the eyes are _____ _____ _____ _____, and obstacles are _____. Episodes usually last from ____ to ____ minutes. (p. 481)

43. The causes of sleepwalking are not fully understood, but it takes place during _____ sleep and appears to be related to some _____-_____ situation that has just occurred or is expected to occur. (p. 481)

44. A tic is a persistent, intermittent muscle twitch or spasm, usually limited to a _____ muscle group. (p. 481)

45. Tics occur most frequently between the ages of ___ and ___. (p. 481)

46. An extreme tic disorder involving multiple motor and vocal patterns is called _____ syndrome. (p. 482)

47. About one-third of individuals with Tourette's syndrome manifest _____, which is a complex vocal tic involving the uttering of obscenities. (p. 482)

48. Complete the following chart summarizing the clinical picture in autism disorder by writing a brief description of autistic children's behavior in each area: (pp. 483-485)

Area of Behavior	Characteristics
Social deficit	
Use of speech	Speech is absent or severely restricted. Echolalic repetition of a few words may be observed. There are suggestions that some autistic children do comprehend language, but they do not use it to express themselves.
Self-stimulation	
Intellectual ability	Autistic children show a particular deficit in representing mental states. As compared to normal and retarded children, autistic children display impaired memory and adaptive behavior. This cognitive impairment may be due to motivational deficits.
Maintaining Sameness	

49. Circle YES, NO, or MAYBE as appropriate to indicate whether each of the following factors is currently thought to be an important cause of autism: (pp. 485-486)

Genetic factors	YES	NO	MAYBE
Chromosomal abnormalities	YES	NO	MAYBE
Inborn defect in perceptual-cognitive functions	YES	NO	MAYBE
Personality characteristics of parents	YES	NO	MAYBE

50. Ivar Lovaas' behavior therapy for autism has garnered impressive support. In this therapy, conducted in a(n) _____ setting, aims are to eliminate _____-_____ behavior, to teach mastery of the fundamentals of _____ behavior, and to aid in the development of some _____ skills. (p. 486)

51. The prognosis for autistic children who show symptoms before the age of 2 is poor. True or False? (p. 487)

52. One important factor limiting treatment success is the difficulty autistic children experience in _____ behavior outside the treatment context. (p. 487)

Planning better programs to help children and adolescents

53. Among the special factors associated with treatment for children and adolescents are the child's _____ to seek assistance, the need for treating _____ as well as children, the problem of placing a child _____ _____ _____, and the value of intervening before problems become _____. (pp. 488-490)

54. Describe how play therapy works and why it is necessary. (p. 490)

55. List some of the effects of child abuse: (p. 491)
    a. Impaired cognitive ability and memory
    b.
    c. Belief that outcomes of events are beyond own control
    d.
    e.
    f. Deficit in interpersonal sensitivity
    g.
    h. Self-destructive behavior

56. What common factors have been found among families with abusive parents? (p. 492)

57. Describe the various approaches to the treatment and prevention of child abuse that are currently available: (pp. 492-493)
    a.

    b.

    c.

    d.

    e. Parent-focused interventions (describe):

◊ CRITICAL THINKING ABOUT DIFFICULT TOPICS

1. In the chapter on substance abuse, you saw that long-term substitution of methadone for opium is sometimes used as a treatment, even though methadone and heroin are similar drugs. In the present chapter, you have seen that long-term use of cerebral stimulants such as the amphetamines (e.g., Ritalin) is viewed by many as the treatment of choice for ADHD (see p. 468). Some psychiatrists see the use of Ritalin as a medication that corrects a "chemical imbalance" and have no misgivings about the long-term use of the drug. Others have expressed alarm about "the possibility of adverse long-range effects resulting from sustained use during early growth and development" (Highlight 14.1, p. 469). What is your evaluation of this issue? Note that both methadone and Ritalin share many properties of street drugs of abuse (heroin in the case of methadone; amphetamines in the case of Ritalin). Is it right to take a drug when prescribed as "medicine" under medical supervision but not to take it when purchased as a street drug without medical supervision? If so, why? At least some drugs, such as alcohol and the phenothiazines (used to treat schizophrenia) have adverse neural effects when used in large doses for long periods of time. Does the concept of correcting a chemical imbalance imply that there should be no adverse side effects, since the brain's neurochemistry is being adjusted to a more normal state? How might you resolve the competing views about Ritalin?

2. In what ways do you think that autism is similar in its clinical features to obsessive-compulsive disorder (OCD)? In what ways do you think that the two disorders are fundamentally different? Do you think that knowledge about one disorder might inform knowledge about the other? Consider autistic self-stimulation behaviors as you answer this question (p. 484). Might echolalia (p. 484) be obsessive as well? There are also interesting and reasonably strong links between OCD and Tourette's syndrome, detailed on p. 482. Describe these links. In general, are you more impressed by the similarities across all kinds of psychological disorders, or the differences?

Circle the best of the four answers provided and check them according to answers provided at the back of this study guide. Be sure you understand why each answer is correct.

1. In multi-site studies in several countries, estimates of childhood disorder ranged from __ to __ percent. (p. 464)
   a. 5; 8   c. 17; 22
   b. 8; 12   d. 21; 26

2. Which of the following is not a usual characteristic of children with ADHD? (pp. 466-467)
   a. low frustration tolerance
   b. less intelligence than children without ADHD
   c. great difficulty in getting along with their parents
   d. higher anxiety than children without ADHD

3. Pelham and colleagues (1993) concluded that in the treatment of children with ADHD: (p. 468)
   a. only medication was effective.
   b. only behavior modification was effective.
   c. both medication and behavior modification were effective, but the latter was better.
   d. both medication and behavior modification were effective, but the former was better.

4. Which of the following is the most common developmental sequence for conduct disorder (CD), antisocial personality disorder (ASPD), and oppositional defiant disorder (ODD)? (pp. 471-472)
   a. CD, ODD, ASPD
   b. ODD, CD, ASPD
   c. CD, ASPD, ODD
   d. ASPD, ODD, CD

5. Which of the following is NOT true of conduct disorder (CD)? (pp. 472-474)
   a. Children with onset of CD in adolescence are much more likely to develop ASPD than are those with earlier onset of CD.
   b. The essential symptomatic behavior in CD involves a persistent, repetitive violation of rules and a disregard for the rights of others.
   c. CD has been associated with obesity in adulthood.
   d. One interesting and often effective treatment for CD is the cohesive family model.

6. Children diagnosed as suffering from an anxiety disorder typically attempt to cope with their fears by: (p. 474)
   a. becoming overly dependent on others for support and help.
   b. denying the existence of anything provoking fear.
   c. developing compulsive behaviors.
   d. indulging in "guardian angel" fantasies.

7. Dawson and colleagues (1997) found that during the expression of negative emotionality by their mothers, infants: (p. 478)
   a. cried inconsolably.
   b. refused to eat.
   c. showed higher levels of cortisol.
   d. showed greater frontal lobe activity.

8. What is the treatment of choice for enuresis? (p. 480)
   a. use of the drug imipramine
   b. use of the hormone replacement intranasal desmopressin (DDAVP)
   c. conditioning procedures
   d. stress inoculation training

9. Which of the following childhood disorders is more prevalent among girls than boys? (pp. 466-469; 474-477; 479-480)
   a. enuresis
   b. encopresis
   c. anxiety disorder of childhood and adolescence
   d. ADHD

10. Sleepwalking takes place during: (p. 481)
    a. REM sleep.
    b. NREM sleep.
    c. stage 1 sleep.
    d. stage 4 sleep.

11. Tics appear to be particularly closely associated with: (p. 482)
    a. separation anxiety disorder.
    b. epilepsy.
    c. obsessive-compulsive disorder.
    d. social phobia.

12. All of the following are true of autism EXCEPT: (p. 483)
    a. it afflicts about 6.5 children in 10,000.
    b. it is usually identified before a child is 30 months old.
    c. it occurs much more frequently among boys than girls.
    d. most cases are found among the upper classes.

13. A cardinal and typical sign of autism is that: (p. 483)
    a. a child seems apart or aloof from others, even in the earliest stages of life.
    b. a child shows poor performance on spatial tasks like puzzles.
    c. a child shows a markedly discrepant and relatively isolated ability.
    d. a child strongly prefers novel environments.

14. Autism is thought to be caused at least in part by: (pp. 485-486)
    a. poverty.
    b. parental indifference and neglect.
    c. genetic factors.
    d. a cold and unresponsive mother.

15. Who has been a pioneer in the behavioral treatment of autistic children? (p. 486)
    a. Patterson
    b. Lovaas
    c. Beck
    d. Lewinsohn

16. One of the major factors that must be taken into account when treating children and adolescents is: (pp. 487-490)
    a. parents are unwilling and/or unable to act as effective assistants in treatment.
    b. children are dependent on those around them.
    c. drug therapy is usually warranted.
    d. children are simply smaller adults.

17. Treatment without parental consent is permitted in all of the following cases EXCEPT: (p. 488)
    a. immature minors.
    b. emancipated minors.
    c. emergency situations.
    d. court-ordered situations.

18. Play therapy for children is: (p. 490)
    a. as effective as psychotherapy with adults.
    b. as effective as behavior therapy for children.
    c. less effective than behavior therapy for children.
    d. as effective as adult psychotherapy and behavior therapy for children.

19. All of the following are true of parents who physically abuse their children EXCEPT: (p. 492)
    a. they show a higher-than-average rate of psychological disturbance.
    b. they tend to be young, with most under 30 years old.
    c. many come from the lower socioeconomic levels.
    d. they tend to be highly over-controlled and inhibited outside of the home.

20. Wolfe and colleagues (1988) found that which of the following procedures reduced the risk among mothers at high risk for child abuse? (p. 493)
    a. use of antidepressant drugs
    b. behaviorally oriented parent training
    c. placing the children in temporary foster homes
    d. stress inoculation training

6. Distinguish among the biological, psychosocial, and sociocultural types of universal interventions. (pp. 508-509)

7. List several national and international organizations involved in mental health efforts. (p. 514)

8. Discuss the challenges facing mental health efforts now and in the future, and identify ways in which individuals can help. (pp. 514-517)

◊ TERMS YOU SHOULD KNOW

forensic psychology (psychiatry) (p. 496)

Tarasoff decision (pp. 499-500)

insanity defense (pp. 500-501)

NGRI defense (pp. 500-501)

guilty but mentally ill (GBMI) (p. 503)

deinstitutionalization (pp. 504-506)

Health Maintenance Organizations (HMOs) (p. 506; pp. 515-516)

universal interventions (pp. 507-509)

selective interventions (p. 507; pp. 509-512)

indicated interventions (p. 507; pp. 512-514)

short-term crisis therapy (p. 512)

managed health care (pp. 515-516)

◊ NAME YOU SHOULD KNOW

Tatiana Tarasoff (pp. 499-500)

1. List four conditions that must be met before involuntary commitment to a mental institution can occur, and describe the legal process that precedes and follows involuntary commitment. (p. 497)

2. Summarize the findings regarding violence and mental disorder, and discuss the following two problems associated with predicting dangerousness: the role of situational circumstances, and the pressure to err on the conservative side. (pp. 497-498)

3. Describe some methods for assessing potential for dangerousness, and explain the difficulty in assessing dangerousness in an over-controlled offender. (pp. 498-499)

4. Discuss the Tarasoff case, and explain the implications of the Tarasoff decision for a therapist's duty to warn or protect those whom a client plans to harm. (pp. 499-500)

5. Explain what is meant by the insanity or NGRI defense in criminal cases. (pp. 500-501)

6. List and describe five established precedents defining the NGRI defense. (pp. 501-502)

7. Summarize the controversy surrounding personality disorders (e.g., dissociative identity disorder) as grounds for the insanity defense. (Highlight 15.2, p. 503)

8. Discuss variations from state to state in law regarding the insanity defense, note conceptual problems with this defense, and explain the role of "guilty but mentally ill" (GBMI) in this context. (pp. 502-503)

9. Define deinstitutionalization. Summarize the factors that drove deinstitutionalization, and describe the unforeseen problems that arose as a result. (pp. 504-506)

10. Describe the facilities that currently serve (or under-serve) chronic mental patients. (p. 506)

11. Define the current conceptualization of prevention and list the three categories of prevention, according to the IOM report. (p. 507)

12. Define universal intervention, and describe strategies for biological, psychosocial, and sociocultural universal intervention. (pp. 508-509)

13. Define selective intervention, and list and explain three broad government strategies for preventing teen drug and alcohol abuse that have proven insufficient. (pp. 509-510)

14. List seven selective intervention programs that have shown promise in preventing teen drug and alcohol abuse. (pp. 510-512)

15. Define indicated intervention and crisis intervention. Describe two types of crisis intervention, explain how they differ in the immediacy and duration of services, and indicate what types of personnel are involved. (pp. 512-513)

16. Describe the three types of indicated intervention services that have been shown to be effective in dealing with psychological problems subsequent to air disasters. (pp. 513-514)

17. Discuss the controversy over the effects of managed health care on the treatment and prevention of mental illness. (pp. 515-516)

18. Describe several ways in which individuals can contribute to the advancement of mental health. (pp. 516-517)

Controversial legal issues and the mentally disordered

1. List the four conditions (beyond mental illness) that usually must be met before formal (involuntary) commitment can occur. (p. 497)
   a. Dangerous to oneself or others
   b.
   c.
   d.

2. Filing a _____ for a commitment hearing is the first step in the process of committing a person involuntarily. (p. 497)

3. If there is no time to get a court order for commitment or if there is imminent danger, the law allows emergency hospitalization without a formal commitment hearing. In such cases, a physician must sign a statement saying that an imminent danger exists. The patient can then be picked up (usually by the police) and detained under a _____ _____, usually not to exceed 72 hours. (p. 497)

4. One recent study from Finland reported that homicidal behavior among former patients was increased eight-fold with the diagnosis of _____ and ten-fold with the diagnosis of _____ _____ or _____. (p. 498)

5. Violent acts are particularly difficult to predict because they are apparently determined as much by _____ circumstances as they are by an individual's personality traits or violent predispositions. (p. 498)

6. One obvious and significantly predictive risk factor for violence is a _____ _____ _____ _____. (p. 498)

7. What is the equation for an aggressive act? (p. 499)

8. The two major sources of personality information for the prediction of dangerousness are data from _____ _____ and the individual's _____ _____. (p. 499)

9. The prediction of violence is even more difficult in the case of a(n) _____ offender. (p. 499)

10. The duty-to-warn ruling (also known as the _____ decision), while spelling out a therapist's responsibility in situations where there has been an explicit threat on a specific person's life, left other areas of application unclear. The California Supreme Court later ruled that the duty is to _____, rather than specifically to warn. (p. 500)

11. In technical legal terms, the insanity defense suggests the ancient doctrine that one's acts, while guilty ones (_____ rea), lack moral blameworthiness, because they were unaccompanied by the corresponding (and, for a guilty judgment, legally mandated) intentional state of mind (_____ rea). (p. 500)

12. Studies have confirmed the fact that persons acquitted of crimes by reason of insanity spend _____ time, on the whole, in a psychiatric hospital than persons who are convicted of crimes spend in prison. (p. 501)

13. The established precedents that define the insanity defense are listed below. Briefly describe each one. (pp. 501-502)

    a. The M'Naughten Rule

    b. The Irresistible Impulse Rule

    c. The Durham Rule

    d. The ALI Standard

    e. The IDRA

14. An extremely common reform instituted by the states in the wake of protests of excessive laxity provoked by the Hinckley acquittal was the shifting of the burden of proof for the insanity defense to the _____. (p. 502)

15. An NGRI plea is most likely to be successful if what four factors are present? (p. 502)
    a.
    b.
    c.
    d.

16. Several states have adopted the optional plea/verdict of _____ _____ _____ _____. Outcomes from use of this plea have been _____. (p. 503)

319

17. Complete the list of five unforeseen problems that have arisen in the effort to deinstitutionalize the mentally ill. (p. 504)
   a. Many residents of mental institutions had no families or homes to go to.

   b.

   c.

   d. Many patients had not been carefully selected for discharge and were not ready for community living.
   e.

18. Rossi (1990) estimated that ____ percent of homeless individuals suffer from chronic mental disorder. (p. 506)

19. The demographics of the inpatient population have shifted in favor of a(n) _____ _____ _____ group. _____ _____ have become the largest single setting to care for the chronically mentally ill. (p. 506)

Perspectives on prevention

20. The three categories of prevention efforts, according to the IOM report, are _____, _____, and _____ interventions. (p. 507)

21. Universal interventions are efforts aimed at influencing the general population. Fill in the missing information on the following chart showing types of universal interventions: (pp. 508-509)

Type of Universal Intervention	Example
Biological	Biologically based universal intervention begins with developing _____ lifestyles. Many of the goals of health psychology can also be viewed as universal prevention strategies. To the extent that physical illness always produces some sort of _____ _____ that can result in such problems as depression, good health is preventive with respect to good mental health.
Psychosocial	The first requirement for psychosocial health is that a person develop the skills needed for effective _____ _____, for expressing _____ constructively, and for forming satisfying _____ with others. The second requirement is that a person acquire an accurate _____ _____ _____ on which to build his or her identity. Third, psychosocial well-being also requires that a person be _____ for the types of problems likely to be encountered during given life stages.
Sociocultural	Sociocultural prevention is focused on making the _____ as safe and attractive as possible for the individuals within it. Examples of sociocultural prevention include a broad spectrum of social measures ranging from public _____ and _____ _____ to economic planning and social legislation directed at ensuring adequate health care for all citizens.

22. _____ interventions are efforts aimed at a specific subgroup of the population considered at risk for developing certain mental health problems. List three strategies proposed by the government to tackle drug and alcohol abuse among teens: (p. 507; p. 510)

a.

b.

c.

23. List seven selective intervention programs that have shown promise in the treatment of drug and alcohol abuse among teens. (pp. 510-512)

    a.

    b.

    c.

    d.

    e.

    f.

    g.

24. Crisis intervention is one form of a(n) _____ intervention that emphasizes the early detection and prompt treatment of maladaptive behavior in a person's family and community setting. Complete the list of types of crisis intervention: (pp. 512-513)

    a.

    b. Telephone hotline

25. Most individuals and families who come for short-term crisis therapy do not continue in treatment for more than ___ to ___ sessions. (p. 512)

26. Explain why crisis therapy can be the most discouraging of any intervention approach for a therapist or volunteer counselor. (p. 513)

27. List the three types of indicated prevention efforts shown to be effective in dealing with the psychological problems related to air disasters: (pp. 513-514)

    a.

    b.

    c.

Challenges for the future

28. _____ _____ _____ has resulted in programs that differ widely in the type and quality of mental health services provided. (p. 515)

29. Lazarus (1996) suggested that _____-_____ psychotherapy has been virtually eliminated for all but a small number of wealthy private clients. Most managed health care organizations approve only short inpatient stays (less than _____ days) and ___ to ___ sessions of outpatient mental health treatment at a time. (p. 515)

30. Critics of managed care argue that there is no convincing evidence that current efforts are actually controlling _____ and no _____ support for the limited benefit options currently being exercised. (p. 515)

31. Beyond the need for better individual care, it seems imperative that more effective _____ be done at community, national, and international levels if mental health problems are going to be reduced or eliminated. (p. 516)

32. Describe some constructive courses of action open to each citizen to work for improved mental health in society. (p. 516)

33. Indicate whether each of the following is true or false by circling the appropriate response: (pp. 516-517)
    a. From time to time, each of us has serious difficulty coping with problems.   True False
    b. During such crises, professional assistance may be needed.   True False
    c. Such difficulties can happen to anyone if stress is severe.   True False
    d. Early detection and treatment help to prevent chronic conditions.   True False

1. Do you think that the duty-to-warn or duty-to-protect doctrine (pp. 499-500) holds therapists to too high a standard of care? Does there seem to be any way to resolve the conflict between the protection of the client's confidentiality and the duty to warn or protect prospective victims of that client? If you had been the psychologist treating Prosenjit Poddar, how would you have acted? Why? Put another way, if your roommate threatened to kill his ex-lover, what specific course of action would you take?

2. Think again about the concepts of free will versus determinism as they arise in discussions of abnormal behavior. Can you apply these concepts to issues surrounding the insanity defense? For example, according to the irresistible impulse rule, "accused persons might not be responsible for their acts, even if they know that what they were doing was wrong, if they had lost the power to choose between right and wrong. That is, they could not avoid doing the act in question because they were compelled *beyond their will* to commit the act (Fersch, 1980)" (p. 501; emphasis added). Does this imply that "free will" guides most people's actions? If so, do you think that this view of human behavior is compatible with the deterministic framework usually adopted in psychology?

3. The current crisis in mental health care is described as a conflict between containment of costs and the provision of quality mental health services (pp. 515-516). Can you think of ways in which one could contain costs while providing high-quality mental health services? One approach that has been recommended is to restrict mental health care to "empirically validated treatments" (i.e., those treatments proven by research to be effective for patients with specific diagnoses). Describe what you believe to be the pros and cons of this approach.

Circle the best of the four answers provided and check them according to answers provided at the back of this study guide. Be sure you understand why each answer is correct.

1. Typically, the first step in committing an individual to a mental hospital involuntarily is: (p. 497)
   a. appointing a physician and a psychologist to examine the individual.
   b. filing a petition for a commitment hearing.
   c. holding a commitment hearing.
   d. notifying the police.

2. Prediction of violent acts is particularly difficult because: (p. 498)
   a. violent acts are determined in part by situational circumstances.
   b. violent acts are determined in part by an individual's personality traits.
   c. violent acts are determined in part by past history of violence.
   d. violent acts are determined in part by violent predispositions.

3. The strongest implication of the Tarasoff decision is that a therapist must: (pp. 499-500)
   a. inform the police when a client has made global threats.
   b. warn a person whom his or her client has specifically threatened to harm.
   c. warn anyone whom he or she believes might be in danger from a client.
   d. warn the authorities when a client threatens suicide.

4. Studies have confirmed that individuals acquitted of crimes by reason of insanity typically spend _____ time in psychiatric hospitals as (than) individuals convicted of crimes spend in prison. (p. 501)
   a. less
   b. about the same amount of
   c. about the same amount or more
   d. much more

5. Under which of the following precedents did the law hold that individuals might not be responsible for their acts, even if they knew that what they were doing was wrong, if they had lost the power to choose between right and wrong? (pp. 501-502)
   a. the M'Naughten Rule (1843)
   b. the Irresistible Impulse Rule (1887)
   c. the Durham Rule (1954)
   d. the federal Insanity Defense Reform Act (1984)

6. All of the following factors make an NGRI plea more likely to be successful EXCEPT: (p. 502)
   a. the defendant is female.
   b. the defendant has a diagnosed (major) mental disorder.
   c. the violent crime was murder.
   d. there have been prior mental hospitalizations.

7. Between 1970 and 1992, the patient population at state mental hospitals was reduced by __ percent. (p. 504)
   a. 73
   b. 53
   c. 23
   d. 10

8. All of the following are true of homeless people EXCEPT: (pp. 505-506)
   a. a greater percentage of homeless people than of people with homes have significant psychopathology.
   b. deinstitutionalization has contributed substantially to the number of homeless people.
   c. all homeless people are former mental patients.
   d. 84% of the homeless people in one study abused various substances.

9. What type of institution has become the largest single setting to care for the chronic mentally ill? (p. 506)
   a. homeless shelter
   b. nursing home
   c. mental hospital
   d. general hospital

10. Over the years, most efforts geared toward improving mental health have been largely aimed at helping people only after they have already developed serious problems. An alternative to this is: (p. 507)
    a. crisis intervention.
    b. in vivo treatment.
    c. prevention.
    d. retrospective research.

11. Any effort aimed at improving the human condition, at making life more fulfilling and meaningful, may be considered part of _____ prevention of mental disorder. (p. 508)
    a. universal
    b. selective
    c. indicated
    d. secondary

12. Adequate preparation for potential problems likely to be encountered by anyone during a given life stage is a requirement for _____ health, at the _____ level of prevention: (p. 508)
    a. biological; universal
    b. psychosocial; universal
    c. biological; selective
    d. psychosocial; selective

13. All of the following are sociocultural measures for universal prevention of mental disorders EXCEPT: (p. 509)
    a. economic planning.
    b. penal systems.
    c. public education.
    d. Social Security.

14. Prevention resources aimed at curtailing or reducing the problem of teenage alcohol and drug abuse exemplify: (p. 509)
    a. indicated intervention.
    b. selective intervention.
    c. universal intervention.
    d. psychosocial intervention.

15. Crisis intervention is one form of a(n) _____ intervention. (p. 512)
    a. selective
    b. universal
    c. indicated
    d. generalized

16. People who appear to be functioning well at a disaster site may experience difficulties after the immediate crisis has subsided. Such people may derive particular benefit from: (p. 514)
    a. telephone hotline crisis counseling services.
    b. immediate crisis intervention services.
    c. short-term crisis therapy.
    d. post-disaster debriefing sessions.

17. What form of treatment is NOT encouraged by HMOs? (p. 515)
    a. long-term psychotherapy
    b. group psychotherapy
    c. pharmacotherapy
    d. somatic therapy

18. Critics of managed care might agree with all of the following statements EXCEPT: (p. 515)
    a. There is no convincing evidence that current efforts are actually controlling costs.
    b. Psychoactive drugs are no longer available to those who need them.
    c. Few, if any, of the decisions regarding amount and type of services provided are directly guided by empirical criteria.
    d. Administrative costs for managed care are exorbitant.

ANSWER KEY FOR CHAPTER QUIZZES

◊ CHAPTER 1

1. c. is away from the normal
2. b. reliable
3. d. configural
4. d. comorbidity
5. c. the person's present condition
6. b. Axis II
7. d. Axis IV
8. c. acute
9. a. lifetime prevalence
10. b. high socioeconomic status and older age
11. b. Hippocrates
12. d. There are basically four types of body fluids.
13. a. the anatomy of the nervous system
14. c. The Black Death
15. d. the result of severe psychological stress
16. c. Patients' psychological and social needs were well met during this movement.
17. b. categorical
18. c. catharsis
19. d. whether the outcome (reinforcer) is dependent on the animal's behavior
20. c. inadvertent early conditioning
21. d. random selection
22. a. analogue
23. d. the difficulty in retaining study participants for multiple assessments across many years
24. c. prospective
25. a. Its categories establish groupings that are clearly and cleanly separated at the boundaries.

◊ CHAPTER 2

1. b. inoculation effect
2. a. re-uptake
3. b. gene-environment correlation
4. b. peer group
5. a. Strong genetic effects do not limit the strength of environmental influences.
6. d. increased vulnerability to accidents
7. b. id
8. d. oral, anal, phallic, latency, genital
9. a. displacement
10. b. introjection
11. d. John Bowlby
12. b. instrumental (operant) conditioning
13. a. generalization
14. a. dysfunctional attributional style
15. a. accommodation
16. c. permissive-indulgent
17. a. authoritative
18. a. more overcontrolled problems but the same number of undercontrolled problems
19. c. antisocial personality disorder
20. d. biopsychosocial

◊ CHAPTER 3

1. b. counseling psychologist
2. a. PET scan
3. d. Hamilton Rating Scale for Depression
4. c. assess the way a patient perceives ambiguous stimuli
5. c. They are highly structured.
6. a. mechanistic
7. d. insufficient validation
8. c. the advent of the major antipsychotic drugs
9. d. psychotropic
10. d. reduce the intensity of delusions and hallucinations
11. d. increase the availability of serotonin and norepinephrine in the synapses
12. c. manic disorders
13. d. client's emotional reactivity
14. d. analysis of projection
15. b. interpersonal functioning

16. c. punishment
17. d. modeling
18. c. Beck's CT
19. b. mania
20. c. Unconditional positive regard from the therapist is critical.
21. a. using less nonverbal communication
22. c. anorexia nervosa

◊ CHAPTER 4

1. d. eustress
2. a. protect the self from psychological damage and disorganization
3. c. mourning
4. c. pupils constricting
5. a. emotional arousal, increased tension, and greater alertness
6. d. delayed post-traumatic stress disorder (delayed PTSD)
7. c. exhaustion stage
8. b. more...than
9. c. socioeconomic class of victim
10. b. anger
11. c. In one study, 90% of former POWs met PTSD criteria 40-50 years after their release.
12. d. the conditions of battle that tax a soldier's stamina
13. d. There might be other adjustment problems involved.
14. b. Southeast Asia
15. d. ignorance about upcoming torture
16. a. uncontrollable
17. b. stress-induced analgesia (SIA)
18. a. both psychotherapy and medication
19. c. stress-inoculation training
20. b. is exceedingly difficult

◊ CHAPTER 5

1. c. anxiety
2. d. phobias
3. b. reduction in anxiety
4. c. direct traumatic conditioning
5. a. innate
6. b. exposure and participant modeling
7. b. specific social phobia
8. c. behavioral inhibition
9. c. false alarm
10. d. weaker; less
11. d. carbon dioxide inhalation and/or lactate infusion
12. c. anxious apprehension
13. c. repression and displacement
14. a. their attention drawn away from threat cues
15. b. GABA
16. d. avoidant and dependent
17. a. nonverbal memory
18. b. serotonin
19. d. social phobia

◊ CHAPTER 6

1. c. 21%
2. c. anaclitic depression
3. b. Dysthmics show fewer symptoms, on average, than do major depressives.
4. b. denial and rejection of the dead person
5. b. low in positive affect and high in negative affect
6. a. relapse
7. c. a depletion of norepinephrine and/or serotonin
8. c. Chronic stressors are associated with increases in both depressive symptoms and in major depressive disorder.
9. d. response-contingent positive reinforcement is no longer available
10. a. dichotomous reasoning
11. b. there is no control over aversive events

12. b. external, specific, and stable
13. d. some combination of biological, psychosocial, and sociocultural factors
14. d. cyclothymia
15. a. at least one episode of mania
16. d. deflated self-esteem
17. d. norepinephrine depletion
18. d. It is ineffective for the treatment of depression of the melancholic type.
19. c. as; as
20. c. one year
21. d. recovery

◊ CHAPTER 7

1. a. somatization disorder
2. d. antisocial personality disorder
3. c. "I deserve more of your attention and concern."
4. c. current level of stress
5. b. ability to talk only in a whisper
6. c. conversion disorder
7. a. a conscious plan to use illness as an escape
8. c. prolonged physical illness of a parent
9. a. escape from one's personal identity
10. c. generalized
11. d. defense by actual flight
12. d. dissociative identity disorder
13. d. 15
14. b. increased
15. b. Derealization
16. b. antisocial personality disorder
17. b. traumatic childhood abuse

CHAPTER 8

1. b. behavioral medicine
2. d. a, b, and c are all true.
3. b. decreased sweating
4. c. humoral and cellular
5. b. more extensive
6. a. aerobic exercise
7. c. there exists direct neural control of immunological agents.
8. d. poor metabolic retention of sodium
9. d. decelerated speech and motor activity
10. a. the absence of positive human relationships
11. c. suggestion
12. c. has shown modest success in treating headache
13. c. preventing pathogenic lifestyle behaviors at the group level
14. b. anorexia nervosa, binge-eating/purging subtype
15. c. borderline
16. a. only eating-disordered women rated their ideal figure as substantially thinner than the figure thought most attractive by the opposite sex.
17. b. binge-eating disorder
18. a. lack of conformity and oppositional style
19. b. encouragement of autonomous strivings

◊ **CHAPTER 9**

1. d. maladaptive ways of perceiving, thinking, and relating
2. b. II
3. a. Too few examples of traits associated with each personality disorder are listed.
4. b. schizotypal
5. b. schizotypal
6. a. histrionic; narcissistic
7. d. borderline
8. c. avoidant
9. b. obsessive-compulsive
10. c. borderline
11. a. mirror
12. d. borderline

13. a. DSM-IV diagnostic criteria describe psychopathy better than ASPD.
14. b. inability to form friendships
15. d. reactivity of the behavioral inhibition system
16. b. oppositional defiant disorder followed by early-onset conduct disorder
17. d. ineffective parenting, especially discipline and supervision
18. a. ASPD is more difficult to treat than psychopathy.

◊ **CHAPTER 10**

---

1. b. psychoactive substance dependence
2. c. 12
3. a. being male versus female
4. a. 0.1
5. d. heightened sexual performance
6. a. alcohol amnestic disorder
7. c. size of the mesocorticolimbic dopamine pathway (MCLP)
8. b. socioeconomic status
9. c. is associated with the common use of alcohol as a means of coping with stress
10. d. aversive conditioning
11. d. 54
12. c. small, apparently irrelevant decisions
13. d. opiate use cannot lead to physiological dependence.
14. c. endorphins
15. a. antisocial
16. a. methadone is less physiologically addictive than heroin.
17. d. stimulant
18. b. amphetamine psychosis
19. d. a middle-aged person who abuses barbiturates only at home
20. a. being born to an alcoholic parent

◊ CHAPTER 11

1. d. transvestic fetishism
2. c. an adolescent male who is shy and feels inadequate in his relations with women
3. b. exhibitionism
4. d. transvestic fetishism
5. a. homosexuality
6. b. homosexual male-to-female transsexuals
7. c. transvestic fetishism
8. c. 44; 2.5
9. d. trained professionals can easily distinguish them from normal "unrepressed" memories
10. c. pedophiles show sexual arousal to girls, but also to adult women
11. a. of lower intelligence
12. d. have both aggressive and sexual motives, but to varying degrees
13. b. most rapists rape only once
14. b. impulsive, antisocial behavior
15. a. 3; 50
16. c. plateau
17. b. one-half
18. b. premature ejaculation

◊ CHAPTER 12

1. a. .2
2. d. higher in women than in men
3. d. cognitive slippage
4. c. delusions
5. b. confused sense of self
6. a. undifferentiated
7. b. catatonic
8. a. disorganized
9. d. both persecution and grandeur
10. d. schizophreniform disorder
11. c. higher concordance rates for identical twins

12. d. genetic vulnerability and parental inadequacy
13. d. Dopamine-stimulating drugs cause hallucinations.
14. c. SPEM involves the participation of numerous widely disseminated brain processes.
15. b. loss of brain tissue mass
16. a. frontal and prefrontal regions
17. c. cognitive slippage
18. a. double-bind communication
19. b. EE may be especially intense when family members believe that schizophrenic symptoms are involuntary.
20. a. 10

◊ CHAPTER 13

1. a. psychopathological symptoms, such as panic attacks or dissociative episodes
2. c. occipital
3. c. III
4. d. delirium
5. c. memory for the recent past
6. b. remains relatively intact
7. c. 40
8. a. simple deterioration
9. c. 6
10. c. the depletion of the neurotransmitter norepinephrine
11. b. series of circumscribed cerebral infarcts
12. c. events immediately preceding the injury
13. a. frontal
14. a. being relatively older at the time of injury
15. b. dementia
16. c. severely retarded
17. a. mild
18. c. 75
19. c. hydrocephalus
20. a. insufficient economic contributions from the community

CHAPTER 14

1. c. 17; 22
2. d. higher anxiety than children without ADHD
3. d. both medication and behavior modification were effective, but the former was better.
4. b. ODD, CD, ASPD
5. a. Children with onset of CD in adolescence are much more likely to develop ASPD than are those with earlier onset CD.
6. a. becoming overly dependent on others for support and help
7. d. showed greater frontal lobe activity
8. c. conditioning procedures
9. c. anxiety disorder of childhood and adolescence
10. b. NREM sleep
11. c. obsessive-compulsive disorder
12. d. most cases are found among the upper classes.
13. a. a child seems apart or aloof from others, even in the earliest stages of life.
14. c. genetic factors
15. b. Lovaas
16. b. children are dependent on those around them.
17. a. immature minors
18. d. as effective as adult psychotherapy and behavior therapy for children
19. d. they tend to be highly over-controlled and inhibited outside of the home.
20. b. behaviorally oriented parent training

CHAPTER 15

1. b. filing a petition for a commitment hearing
2. a. violent acts are determined in part by situational circumstances
3. b. warn a person whom his or her client has specifically threatened to harm
4. a. less
5. b. the Irresistible Impulse Rule (1887)
6. c. the violent crime was murder
7. a. 73
8. c. all homeless people are former mental patients
9. b. nursing home
10. c. prevention
11. a. universal
12. b. psychosocial; universal
13. b. penal systems
14. b. selective intervention
15. c. indicated
16. d. post-disaster debriefing sessions
17. a. long-term psychotherapy
18. b. Psychoactive drugs are no longer available to those who need them.

NOTES

NOTES